Late Antiquity:
Crisis and Transformation
Part II

Professor Thomas F. X. Noble

THE TEACHING COMPANY ®

PUBLISHED BY:

THE TEACHING COMPANY
4151 Lafayette Center Drive, Suite 100
Chantilly, Virginia 20151-1232
1-800-TEACH-12
Fax—703-378-3819
www.teach12.com

ISBN 1-59803-492-8

Thomas F. X. Noble, Ph.D.
Professor of History, University of Notre Dame

Thomas F. X. Noble is a Professor of History and chair of the Department of History at the University of Notre Dame. From 2000 to 2008, he was the Robert M. Conway Director of the Medieval Institute at Notre Dame. From 1980 to 2000, he was a Professor of History at the University of Virginia.

Professor Noble earned his B.A. in History at Ohio University and his M.A. and Ph.D. in Medieval History at Michigan State University, where he studied with the distinguished medievalist Richard E. Sullivan. A Fulbright Fellowship afforded him further study in Belgium with François-Louis Ganshof and Léopold Génicot.

Professor Noble is the author, coauthor, or editor of 10 books and has published more than 40 articles, chapters, and essays. His coauthored textbook, *Western Civilization: The Continuing Experiment*, is in its fifth edition. His research has concentrated on late antiquity and the early Middle Ages, focusing on the history of the city of Rome, the history of the papacy, and the age of Charlemagne.

Professor Noble has held fellowships from the National Endowment for the Humanities and research grants from the American Philosophical Society. He is an elected fellow of the Medieval Academy of America and the International Society for the Study of the Latin Middle Ages. He has been an elected member and visitor of the Institute for Advanced Study (Princeton) and a fellow of the Netherlands Institute for Advanced Study. He is a life member of Clare Hall, University of Cambridge. He currently serves on the editorial boards of *Speculum* and *Church History* and has held offices and/or served on committees of the American Academy of Religion, the American Catholic Historical Association, the American Historical Association, and the Medieval Academy of America.

In 2008 Professor Noble received the Edmund P. Joyce, C.S.C., Award for Excellence in Teaching from the University of Notre Dame. In 1999 he was awarded the Alumni Distinguished Professor Award by the University of Virginia, that university's highest award for teaching excellence, and a David Harrison III Award for outstanding undergraduate advising. Professor Noble has supervised 11 doctoral dissertations; his Ph.D. students now teach at colleges and universities across the country.

Table of Contents
Late Antiquity: Crisis and Transformation
Part II

Late Antiquity: Crisis and Transformation

Scope:

Since the publication (1776–1787) of Edward Gibbon's justly famous *The History of the Decline and Fall of the Roman Empire*, knowledgeable people have believed that the Roman Empire suffered a long, debilitating decline that culminated in an agonizing death at the hands of barbarian savages. Gibbon suggested that ancient civilization succumbed to "barbarism and religion," but that is no longer how serious historians view the period from about 200–750 A.D. Instead the period is viewed as one of intense dynamism, some of whose forces were destructive but more of whose forces were creative.

The western half of the Roman Empire ceased to exist after 476. But the eastern lived on for a millennium, albeit in a new geographical and political shape that we call Byzantium. Moreover, from the Pyrenees to the frontiers of China, a new faith and regime—Islam and the caliphate—emerged violently and unexpectedly.

We will discuss the barbarians, but we will take care to learn who they actually were and how we talk about them today. We will explore their long and complex relations with the Roman state. We will also try to understand how Rome's former western provinces evolved into a series of barbarian kingdoms. Having situated those kingdoms on the map, we will look inside them to see what they were like, paying particular attention to how Roman they remained.

Nevertheless, the startling transformation of a particular institutional regime, the Roman Empire, cannot really be equated with the end of a civilization. This course will look at the late antique centuries with a rather different perspective from that of the traditional gloom-and-doom approach. We shall discern dramatic changes, but also remarkable continuities, especially in the lives of ordinary people. We shall watch the Roman Empire reinvent itself institutionally three times, displaying in the process great creativity and energy.

Religion will occupy us constantly: new Christian theologies, the rise of monasticism, the emergence of Orthodoxy, and the dramatic rise of Islam. We will ask what it was like to live in the late antique world. How did people earn their slender livings? How did the lives of rich and poor differ? What were the great cities—say, Rome and

Constantinople—like? What did people in the dawning European, Byzantine, and Islamic worlds inherit from the Roman Empire, and how did they manage their inheritance?

In other words, those who speak of "late antiquity" address themes of growth, creativity, originality, and dynamism, not themes of decline and fall.

Lecture Thirteen
Barbarian Kingdoms—Italy

Scope:

After the collapse of Roman imperial authority in Italy, the government in Constantinople sent the Ostrogoths to Italy to restore order. Under their great king Theodoric, the Ostrogoths created a remarkable kingdom that might well have had a bright future. When Theodoric died his successors battled among themselves and provided Constantinople with a pretext to intervene. After 20 years of brutal warfare, the Ostrogoths were defeated but Italy was devastated. Into the breach stepped the Lombards in 568. They reigned there until the Charlemagne defeated them in 774. By the time the former Roman world had become recognizably medieval, only one of the dozen or so barbarian kingdoms survived: that of the Franks.

Outline

I. Having worked our way around the periphery, we come now to the Roman Empire's heartland: Italy.

    A. Although attacked and crossed by many peoples, the Ostrogoths founded the first barbarian kingdom in Italy.

    B. After the tragic failure of the Ostrogothic kingdom, the Lombards entered Italy and created a kingdom that lasted for two centuries.

II. The Ostrogoths were a people who coalesced around the leader Valamer after the collapse of the Huns, who had held them in subjection for some decades.

    A. Some of the peoples who formed the Ostrogoths had lived in southern Russia, the Ukraine, and along the Black Sea from, probably, the late 3rd century.

        1. The Huns attacked the Ostrogoths around 350, precipitating, eventually, the Visigothic push across the Danube in 376.

    2. The Ostrogoths pressed into the Danube basin when the Visigoths crossed into the empire but generally lived under Hunnic domination.

B. Valamer fell in battle against the Gepids, but his leadership passed in turn to his son Theodemer and then to Theodoric.

C. Under pressure from the Gepids, Heruls, and Avars, the Ostrogoths crossed into imperial territory in 473.

    1. Two groups of Goths fell to battling one another, and each tried to get recognition from the emperor.

    2. Theodoric won out but could not get an eastern settlement from Emperor Zeno, who sent him to Italy in 488.

D. Theodoric entered Italy in 489 and struggled for four years to gain the upper hand.

E. Theodoric had spent a decade at Constantinople as a hostage, was well educated, had been named to several impressive offices and titles, and was adopted by Zeno.

III. The regime of Theodoric in Italy was on the whole successful and promising.

A. In 497 Theodoric was formally recognized by Emperor Anastasius, perhaps as master of the soldiers.

B. He brought peace, order, and tremendous security to Italy—something unknown there for decades.

C. He engaged in a massive program of public works in Ravenna, Rome, and elsewhere.

D. Theodoric restored the grain supply and the corn dole in Rome after a long disruption because of the Vandal conquest of Africa.

E. Theodoric drew the senate into his government. One of our key sources for Ostrogothic Italy is the *Variae* of Cassiodorus, a noble Roman senator who served Theodoric three times in key public offices and kept his official documents.

F. Theodoric formed marriage alliances all over the west with Visigoths, Burgundians, Franks, and Vandals.

G. The Ostrogoths were Arians but were not militant.

IV. Theodoric had no sons, and when he died many Goths refused to accept the rule of his daughter Amalasuntha.

    A. From 526 to 534, Amalasuntha ruled as regent for her son Athalaric. who was perceived to be too Roman in his leanings.

    B. When Athalaric died in 534, Amalasuntha ruled briefly as queen, but she was compelled to marry Theodohad.

    C. When Theodohad was declared king, he exiled his wife (who was then strangled).

    D. The fall of Amalasuntha provided Justinian with a pretext to invade Italy.

    E. Justinian "won" the Gothic war, but it subjected Italy to 20 years of brutal warfare and devastation.

    F. The end of the Ostrogothic kingdom resulted from a disastrous shift in Roman policy.

V. Justinian defeated the Ostrogoths but was unable to reestablish peace and order in Italy. This fraught situation provided an opening for the Lombards.

    A. The Lombards were another confederation of people who in the late 5th century were living in what is now lower Austria. The confederation included Sueves, Heruls, Gepids, Bavarians, Bulgars, Avars, Saxons, Goths, Thuringians, and Romanized Pannonians.

    B. In c. 507–508 they defeated the Heruls and then moved across the Danube and settled in Noricum and Pannonia. There was no effective Roman force in the west to oppose them.

    C. In c. 546–547 they obtained a treaty and fought for 20 years against the Gepids under their kings Audoin and Alboin.

    D. In 568–569 Alboin led the Lombards into Italy, where they soon took the major northern cities. Pavia held out until 572 and then became the capital of the Lombard kingdom.

        1. Alboin was murdered in 572, probably with the connivance of his wife Rosamund. (Alboin had murdered her father, the Gepid king.)

        2. The Lombards chose Clef as their king, but he was murdered in 574.

3. For 10 years the Lombards had no kings.
4. Aggressive dukes moved south and created vast duchies in Spoleto and Benevento.

VI. The Lombard kings of the 7th and 8th centuries were often highly accomplished rulers and developed a sophisticated legal culture. Nevertheless, they faced a series of challenges.

A. The kings could never get control of the southern dukes.

B. The Roman administration in Constantinople never accepted the Lombards, and their local officials in Ravenna were a constant challenge.

C. The Lombards were Arian until around 680 and had uneasy relations with the local population and constant antagonism from the popes.

D. In efforts to control the southern dukes, the Lombards had to cross papal territory in central Italy, and eventually the popes asked the Franks to help them.

1. Pippin III campaigned twice against the Lombards in 755 and 756, forcing them to cede lands to the papacy.
2. After the Lombards reneged on their promises, Charlemagne conquered them in 774.

VII. In the end only the Franks had a long-lived dynasty, were Catholic, were stronger than all their neighbors, and got on well with the Roman authorities.

Suggested Reading:

Amory, *People and Identity in Ostrogothic Italy*.

Christie, *The Lombards*.

Questions to Consider:

1. Compare the Ostrogothic kingdom with the other barbarian kingdoms we have studied. What were its relative advantages and disadvantages? What were its strengths and weaknesses?

2. The Lombard kingdom lasted for just over two centuries but finally failed. Why? What might the Lombards have done to ensure long-term success?

Lecture Thirteen—Transcript
Barbarian Kingdoms—Italy

Welcome once again to this series of lectures on late antiquity. This time, in Lecture Thirteen, we're going to look at some barbarian kingdoms again, but this time in Italy. We're going to look at peoples called the Ostrogoths and then the Lombards. You may recall in our last couple of lectures, we've been sort of working our way around the periphery of the west. We talked about Gaul— Franks, Burgundians, Visigoths, for example. We talked about Spain—Vandals, Alans, Sueves, Visigoths, for example. And then we talked about North Africa—Vandals. Essentially, we moved more or less counterclockwise around the Western Empire looking at these various peoples who settled inside the territory of what had been the Roman Empire.

We come now then to the empire's heartlands, to Italy itself. Right away it's worth pausing for just a second and reflecting on the fact that none of these early barbarian peoples settled in or coveted the old sentimentally and ideologically significant land of Italy. It's only actually after, as we'll see in just a few minutes, there is no longer an effective Roman administration, or even an ineffective Roman administration for that matter, in Italy that finally Italy was settled by a barbarian people. Although we're going to see that once again imperial policy plays as large or larger a role in settling these people, the Ostrogoths, in Italy, than did indeed any particular aspirations or interests of the Ostrogoths themselves. Having introduced them then, let's talk a little about Ostrogoths. We've obviously been much concerned in recent lectures with Visigoths, so now we'll talk about some other Goths, Ostrogoths.

After the failure of the Ostrogothic kingdom—so we'll build it and then we'll destroy it—(and I think we're going to see that in many respects it was a tragic failure. This was really a very bright, promising, interesting kingdom. One would love to be able to do "what if" history and imagine what if the Ostrogothic kingdom had persisted for some decades, or even for some centuries, but it didn't), after the failure, after the fall, the disappearance, the defeat of the Ostrogothic kingdom, the Lombards entered Italy. They created a kingdom, which lasted for some two centuries and which was very effective and very successful in a variety of ways, while also challenged in other ways. The Lombards eventually, of course, ran into a much more powerful foe, namely the Franks of the dynasty of Chardonnay. We'll come to that toward the end of this lecture.

So now, let's go back and introduce the *dramatis personae*. Ostrogoths—who are the Ostrogoths? These are people who are sometimes called the East Goths, sometimes called the Bright or the Shining Goths, sometimes there's a tendency to call the Visigoths the "Western Goths"; it isn't clear whether actually any of these particular derivations of their names are valid or not. It's probably safest just to say Ostrogoths and Visigoths, which is generally the terminology used in the ancient sources and also the terminology with which we're most familiar today. Whether these folks were easterners or bright or shining or something, I don't know, but anyway, Ostrogoths they are.

These were a people who coalesced around a leader whose name was Valamer, after the collapse of the Huns. The Huns—I'll come to this in a little bit more detail in just a second—had held the Ostrogoths in subjection for some decades. Then, after the death of Attila—we talked about this a lecture or two back—in 453, the Ostrogoths came out from under Hunnic domination, and then they really emerged in a fairly clear way for us historically. Yes, it's true that the ancient sources had known something about them, going back even to the late 3rd to early 4th century, but it's really in the second half of the 5th century that the Goths kind of come up on the screen, as it were, and we know a lot about them.

Some of the peoples who formed the Ostrogoths—let's just remember our notion of ethnogenesis, the making of a people. Ostrogoths are not a kind of a nice, tidy, biological community who have been on the planet earth since the beginning of time; they are a people formed in a historical time. As I was suggesting a moment ago, they formed around Valamer. You may remember I read a couple of quotations the other day about the Goths leaving Scandinavia with their king Berig. I read another quotation from the Turkish peoples out on the steppe lands where the khagan formed a group of warriors around himself. This Valamer indeed formed a group of warriors around himself after the middle of the 5th century. But, even earlier than this, there will have been leaders of the Goths who had coalesced a fairly diverse group of people around themselves.

The Huns attacked the Ostrogoths round about 350. That's not a precise date, but that's about right. Eventually, of course, as we've seen in some earlier lectures, this precipitated the Visigothic push across the Danube in 376. I don't want to push it too far, but you can almost imagine balls on a billiard table. The Huns banged into the Ostrogoths, the Ostrogoths banged into the Visigoths, and the Visigoths crossed the Danube and banged into the Romans. That's a way of kind of visualizing what was going on here, but again I don't want to press too hard the idea of a billiard-ball effect out there in the barbarian world.

When the Visigoths crossed the Danube, 376–378, with all the various consequences that we've discussed in some earlier lectures, the Ostrogoths essentially moved south toward the northern bank of the Danube and settled in the area where the Visigoths had been for some considerable period of time. The Huns who lived north and a bit east and west of the Ostrogoths, basically held them in subjection. I was referring to this a few minutes ago. For some decades then, so from the 370s, 380s, 390s thereabouts, until 450s when Attila dies, the Ostrogoths are, generally speaking, under Hunnic domination. Attila the Hun dies, the Hunnic confederation collapses almost immediately. This is really an ethnogenesis, if you will, that was held together by these remarkably charismatic leaders, Attila and his brother and perhaps their father, for a few decades. Absent these leaders, the Hunnic confederation simply collapsed. They didn't have any other, we might say, strong glue to hold it together. Valamer then emerges as the leader of the Ostrogoths, but he himself fell in battle against the people whom we call the "Gepids."

Let me just pause here and say that we're going to meet in the next few minutes a bunch of people—Gepids and Heruls and Avars and what have you. Out here in this land to the north of the Danube and extending lower, probably a couple of hundred miles to the north of the Danube outside the Roman world, we're dealing with an area which for us today is still very much the dark side of the moon. There are a lot of people out there. Our sources are full of all different names of people. They're encountering each other. They're fighting with each other. They're allying with each other. We don't actually know, in most cases, very much about who these people are, but this does serve to reiterate a point that I had made a couple of times in some earlier lectures; that is that if we were going to really try to build a comprehensive picture of everything that was going on as those people from the barbarian world moved from out there, outside the Roman world, to in here, inside the Roman world, we'd have to go through one people after another, again and again and again, in order to form a full picture.

Valamer falls against one of these peoples who we're not going to concern ourselves with, the Gepids, and his leadership then passed to his son Theodemer and then to Theodoric. Under pressure from Gepids, Heruls, Avars, a number of these people whom I've just been mentioning, they crossed into imperial territory in 473. In other words, they crossed the Danube into the northern Balkans. This is in certain respects a replay of the situation that had existed with the Visigoths almost exactly a century earlier when the Visigoths pressured, in that case by the Huns and the Ostrogoths, had themselves crossed the Danube and entered imperial territory.

At this time, the sort of Gothic confederation was not terribly tight and there were at least two fairly significant groups of Goths who fell to battling with one another. Each of them tried to get recognition from the emperor. How many times now have we seen that story play out? You're along the imperial frontier or you cross the imperial frontier, and the first thing you try to do, or maybe the second or third anyway, one of the early things you to try to do, is get official recognition from the Roman Empire, from the ruler. The various contending groups of Goths are attempting to gain recognition from the eastern emperor, who at this moment is named Zeno. Zeno, for a while, temporizes; he's not particularly interested in making a deal with these guys. Then—and here again we have a replay of a situation, which we talked about in earlier lectures—Zeno basically thinks, look, I've got these Goths, living now effectively on both sides of the Danube, but some of them are inside my empire, they're in the east, I'm going to send them west. You will recall perhaps that even where the Visigoths were concerned, the eastern court wanted to send them west, and the western court wanted to use them to lop off a chunk of the east. We're seeing kind of a replay of this particular situation.

Zeno decides what he'll do is he'll send the Ostrogoths to Italy. It may occur to you to ask, why Italy? Italy, after all, as I said at the outset of this lecture, was an old, prestigious, sentimentally significant land. None of the other barbarian peoples had coveted Italy. Yes, to be sure, for instance the Visigoths entered Italy, fetched up outside Rome in 408, sacked the city of Rome in 410, but you'll recall they wanted to go to North Africa and they wound up going to southern Gaul. They didn't lay claim to Italy itself. So why Italy in 488? Here's why: In 476, an obscure military officer by the name of Odovacer deposed the last western emperor. His name was Romulus Augustulus; we're going to come back to all of these events in a little bit more detail in Lecture Fifteen of this series. Anyway, Odovacer deposed the last of the western Roman emperors—Romulus Augustulus was his name—and sent the imperial insignia to Constantinople, thereby effectively signaling that the west didn't need an emperor anymore, thank you very much. Barbarian generals had essentially been ruling in the west under Roman auspices to be sure, but they had been ruling in the west now for a very long time. Then Odovacer takes the rather bold step of simply sending the imperial insignia to Constantinople, thereby signaling that we don't need an emperor over here anymore.

It won't surprise you to hear that this didn't sit very well with the imperial authorities of Constantinople. Would they on their own, for example, have countenanced an end of the Western Empire? Might they have put an end to the Western Empire? Might they have wished to put another emperor in the west? We'll never know because the story didn't play out that way; but in any case, they thought that Odovacer's actions constituted a mighty affront. At the same time in 476, and for a few years after this, the eastern court simply hadn't the means and hadn't the possibility of doing anything about what had happened in Italy. Now the Ostrogoths present them with a fine opportunity. Here you've got these Goths who had been in various relations with the Romans for a long time. Theodoric, moreover, amongst those contending factions of Goths, Theodoric's faction had actually won out. Theodoric had spent about 10 years in Constantinople as a hostage. He knew the players. They knew him. He spoke Greek. He was fairly well educated. An opportunity was presented to the Emperor Zeno, and then to his successor Anastasius, to use the Goths to displace Odovacer in Italy, to be able to lay claim once again to some sort of imperial authority, what kind we'll come to in just a second, but to restore some kind of imperial authority in Italy, and at the same time to get this potentially threatening group of people out of the Balkans and into the west. From various points of view at Constantinople, this looked like a good deal.

Theodoric entered Italy in 489. It took him about four years of a fairly hard struggle to gain the upper hand; that is to say, to put paid to Odovacer and his forces in Italy. Let's just bear in mind that when we're talking about Theodoric, just to repeat a point I was making a second ago, we're not talking about some wild and woolly barbarian here. He'd spend a decade in Constantinople; he knew Greek; he was a Christian, to be sure an Arian, but he was a Christian; and he was well-educated. He had been named to several impressive offices and titles while he was at Constantinople after he went back to his own people when his peoples were still in the Balkan region—north or south of the Danube as the case might have been at one time or another—and he was even adopted. He was made an adoptive son of the Emperor Zeno. This was a very interesting little step that Roman rulers had begun using over a period of time and that Byzantine emperors would use right through the Middle Ages. As a way of sort of honoring someone, the emperors would adopt them as sons. There was no sense that these people were going to succeed to the emperor; it was really a way of establishing a father-son relationship, so if you stop and think about it, a relationship of dependency, a relationship of superiority and inferiority, but there was a measure of respect, admiration, and possibly even affection involved in these relationships. The point I'm simply making is that Theodoric is somebody who is in very close relations with the eastern regime. That's the crucial point to retain here.

What kind of a regime then did Theodoric establish in Italy after about 492, 493, when he finally removed Odovacer from the scene and was in a position to operate on his own behalf? He was formally recognized by the Emperor Anastasius. You'll remember Theodoric's earlier relations had been with the Emperor Zeno, Anastasius's predecessor. The Emperor Anastasius recognizes him. At this point, things get for us a little bit obscure. That is to say, it certainly seems as if Theodoric had some official position, some official title, some, we might almost say a little bit anachronistically maybe, but some constitutional role here in Italy. The sources never quite specify what that role was. It is generally speculated that he was made master of the soldiers. We've seen, going all the way back to the age of Diocletian and Constantine, that we had these two officers; Constantine in particular creates the master of the foot and the master of the horse. Over the course of the 4th and into the 5th century, there also emerged a kind of a *magister utriusque militiae*, the master of both branches. There was a master of the soldiers who was the chief military officer. It is possible, maybe even likely, that that was the title under which Theodoric was operating in Italy. Again, that's a bit of speculation. We don't know that for sure.

What we do know for sure is that Theodoric brought peace, he brought order, and he brought tremendous security to Italy, something which, after all, Italy had not known for decades. We saw for example that Italy had been attacked during the 3rd-century crisis. We've seen these battles fought at the Frigidus River and at Mursa, just on Italy's northern frontier, contenders inside the Roman Empire. We've seen the Visigoths traipsing through Italy. We saw the Vandals sack Rome in the year 455. Italy had experienced a lot of trouble and a lot of disruption. Even though nobody laid claim to it, Italy had experienced a lot of disruption over a considerable period of time. For Theodoric once again to restore peace in Italy was a big deal, was a major accomplishment. Theodoric engaged in a massive program of public works. One of the things that had been happening of course—well, several of things have been happening and we've noted most of them.

Rome, for example, was very rarely the western capital after the early years of the 4th century. The city of Rome had gotten a bit tatty. Its great buildings and monuments and so forth simply had not been taken care of in the way that they had previously. Yes, there were urban prefects; yes, that would have been part of the responsibility of the urban prefect. But also what had been happening in Italy was that the economic situation had been declining across the 5th century and indeed into the early years of the 6th century. In part, this was occasioned by the Vandal conquest of North Africa, which cut off food and taxes coming into Italy. Theodoric comes along and establishes a program of public works.

Remember on an earlier day I talked about sort of the basic Roman kit of urban amenities as rhetoric in stone. Theodoric understood this rhetoric in stone very, very well—building great buildings, restoring buildings. For instance, say in the city of Rome, one of his achievements was to repair the Aurelian Walls, Rome's great circuit of walls that had been built in the 3rd century. One of the points of doing this was, yes, of course the work needed to be done, but it was also making a very powerful statement. On Theodoric's state visit to Rome in the year 500, mostly he kept his hands off the city of Rome.

He was aware, perhaps, because there were certain sensitivities involved. Anyway, he does make a kind of a great state visit to Rome in 500, and a North African visitor, his name is Fulgentius—that's not important—remarked, "How beautiful must the heavenly Jerusalem be if the earthly Rome shines so brilliantly."

Theodoric also managed to get good relations with the Vandals in Africa, and he was able to restore the grain supply to Rome and the corn dole in the city. He's really getting some very important aspects of the old Roman system up and running again. Theodoric drew the senate into his government. He was very keen to have good relations with the old traditional elites of Italy. One of our key sources indeed for Ostrogothic Italy is a book called the *Variae* written by a man called Cassiodorus. We're going to meet Cassiodorus a couple of times in later lectures. For now let's just say this is a noble Roman, a man of senatorial family, who three different times served Theodoric in high offices and he basically kept Theodoric's official documents. The *Variae* are Cassiodorus's own selection from those official documents. We're enormously grateful to have these.

Cassiodorus himself seems to have had very high hopes for the possibility of an assimilation between Goths and Romans. He really felt that these people could be blended together. He wrote apparently a history of the Goths. It doesn't survive. Jordanes, whom I've mentioned a couple of times in earlier lectures, and I think a few minutes ago in this one, when Jordanes wrote his *Getica*, his history of the Goths, he tells us that he'd actually read Cassiodorus. Cassiodorus had a very keen sense of these Goths and he didn't see them as the enemy, as the alien.

Theodoric also formed marriage alliances all over the west with Visigoths, with Burgundians, with Franks, with Vandals. Some historians speak of a *Pax Gothica*, that basically Theodoric kind of established a general peace around the Western Empire—around the territories that had formerly been the Western Empire. In lots and lots of ways, this was a very bright, very capable, a very effective rule.

Theodoric had no sons. When he died, many Goths refused to accept the rule of his daughter Amalasuntha. From 526 until about 534 (Theodoric died in 526), Amalasuntha ruled as regent for her son Athalaric. Athalaric, though raised to become king, was perceived by many of the Gothic elite as a little too Roman in his leanings. As a result, when he died in 534, Amalasuntha ruled very briefly as queen, the only time amongst the barbarian peoples that a woman ruled, albeit briefly, in her own name. She was then forced to marry a Gothic nobleman by the name of Theodohad. Theodohad then, through Amalasuntha, was declared king. As soon as he was declared king, he exiled Amalasuntha who was then strangled and gotten rid of. The fall of Amalasuntha provided Justinian in Constantinople with a pretext to invade Italy. You'll recall perhaps in our last lecture we talked about Justinian and his great General Belisarius invading North Africa. Now Justinian turns to Italy.

From the 530s to the 550s, the brutal Gothic wars were fought. Justinian "won" the Gothic war in the end, if win we call it. He defeated the Ostrogoths. He put an end to the Ostrogothic regime in Italy. Nominally, he brought Italy back under imperial control. The fact of the matter is, however, these 20 years of Gothic war were devastating to the economic life, and more broadly, even to the social life, to the intellectual life, and to the cultural life of Italy. If we really look for the bad moment in Italy, it's when Justinian's troops are trying to take Italy back from the Ostrogoths, not for example when the Visigoths sacked Rome in 410 or even when the Vandals did so in 455.

Cities were taken and retaken, and oftentimes destroyed. Rome's aqueducts were cut, which cut off the water supply to the city, a very real danger for the city of Rome. Agricultural production declined dramatically. It appears that many members of the senatorial class, the very class of Cassiodorus about whom we spoke a second ago, many of these people left Italy altogether and went to Constantinople. Justinian defeated the Ostrogoths, but he wasn't able to reestablish peace and order in Italy. What we see actually with Justinian is a radical reversal of Roman policy. Let's keep in mind, Theodoric had been sent to Italy by the Roman administration. He behaved capably and loyally, and it was in those circumstances then that Justinian overthrows the Ostrogothic kingdom, and destroys Italy into the bargain. Once again, it's hard to see barbarian invasions here, isn't it?

It was in this fraught situation then that an opening was provided for the Lombards. The Lombards were another confederation of people who in the late 5th century were living basically in what is now lower Austria. This confederation included, at least—here's a good example of these confederations, of this ethnogenesis. The people we call "Lombards" were made up of Sueves, Heruls, Gepids, Bavarians, Bulgars, Avars, Saxons, Goths, Thuringians, and Romanized Pannonians. That's the Lombards. Again, there was no Lombard ethnicity. There's an interesting anecdote about how they got their names. They were, at an earlier point in their history, about to do battle with some of their foes and one of the goddesses who favored the Lombards went to one of the gods who either hadn't made up his mind or may have, but it would have been hostile, he said, when I get up in the morning, the people I see, those are the ones that I will favor. The goddess goes to the people who would become the Lombards, the "Winnili" they were then called, and tells them all to array themselves on a great field of battle, sort of outside the window that the god will wake up and look out and see them. All of the Lombard women gathered up amongst the Lombard men and they pulled their hair down and arranged it across their face so it looked like they had beards. The god wakes up and says, who are these Longbeards, Langobardi, Lombards. Who are these Longbeards? Probably that story is not true, but again, it's an example of the kinds of stories that these people tell about themselves, and it helped to form them as a people.

In 507 or 508, the Lombards defeated the Heruls, then moved across the Danube and settled in Noricum and in Pannonia—two old, Roman, Danubian provinces. There was no effective Roman force any longer in the west to stop them. Keep in mind where we are. We're in the late years of the 5th century, the early years of the 6th century, so there were basically no Roman forces.

By 546 or 547, they got a treaty. They fought for 20 years against the Gepids under their kings Audoin and Alboin. We know a fair amount about Audoin and Alboin. They seem to have been fairly effective rulers. The Romans were attempting to use them as auxiliary troops along the Danube. We know that Lombard, bear in mind what I said a minute about who Lombards are, Lombard contingents served against the Persians. We also know that Lombard contingents served in the Gothic wars. It's probably in that context that they learned something about the unstable situation in Italy. In 568 and 569, Alboin led the Lombards into Italy. They pretty soon took most of the great major cities, except Pavia, which held out until about 572, but once they finally took Pavia, they made it their capital, and Pavia would remain from now until the end of the 8th century the capital of the Lombard kingdom.

Unfortunately, Alboin was murdered by his chamberlain Peredeo in 572, who was a courtier, who appears to have been the lover of Alboin's wife Rosamund. Alboin had murdered Rosamund's father, the Gepid king. It's a gruesome story: He'd made a drinking cup out of the dead king's head and forced Rosamund to drink from it, so she was always kind of biding her time until she could get even, and she finally did. The Lombards chose Clef as their king. He was murdered in 574. Then, for about 10 years, the Lombards had no kings at all. A couple of aggressive dukes moved south in Italy and created vast duchies in Spoleto and Benevento, so to the south of Rome in both the east and to the south of Rome.

The Lombard kings in the 7th and 8th centuries were often highly accomplished rulers. They developed a very sophisticated legal culture, something that we've talked about in connection with some of the other barbarian peoples. But the Lombard kings faced a series of insurmountable challenges in the long run. First, they could never get control of the southern dukes, the dukes of Spoleto and Benevento. They simply could never get control of those dukes. Moreover, let's bear in mind we're after the Gothic wars; when Justinian won the Gothic war, he basically established and his successors did the capital, if you like, of the East Roman administration of Italy at Ravenna in the north under officers called "exarchs." The Roman administration at Constantinople never accepted the Lombards; therefore, the East Roman officials at Ravenna were always a problem for the Lombards, as indeed the Lombards were a problem for them. There was always hostility and tension.

On July 4, 751—thus making that day historically significant—the Lombards took Ravenna. But, by then, in lots of ways it was too late. The Lombards had been Arians. By about 680, they had converted to Catholicism, but they always had rather uneasy relations with the local population and constant antagonism from the popes. This antagonism with the popes played out in a whole variety of ways. The popes saw themselves as the protectors of the people of Italy and so on. But the lands that the papacy lay direct claim to, extending in a kind of a diagonal band across Italy, separated the Lombard kingdom in the north from the duchies of Benevento and Spoleto in the south. Whenever the kings tried to go south to suppress their unruly dukes, they crossed papal land. Every time they crossed papal land, the popes would oppose them. The popes would ask the government in Constantinople for assistance, and again and again and again, the government in Constantinople basically said, look to your own interest, we can't spare troops, money, or anything else to fight in Italy. Consequently, the popes turn to the Franks. They turn to Charles Martel, Charlemagne's grandfather, and to Pippin III, Charlemagne's father.

Pippin campaigned—and we'll talk about these issues in a little bit more detail in some later lectures—in Italy in 755 and 756. He defeated the Lombards and he forced them to hand over a great deal of land to the popes. After the Lombards had reneged on their promises, Charlemagne finally decided the only thing we can do here is put paid to these Lombards. They're going to be a constant provocation. In 773, he marches into Italy; in 774 he defeats the Lombards and puts an end to the Lombard kingdom, indeed naming himself Rex Langobardorum, "king of the Lombards." The Lombards are now off the scene, as indeed the Ostrogoths are off the scene. At the end of the day, only the Franks had a long-lived dynasty. The Merovinigians, followed by the Carolingians, the family of Charlemagne, were Catholic, were stronger than all their neighbors, enjoyed social cohesion inside their kingdom, and got on well over the long term with the Roman authorities.

One kingdom after another formed on Roman soil. Referring once again to the quotation I mentioned a lecture or two back, it was a series of imaginative experiments that got a little out of hand. Yes, by now there are kingdoms where once there were provinces, but Roman policy played every bit as much of a role as barbarian aspirations.

Lecture Fourteen
The Eastern Empire in the 5th Century

Scope:

The long reign of Theodosius II saw a great codification of Roman law, military successes in the Balkans, and continuing religious strife. The great Council of Chalcedon settled theological quarrels among the orthodox, but its formulations were rejected by Rome's eastern provinces. Theodosius was followed by a series of rather nondescript military men who maintained the Danube frontier against repeated attacks by the fearsome Huns. The 5th century also witnessed the rising prominence of court eunuchs and of the women of the imperial house.

Outline

I. In the last few lectures, we have been in the Roman Empire constantly, but we have not been looking at the empire itself. In this lecture we will turn specifically to the Eastern Empire.

   A. It should be recalled that when Theodosius died in 395 he divided the empire between his sons Arcadius and Honorius.

   B. The brothers were fierce rivals, and that rivalry had disastrous consequences.

II. Four themes will help us to organize our thoughts on the Roman east.

   A. First, let us look at the imperial succession.

      1. When Theodosius died in Italy, he left his 17-year-old son, Arcadius, as augustus in the Eastern Empire.

         a. He was under the domination of the master of offices, Rufinus, and the eunuch chamberlain, Eutropius.

         b. Eutropius persuaded Arcadius to marry Aelia Eudoxia, the daughter of the Frankish officer Bauto.

         c. The first in a long line of powerful women in the Eastern Empire, she produced five children.

2. Arcadius died in 408, leaving a seven-year-old son, Theodosius II.

   a. Theodosius II was made augustus at age one. He was well educated, bookish, pious, and not at all political.

   b. Theodosius II issued the Theodosian Code and built Constantinople's vast landward walls.

   c. As a boy and young man, he was under the influence of his two-years-older sister, Pulcheria. He made her augusta in 414.

3. Theodosius II died in 450 without a male heir. Marcian (an obscure courtier and soldier) was selected to marry Pulcheria, giving him thereby the legitimacy of a connection to the Theodosian house.

   a. When Marcian died the senate passed over his son-in-law and appointed another military man, Leo.

   b. Leo was acclaimed by his troops in Germanic fashion and was crowned by the patriarch of Constantinople.

   c. Leo chafed under the Roman general Aspar's influence and turned to the Isaurian Zeno, to whom he married his daughter Ariadne.

4. In 474 a baby son of Zeno and Ariadne was accepted as successor, but he died suddenly and Zeno himself became augustus.

5. On Zeno's death his widow Ariadne got the 60-year-old Anastasius accepted, and she married him to strengthen his position.

B. The Eastern Empire experienced new or disruptive political forces.

   1. Generals were highly influential.

   2. Palace eunuchs gained power and influence for the first time. They rarely maintained their positions for long and were roundly hated.

   3. Imperial officers and members of the senatorial aristocracy were more prominent than ever before.

   4. The women of the imperial family were intelligent and resourceful.

C. Foreign policy and war saw both old and new developments.

  1. The Persian frontier was, fortunately, peaceful most of the time.

  2. The emperors were free to concentrate on the Balkans.

    a. The Huns began plundering, crossing the Danube in 405–408, 422, and 434.

    b. The ambitious Attila became king in 434 and demanded a doubling of the tribute from 350 to 700 pounds of gold.

    c. The Huns claimed the Romans broke their agreements and raided in 440, 441, 442, and 447.

    d. Marcian was immensely lucky and got to reduce taxes significantly.

  3. The Goths were another serious Balkan threat.

    a. The Visigoths moved west between 408 and 412.

    b. For a time the Ostrogoths were seen as useful because they shared a common foe with the Romans: the Huns.

  4. As the Ostrogoths departed the Balkan frontier region, the Bulgars moved in and defeated local armies in 493, 499, and 502.

D. Constant religious strife created a number of problems.

  1. The problem of Arianism wound down for the Eastern Empire because almost all Arians were in the west.

  2. Theologians in Alexandria, Antioch, and Constantinople had fierce disputes on basic issues of Christology.

  3. Pulcheria and Pope Leo I collaborated on a new church council at Chalcedon in 451.

    a. Key problems surrounded the Monophysites, who emphasized Christ's divine nature, the Nestorians, who emphasized his human nature, and the orthodox (or Chalcedonians) who emphasized both simultaneously.

    b. Large areas of the Eastern Empire rejected the Chalcedonian formulation and were more or less permanently disaffected.

    c. Emperors struggled ineffectively for more than two centuries to find a theological formula that would reconcile all parties.

III. In sum, the situation in the east was complex and precarious.

    A. How important was the emperor? Some had been great, some ineffective, some nonentities.

    B. Shifting groups of nobles, eunuchs, military men, and imperial women contested for influence.

    C. The empire seemed little interested in the west and had minimal influence there, had a tense stalemate along the Danube, and was perhaps vulnerable to renewed trouble with Persia.

    D. Religious problems threatened relations with old, rich provinces.

Suggested Reading:

Holum, *Theodosian Empresses.*

Williams, *Later Roman Empire*, p. 101–124.

Questions to Consider:

1. Construct a balance sheet for the Eastern Empire: What were its key strengths and weaknesses? How promising were its prospects as the 6th century dawned?

2. Can you think of ways to account for the seemingly powerful position of women in the Eastern Empire?

Lecture Fourteen—Transcript
The Eastern Empire in the 5th Century

Welcome back once again to this series of lectures on late antiquity. This time, in Lecture Fourteen, we'll look at the Eastern Empire in the 5th century. In the last few lectures when we've been building and unbuilding these various kingdoms inside the Western Empire, we have actually been on imperial soil, and for a very long time, under imperial rule all the time, but we haven't actually been looking at the empire itself. We'd started off, of course, with a series of lectures on Diocletian and Constantine and the House of Constantine and so on and then the Roman government, and we looked at the empire. Now let's take a step back once again and look at the empire, in particular, the empire in the east.

I think you'll remember that when Theodosius died in 395, he divided the empire between his two sons, Arcadius and Honorius—Arcadius in the east, Honorius in the west. We've also noticed on a number of occasions that the brothers were fierce rivals, and in the end, their rivalry had some fairly serious, and indeed in some cases almost disastrous, consequences. What we want to do then is look at the Eastern Empire from the age of Arcadius very briefly, and then in a little bit more detail across the course of the 5th century.

I'm going to sort of organize my remarks, organize my reflections, on the empire in the east around a series of four themes. First of all, then, let's look at the imperial succession. Who became emperor and who were these people? When Theodosius died in Italy, he left his 17-year-old son, Arcadius, as augustus in the east. Arcadius was under the domination of the master of the offices—remember we've talked about all these great officers of the government. The master of offices is sort of the chief official administrative officer in the palace. He's under the domination of the master of the offices, a man by the name of Rufinus, and under the eunuch chamberlain, a man by the name of Eutropius. Eutropius was—and I'll have a little bit more to say about these eunuchs in just a minute—particularly influential. As far as we can tell, he's really the first of the eunuchs in the east to become a kind of a personality on the historical scene and to exercise considerable authority. Anyway, Eutropius persuaded Arcadius to marry a woman by the name of Aelia Eudoxia, the daughter of a Frankish military officer named Bauto. Again, we see these barbarian military officers holding very high positions, east and west, inside the empire. It's also interesting to notice that this man with a perfectly good Frankish name, Bauto, has a daughter with the beautiful Greek name Eudoxia. This is a sign I think of sort of the blending of cultures.

Aelia was herself the first in a long line of very powerful women in the east. She produced five children and we're going to encounter several of these very powerful women of the Theodosian House as we go along here in the next few minutes. Arcadius died in 408. He left a seven-year-old son, Theodosius II. Theodosius, born 401, died in 450, had been made augustus at the age of one. He succeeds to his father sort of at the tender age of seven. His was the longest reign in Roman imperial history. Of Theodosius himself we can say a number of things. He was very well educated, he was bookish, he was pious, and he wasn't at all political. He really was not a man who had a kind of a keen sense of all the swirling intrigue around him. He was not a nonentity. We've had occasion, for instance, in an earlier lecture to talk about the Theodosian Code, the great compilation of Roman law, effected by Theodosius. He didn't do it himself, but he caused it to be done. We might also notice that it was Theodosius II who vastly expanded and built the landward fortifications of Constantinople. The city of Constantinople, of course, sits on a narrow peninsula. It is virtually unattackable by sea, but of course it was wide open at the back door, so to speak, by land. Walls had been built across that landed strip in the 4th century, and now Theodosius vastly expands those walls during the course of his reign. He was not an utterly ineffective ruler.

As a boy and as a young man, he was very much under the influence of his two-years-older sister whose name was Pulcheria. He took the extraordinary step of making her augusta in the year 414. Since the inception of the tetrarchy, sources from time to time refer to the emperor's wife as augusta. The emperor of course is augustus, so occasionally the emperor's wife is referred to as augusta. This was not always the case, and it's perfectly clear that as augusta, the emperor's wife didn't have any specific area of responsibility, any jobs, any duties, or any legal position in the empire. Clearly some emperors' wives were very influential and important advisors, they had an important influence on their husbands, but they didn't have an official position. But for Theodosius to name his sister as augusta was really a very unusual step.

Pulcheria decided that she was going to look around for a suitable wife for her brother, and she eventually settled on the beautiful Athenais, the daughter of an Athenian philosopher. She was raised as a pagan. On her baptism—she was required to become Christian to be baptized in order to marry the emperor—she took the name Eudokia, another of these lovely Greek names and a name that passed very often through the women of the Theodosian House. Made augusta herself in 423, Athenais had three children. One of them was Licinia Eudoxia who married the western augustus Valentinian III. We're going to meet Valentinian III in our next lecture, so I'm not going to pause over him at this moment. But it is interesting to think about this marriage between the eastern imperial family and the western imperial family, which in better times might just have led to a restoration of imperial unity. In the end, that didn't happen, but again and again and again I've sort of played "what if" here, and so here's another really good sort of "what if." What if this marriage alliance had procured an heir who would succeed east and west? Well, that didn't happen.

Theodosius died in 450 without a male heir. A barbarian general yet again, a man by the name of Aspar, along with Pulcheria, Theodosius's sister, selected an obscure courtier and soldier, a man by the name of Marcian, who then reigned for about seven years from 450–457. In order to give him a connection to the Theodosian House, and also to confer upon him an element of legitimacy, Pulcheria actually married him. When Marcian died, the senate passed over his own son-in-law and offered the office to Aspar. Aspar declined, so the senate appointed another military man whose name was Leo. Leo reigned from 457 until about 474. It's interesting that Leo was acclaimed by his troops in Germanic fashion, presumably this means *acclamatsio*. They shouted out their approval at his becoming emperor, and perhaps also banged their swords upon their shields, which would have been a typical way for Germanic peoples to acknowledge, to acclaim their new ruler.

It's also the case, however, that Leo was crowned by the patriarch of Constantinople. It was the first time for this. Let's just look at this for a second. What we have here is an individual who doesn't really have an obvious claim to authority, he isn't connected to the Theodosian House, he doesn't have a wide backing, and he doesn't come from an old elite family. On the one hand, he gets legitimized by his troops; on the other hand, he gets legitimized by the patriarch.

It's rather interesting here that this attempt is being made to make this guy, as it were, look as good as possible, to make him seem as acceptable as possible as the imperial successor.

Leo chaffed under Aspar's influence and here let's just pause to say that isn't it interesting that even the senate wanted Aspar to accept the imperial title and Aspar declined. We don't find these barbarian generals, these barbarian military officials, ever trying themselves to take over the imperial office. There had been a few instances when usurpers had tried to do so without success. Here Aspar has a perfect opportunity and he turns it down.

Leo chafes under Aspar's influence and he turned to an Isaurian, a man from the east, from Asia Minor, whose name was Zeno. Leo married his own daughter Ariadne to Zeno, so this then attempts to kind of bring Zeno into the family—not the Theodosian House, mind you, but into the family. In 474, a baby son of Zeno and Ariadne was accepted as successor, but the baby died almost immediately and Zeno himself became augustus. He reigned a fairly long time actually, from 474–491. On Zeno's death, his widow Ariadne got the 60-year-old Anastasius, who reigns for 20 years then, from 491–511, she gets Anastasius accepted, and to shore up his position she married him.

This is very interesting. Going all the way back to Pulcheria choosing a wife for her brother Theodosius, on again and again and again over the course of the 5th century, the women of the Theodosian House, or after the death of Theodosius and particularly after the death of Pulcheria, the women of the imperial family are playing a decisive role in transmitting the imperial office and in getting men recognized as legitimate emperors. You might say, why didn't one or another of these women simply take over on their own? This had not het happened in Roman history. It wouldn't happen, as we'll have occasion to see, until the very end of the 8th century when a woman, Irene, did actually rule in her own name for a brief period of time in Constantinople. But at this moment in the 5th century, this is still unthinkable.

Influential right until the very end, Ariadne lived until 515 and she was a real force to be reckoned with. Anastasius himself, perhaps somewhat unexpectedly—he was a fairly obscure fellow when Ariadne kind of plucks him out and makes him ruler, or perhaps Ariadne was herself a very astute judge of character and recognized that Anastasius, despite his obscurity, was actually a man of considerable ability—in any case, Anastasius really does kind of shore up the eastern regime. In a little bit later lecture, we'll talk not in great detail, but we will say some things about what Anastasius himself was actually able to accomplish.

Here's a second theme then to look at. The imperial succession, generally speaking, it moved along fairly smoothly. We get the Theodosian House, this very long reign of Theodosius II. Then we get a series of military men, no one of whom strikes us as terribly attractive, terribly interesting, but all of whom were in their own way reasonably effective. None, at any rate, was a disaster. The first theme is imperial succession; things worked pretty well. In the second place, the east experienced a whole series of new or disruptive political forces. Sometimes the new ones weren't disruptive, sometimes the disruptive ones weren't new, but in any case, there were a variety of forces that we ought to acknowledge, at least briefly. Generals continued to be highly influential. We've mentioned here Bauto, we've mentioned Aspar, for example, and we could mention lots more if we wanted to pursue the subject in great detail.

For the most part, these individuals seem to have been loyal, they seem to have been well-intentioned, they seem to have been focused on the essential interests of the state, but there is a kind of troubling reminder of the military situation of the 3rd century, which we talked about at the very beginning of this course of lectures. Things did not ever descend into the kind of military anarchy that had characterized the 3rd century, but a troubling reminder of that period is formed by these generals.

Palace eunuchs began to gain power and influence for the first time. We hear something of eunuchs in the 4th century already. We hear of various officials in the palace who were responsible for the eunuchs, but it's in the 5th century that eunuchs in the east begin to be quite prominent. They rarely maintain their positions for very long. They were roundly disliked. But from the standpoint of the emperors and those who were closest advisors to the emperors, having these eunuchs around was not an entirely bad idea. They came from obscure backgrounds. They were people of no family whatsoever. Obviously, as eunuchs they were not going to produce heirs of their own. They had no independent power, they weren't wealthy, they didn't come from old elite families, and they were utterly dependent on the emperor. They could be dismissed at any moment and oftentimes they were dismissed after very short periods in office. They were very loyal and they were very efficient.

If you stop and think about it, it's hard to think of any other group of people whom the emperors could have had around themselves who would have been so unquestioningly loyal. It's just occasionally the case—we mentioned Eutropius, for example, who arranged Arcadius's marriage for him—that we find a eunuch who really becomes a kind of a personality in the sources, who becomes really important, but that is pretty rare. On the whole, they were sort of nameless, faceless individuals, but nevertheless, they are a force that begins emerging in the course of the 5th century. It is something somewhat new and potentially at least somewhat disruptive, if only because of all the controversy they occasioned in the Roman administration.

Something else we notice over the course of the 5th century, and some of this may be attributable in part to the fact that Theodosius II himself was (as I mentioned a moment ago) not very political on the one hand, and on the other hand, the fact that the women of the Theodosian House, though interesting, well-connected, and important, were generally speaking involved in projects other than managing the empire day in and day out. We'll come to those women in just a second. What happens is that members of the senatorial aristocracy, the old traditional elite of Rome, and various members of the high imperial administration—think back to an earlier lecture when we sort of detailed that administration—so holders of various high offices, some of these people became much more prominent than they had been in recent Roman history. Recall again that all the way back to the 3rd century, for instance, members of the senate had been gradually marginalized. They were denied high military offices; little by little, they were denied high offices in the state apparatus. What we begin to see in the 5th century is that some of these old traditional elites begin to come back in a fairly prominent fashion in the Roman Empire in the east.

Then there are the women of the imperial family. These women were intelligent, they were resourceful, and they were determined. As we've seen in the second half of the 5th century, they basically settled, time after time after time, the imperial succession. This is something utterly new in Roman history. Yes, of course there had been at various moments in Roman history certain very interesting prominent influential women, but to see this long series of women and their tremendous influences in the course of the 5th century is something quite new. The basis of their authority was, after all, they are connected to the emperors. They are key advisors, they have continuous access to the emperors, but they controlled vast wealth. They used this money in a number of interesting ways. In Constantinople, for example, by dispensing largess by various benefactions to the population of the city, the women built very, very strong relationships with Constantinople's population. These women were also pious and fiercely orthodox. We'll see in a few minutes some of the various consequences of their fierce orthodoxy. They were pious and fiercely orthodox, and they learned how to use the church. Among other things, they were great church builders, they were great church dedicators, but they also were able to work with the patriarchs of Constantinople, other bishops throughout the empire, and to extend their own influence through these means. The women of the imperial house were something new, something interesting, and something distinctive in the course of the 5th century.

In the next place then, the third of our themes is foreign policy and war. Here we have something old and something new. The Persian frontier was, for most of the 5th century, fortunately peaceful. I've emphasized again and again and it bears repeating, the Romans always knew the Persians were the great foe. When the Persians were on the rampage, the Romans had to go and deal with it. When the Persian frontier was peaceful, the Romans were freed, their material resources were freed, and their human resources were freed, to concentrate elsewhere. In the Eastern Empire, where is elsewhere? The Balkans, the Danube Frontier, that's of course always going to be the area that the Romans are going to focus on, are going to emphasize, when they are freed of other concerns, of other distractions that prevent them from focusing on the Danube and on the Balkans. What's the problem in the Danube and the Balkans? We're now into the 5th century, of course, and our Visigothic friends have been shipped west. The Visigoths are not yet an issue. We spoke in our last lecture about the Ostrogoths; the Ostrogoths are not yet an issue either. Right now, the big issue is the Huns. The Huns plundered over the Danube and in the Danubian Provinces between 405 and 408, again in 422, and again in 434. The ambitious Attila became king of the Huns in 434. He audaciously demanded a doubling of the tribute that had been being paid to the Huns, from 350 to 700 pounds of gold—an enormous of money.

I've mentioned this paying of tributes on a couple of occasions. At different times, of course, the Roman administration got other peoples to pay them tributes, and from time to time, the Romans paid tributes to other people. Yes, there was something sort of damaging in terms of reputation, damaging in terms of prestige in paying tributes to other people, but from time to time, as a temporary measure, it was an intelligent policy. If you can buy a little time, you can buy a little peace, because after all, you're otherwise going to focus your tax revenues on raising troops and supporting those troops so the troops could go out and do the work that sometimes a subsidy can do for you.

The Huns claimed, whether with justification or not is hard to say, that the Romans broke their agreements. In 440 and 441 and 442 and then again in 447, the Huns are sort of on the rampage again. In 447, Theodosius II offered an enormous indemnity, 6,000 pounds of gold as a kind of a signing bonus plus 2,000 pounds of gold per year, to get peace with the Huns. Was this a sign of Theodosius's general lack of political acumen? Was he advised to take this step? Why was he so incredibly generous? Basically, he wants to get rid of this Hun problem and apparently this enormous subsidy was able to accomplish this to some degree.

On his accession, however, Marcian refused the tribute. He felt that this was simply disgraceful, and Attila turned to the west. Interestingly enough, Attila seems to have felt that Marcian, having refused the tribute, the pickings might be a little bit better in the west. You'll recall we've mentioned in an earlier lecture that the master of the soldiers in Gaul, Aetius, had been using the Huns as a check upon the Burgundians, as a check on some other peoples too like Saxons and so on, but we needn't concern ourselves with them. The Huns then of course began to figure out, look, if you've got to hire us, we may be stronger than you are, so the Huns then began raiding in the west. In consequence of this, Attila attacked Gaul in 451.

It's very interesting that during this period, the late 440s to early 450s, Honoria, who was the sister of Valentinian III who was ruling in the west, sent Attila a ring. Did she send him this ring as a thank offering, did she send him the ring by way of establishing relations with him, did she send him a ring because she hoped to have his influence, his authority, his support? It's very hard to say. Attila interpreted it as an offer of marriage. This may have been another of the reasons why Attila turned his attentions momentarily from the east to the west in the Roman world. In any case, as we've seen, Attila attacks Gaul in 451 and somewhat surprisingly in the circumstances, he was defeated by this army of *Romanee*, made up of Franks and Burgundians and Visigoths and so forth, which Aetius put together. Attila then ineffectually attacked Italy in 452. Stories are told there that basically Pope Leo I sort of bought him off with an enormous subsidy. He returns to his homelands and died suddenly in 453. This was a great stroke of luck for the Eastern Empire. Marcian was immensely lucky and he immediately got to reduce taxes significantly, as he didn't have to pay tributes to anybody anymore.

Another serious problem in the Balkans of course, another threat, was the Goths. We've seen our Visigoths have moved west between 408 and 412, so they're off the stage. We also talked in our last lecture about how, once the Huns disappear as a significant threat, the Ostrogoths emerge. They've been under Hunnic domination for a considerable period of time. The Romans always had a kind of a love-hate relation with the Ostrogoths. From one point of view, they had a common foe in the Huns. There's always an element in foreign policy where you may kind of have a friendly relationship with somebody with whom you otherwise have no basis for a friendly relationship, precisely because you share a foe. That was really pretty much what was going on here. The Emperor Leo made an alliance with the Ostrogoths and it was in his time that Theodoric, one of their leaders, came to Constantinople as a hostage. Zeno, then—and we saw this in our last lecture so I'll just remind you— sort of solved the Ostrogoth problem by sending the Ostrogoths to Italy, where as we saw they established a kingdom, they worked very effectively and very loyally, until the death of Theodoric in 526, after which things began to go very bad indeed for Italy.

As the Ostrogoths departed the Balkans and the Balkan frontier region, the Danube frontier region, interestingly enough, a people called the Bulgars moved in. They defeated local army contingents in 493 and 499, and again in 502, so the Bulgars gradually blend with the local Slavic population. The Bulgars were a Turkish people, a steppe people who have come from the east to the west. Anyway, the

Bulgars blended with the local population, settled down locally, and began a long and intense relationship with the government in Constantinople. A new problem had risen up in place of the old one, thus far our third thing.

The fourth one is religion. There was constant religious strife and constant attempts in the east to find some way to address this religious strife. The problem of Arianism, which had risen acutely in the early years of the 4th century and which had persisted fairly significantly across the course of the 4th century, was for the most part winding down in the east by the end of the 4th century and into the 5th century for this reason: Almost all the Arians were in the west. Insofar as the Arians were in the west, this was not a big deal then for the government in the east. Theologians in Alexandria, Antioch, and Constantinople, however, the three great sort of intellectual powerhouses of the eastern Roman world, were now beginning to have fierce disputes on basic issues of Christology. When we talk about the fathers of the church, we're going to pick up some of these issues in a little bit more detail and we'll specify again in more detail just what's going on here, but for the moment let's just say this: Arianism had been a Trinitarian problem. How do you explain that God is three and one—Father, Son, and Holy Spirit—not three gods, only one God? How do you explain the doctrine of the Trinity? We saw that Arians were what we call "subordinationists." They subordinated Jesus to his father. Christology is that branch of theology that involves efforts to explain how Jesus Christ could at once be true God and true man. The Trinity is Father, Son, and Holy Spirit; Christology is God and man in Christ.

Pulcheria and Pope Leo I collaborated to get a new church council, which met at Chalcedon in the year 451, one of the great councils of the ancient church. The fundamental problem to which they had to address themselves was just this: There was a group of people who were called, to be sure by their opponents more than by themselves, Monophysites—monophysis, one nature. The Monophysites are "one-naturites." What does that mean? They emphasized Christ's divine nature, saying his human nature was only assumed and not utterly real. At the other end of the spectrum, however, there was a group of people called the Nestorians. The Nestorians, for example, emphasized Christ's human nature and not his divine nature. They said, for example, that Mary could not be the *theotokos*; she could not be the bearer of God.

The orthodox fell, as it were, smack in the middle. This was not because they'd made an enlightened compromise, but because quite simply the orthodox—that is to say, those who held to right teaching, which is what orthodox means—they argued, they believed, and they maintained that Christ was true God and true man. That was the teaching that was enunciated at the Council of Chalcedon, and that was the teaching that has become normative for western Christianity and also for eastern Christianity ever since. But there were large areas of the east that rejected the Chalcedonian formulation and that were more or less permanently disaffected from the regime in Constantinople. This is a matter of real consequence. In many subsequent lectures, we're going to keep bumping into this problem of religious strife in the east. We're going to see emperors again and again and again struggle, ineffectively to be sure in the long run, but struggle to find a theological formula that would somehow reconcile all of these contending parties.

In sum, the situation in the east was complex, precarious, and interesting in a variety of ways. We might ask, how important was the emperor? Some of these emperors had been great, some ineffective, some were nonentities, some were obscure, and some were really significant. We've noticed shifting groups of nobles, eunuchs, military men, and imperial women, contesting for influence. What will be the long-term consequences of this swirl of contention? The empire seemed little interested in the west. It had minimal influence there. It had a very tense stalemate along the Danube—Visigoths gone, Ostrogoths gone, Bulgars have moved in—and always there was a certain vulnerability to renewed trouble from Persia. Religious problems threatened relations with old, rich provinces and sometimes divided councils at the imperial court itself. The Roman Empire in the east was a very interesting, but nevertheless very successful phenomenon still, throughout the 5th century.

Lecture Fifteen
The End of the Western Empire

Scope:

The long reign of Valentinian III marked the beginning of the end. Valentinian was dominated by his mother, Galla Placidia, and by military men. One of the latter, Aetius, struggled mightily to maintain some semblance of Roman authority in Italy and Gaul, but he was able to do so only by means of a shifting set of alliances with various barbarian peoples. With the Western Empire reduced to parts of Gaul and Italy, the tax base dwindled and institutional structures collapsed. In 476 a barbarian general, Odovacer, deposed Romulus Augustulus and sent the imperial insignia to Constantinople, declaring that the west no longer needed an emperor. Rome indeed ended not with a bang but with a whimper. And the west would be without an emperor until Charlemagne was crowned in 800.

Outline

I. Now we finally come to the "fall" of the Roman Empire.

   A. We must bear in mind that no matter how fragile the Eastern Empire appeared, it was still a "going concern" and would remain one until 1453.

   B. As we shall see, the fall of the Western Empire was pretty much a nonevent.

II. In analyzing the fall of the Western Empire, we shall follow three basic themes.

   A. The imperial succession was more complex than in the Eastern Empire.

   1. Theodosius's son Honorius was under the thumb of Stilicho until his death in 408.

   2. After 408 Honorius was under the control of the patrician Constantius.

   a. Constantius married Galla Placidia (Honorius's sister) in 418; she had been married (forcibly) to the Visigoth Atawulf.

   b. Constantius was named augustus in 421.

3. Honorius died in 423 without male heirs. In 424 Theodosius recognized Valentinian III (born in 419 to Galla and Constantius) as caesar and in 425 as augustus.

4. Appearances can be deceiving: Theodosius II really had no influence in the west, and the court was dominated by Galla Placidia, while Aetius, the master of the soldiers, dominated the army and the Gallic nobility.

5. After the collapse of the Huns, Galla decided to try to get along without Aetius, and stupidly—as it seems in retrospect—had him murdered in 454.

6. In 455 a loyal follower of Aetius murdered Valentinian III.

7. The murderers of Valentinian put forward Petronius Maximus, a wealthy senator who married Valentinian's widow, Licinia.

8. Leadership in the west passed to Ricimer, a grandson of the Visigoth Wallia.

   a. Ricimer named a series of relative nonentities as emperors until his death in 472.

   b. It is interesting that—still—no barbarian claimed the imperial office.

B. The territory of the Western Empire continued to shrink.

1. Britain was effectively abandoned in 410, but Stilicho had begun pulling troops out of Britain in 407.

2. Northern Gaul, increasingly under Frankish domination, was effectively abandoned.

3. As the 5th century wore on, Roman control in Spain became a dead letter.

4. After the Vandal conquest, the situation in North Africa was tenuous.

5. Aetius had held things together with his shifting alliance with and against the Huns, but the collapse of the Huns cost him his life.

C. The financial and institutional structure of the Western Empire succumbed.

1. There were for all practical purposes no longer any tax revenues from Britain, northern Gaul, Spain, and Africa.

2. Italy and Sicily continued to "enjoy" old tax exemptions.

3. The rural elites, especially in Gaul, were largely disaffected and began to throw in their lot with the barbarians.
4. Traditional urban institutions were weakened.
5. The Roman Senate was weak and imperiled.
6. The state itself had no military capability.

III. The end when it came was a whimper, not a bang.

    A. Ricimer's last appointment, Olybrius, died almost immediately, and Leo sent Julius Nepos.

    B. Julius appointed Orestes as military commander, and he rebelled.

    C. Orestes named his son Romulus Augustulus as emperor, but troops led by Odovacer rebelled against Orestes and took control.

    D. Odovacer deposed Romulus on September 4, 476, and sent the imperial insignia to Constantinople, saying that the west no longer needed an emperor.

    E. The west would not again have an emperor until Charlemagne was crowned in Rome on Christmas in 800.

Suggested Reading:

Heather, *The Fall of the Roman Empire*.

Ward-Perkins, *The Fall of Rome*.

Questions to Consider:

1. From the 450s to the 470s, the Western Empire kept shrinking in various ways. How? Why?

2. How significant, really, was the deposition of Romulus Augustulus in 476?

Lecture Fifteen—Transcript
The End of the Western Empire

Welcome back once again to our series of lectures on late antiquity. This, the 15th in the series, is the end of the Western Roman Empire. Now we'll talk about the elephant in the room. I've been rather dancing around the question of the "fall" of Rome, lecture after lecture after lecture, throughout this course. We do need to bear in mind, as we saw in our last lecture, that however fragile the east might have appeared, it was still very much a "going concern." It would remain a going concern until 1453 when the city of Constantinople fell to the Turks. You may recall my mentioning in the first lecture or two that Edward Gibbon in his great *Decline and Fall of the Roman Empire* traced that story all the way down to 1453. What we're going to see as we go along here in the next few minutes is that the fall of the west was pretty much a nonevent. If it fell, it didn't make much of a sound. It wasn't particularly noticed by people at the time. It was only long after the fact that the fall of the Roman Empire was somehow seen to be a cataclysmic event, a great turning point in history. It was not so seen at its time.

It has been the subject, of course, of countless novels, movies, and plays, not to mention history books, some good and some bad. It's a story that somehow in its broad outlines seems incredibly familiar. Yet, I think we'll see, as we go along here, it's a story that in its actual details is not so familiar, and perhaps that is part of why I will invite you to think with me about this great nonevent that was the fall of the Western Roman Empire. Let me also signal an issue that I raised at the beginning of this course of lectures, and that is, what we're going to see here is the disappearance of a particular institutional, constitutional, political regime in those areas that had been the two western prefectures of the Roman Empire. We are not going to see here a collapse of civilization. We are not going to see here the end of a way of life. Certainly, those are the kinds of things, I think, that are implied by the fall of the Roman Empire. The whole idea that the glories of classical Greek and Roman civilizations succumbed to the blows of barbarism, that darkness descended, Europe plunged into the Middle Ages, the Dark Ages, and for a thousand years ignorance and superstition and barbarity prevailed. Only with the Renaissance did someone flip the lights back on and things began to improve. I'm caricaturing, of course I am, but at the same time I think probably most people listening to my words would agree that is sort of the way we understand this period. That's not the way we're going to understand it here, no.

We've already anchored into place some elements of not thinking about the period in those traditional ways. We've put a series of kingdoms in place. To be sure, we built a few and unbuilt a few; we mantled some and dismantled some, as it were. We've still got our Franks out there doing quite well, thank you. In a little bit later lecture, we're going to see that over in Britain the Anglo-Saxons are beginning to get themselves established. The Visigoths have still got a while to act upon the stage. They don't really get wiped out until 711, the early 8th century, so these kingdoms that were themselves politically, institutionally, legally, and governmentally the heirs of Rome are already in place. What we're going to do here, just to repeat again, is we're going to dismantle a political regime. We are not going to draw the curtain down on a phase in human civilization.

In analyzing then the fall of the Western Roman Empire, we're going to follow three basic themes. We looked at four themes when we talked about the east. On this particular occasion, we're not really going to talk about religious issues, but we're going to look at the other kinds of issues that we talked about in connection with the Eastern Empire in the 5th century. Broadly speaking, what we're going to talk about in this lecture is the Western Empire in the 5th century. We'll look at imperial succession and war and government and so on, but we won't be looking at religious issues because these, on the whole, are not a primary force or factor or issue for the west as they were for the east.

The imperial succession was more complex than it was in the east. Given what we talked about in our last lecture, the years from 450 when Theodosius II died down until the death of Anastasius in the early 6th century, yes, there was a series of fairly complicated imperial successions. But, on the whole, the east was a lot tidier than the west was. Let's have a little look at the situation in the west and see what we make of it.

Remember that Theodosius dies in 395, leaving his son Arcadius in the east and his son Honorius in the west. Theodosius's son Honorius who reigned from 395–423 was under the thumb of Stilicho, our friend Stilicho—we talked about him in some detail in an earlier lecture—until Stilicho died, indeed until he was murdered, in the year 408. Stilicho, we saw, had actually moved his base of operations to Ravenna in northern Italy when he was contending with the Visigoths. After Stilicho's death, Honorius then basically moved the capital of the Western Empire to Ravenna. Ravenna is going to be, then, sort of the last capital that the Western Empire actually has. You may recall my mentioning in the previous lecture that after Justinian reconquered Italy during the Gothic wars, he and then his successors established the base for Constantinople's rule in Italy in Ravenna, not any longer in Rome. It might have occurred to you to say, well, why is that? It's because from the early years of the 5th century on, Ravenna had actually been, not Rome, the western capital, and not Milan, Trier, or Arles, or the various other cities in the west that had been of real consequence in earlier times. Honorius moves the western capital to Ravenna.

After 408, Honorius was pretty largely under the control of the patrician Constantius. We've bumped into that term patrician a couple of other times. Let me just repeat that occasionally the imperial government would name someone *patricius*, patrician. It was an honorific title, it conferred prestige, it conferred great honor on the person to whom it was given, but it was not an office in the official Roman system. As patrician, you didn't have a job; you didn't have particular responsibilities. There's this man Constantius who has been named patrician, who is a person, in other words, of considerable influence, of considerable prestige, and as we'll see, of considerable authority. Constantius married Galla Placidia. She was Honorius's sister, half-sister actually. Constantius married her in 418. You may recall that she had been forcibly married to the Visigoth Atawulf. Constantius was named augustus by Honorius in 421. This is quite remarkable. We saw in the east the curious phenomenon of Theodosius II naming his sister augusta, but now we have Honorius naming as augustus Constantius, the husband of his half-sister Galla. It may occur to you to ask, why does he do this? In a sense he's trying to shore up the succession. Honorius has no male heirs.

He died in 423, and in 424, Theodosius II in Constantinople recognizes Valentinian III. Valentinian III was born in 419 to Galla Placidia and Constantius. We can see in a sense that there was method to Honorius's madness. Indeed, it wasn't madness at all. By naming Constantius augustus, he's attempting to shore up the western succession. He doesn't have an heir himself. We're attempting to retain the dynastic principle that has been so significant in the Roman world since the time of Constantine.

Valentinian III is recognized by the court at Constantinople as augustus, as legitimate successor. As we saw in our last lecture, Valentinian eventually married Theodosius's daughter Licinia Eudoxia. Here's a very interesting situation. The ruler in the west, Valentinian III, is the son of Galla Placidia, heiress of the Theodosian dynasty, and Constantius not a member of the dynasty. Valentinian is now married to the daughter of Theodosius II ruling in Constantinople. In the last lecture, I looked at this from the "what if" point of view from the standpoint of Constantinople. Now we can, as it were, turn around and look at this from the "what if" point of view from the standpoint of the west. It looks really, doesn't it, like the whole great Theodosian dynasty is kind of consolidating itself. Had there been further heirs of these marriages, it's quite interesting to reflect on what things might have been like. It didn't turn out that way and so we'll never know, but it is interesting to see this sort of consolidation, as it were, of the Theodosian House. It's also interesting to see that in east and west alike there was an awareness of the need to sort of shore up the dynasty.

Appearances can be a little bit deceiving actually when we look a little more closely at this particular situation. Theodosius II really didn't have any influence in the west. His capacity to influence the west, to influence policy in the west, to take serious steps in the west was small indeed, small verging on zero. Moreover, the western court was dominated by Galla Placidia. She is very clearly the dominant player at this time. That compares in quite interesting ways, does it not, with the very, very powerful role played by the women of the Theodosian House in the east at this particular period of time. It's a quite remarkable period when in the Roman world you have this series of very able, very ambitious, very determined women, in effect, calling the shots.

Galla Placidia dominates the western court, sort of the nerve center of government, but in some respects the real power in the west is in the hands of Aetius, this fellow that we've met a couple of times before, the master of the soldiers, the man who is basically dominating what's left of—we'll get to that Roman army in a second—what's left of the Roman army is basically dominated by Aetius. Aetius also is sort of in league with, gets along very well with, is loyal to, the Gallic nobility. The last great provincial nobility of the Roman Empire is still essentially the Gallic nobility. Aetius, on the whole, is in very good odor with those people. Galla Placidia is tending to dominate things at the court and Aetius, the master of the soldiers, is tending to dominate things out in the field, in this particular instance in Gaul. That's the situation in the 420s, 430s, as we move forward across the early decades of the 5th century in the west.

After the collapse of the Huns, Galla decided to try to get along without Aetius. You'll recall Aetius puts together this confederated army and defeats Attila and his Huns on the Catalaunian Field in 451. Galla now basically has come to the view that she doesn't like sort of sharing power with Aetius, she doesn't like all of his influence and his authority, and she was a very able, intelligent women in lots of ways, but she really did make a stupid mistake in basically having Aetius murdered in 454. She wants to consolidate power in her own hands and this was really a very, very foolish step indeed. If we were to look at the various markers along the path to the fall of the Western Empire, certainly one of them we would have to pay some attention to is the murder of Aetius in 454. How about some payback? In 455, a loyal follower of Aetius murdered Valentinian III. The murderers of Valentinian more or less had a plan. What they wanted to do was promote a man by the name of Petronius Maximums. Petronius Maximus was a wealthy western senator. He married Valentinian's widow Licinia. This looks a little like, doesn't it, the situation that had existed after the death of Theodosius II in the east, where a series of individuals married in order to establish their connections to the family, in order to gain legitimacy. Petronius Maximus, who otherwise has no claim on authority, marries Valentinian's widow, Licinia Eudoxia, the daughter of the eastern emperor, and he promised Valentinian's daughter, Eudokia, to his own son. Petronius Maximus promises Valentinian's daughter Eudokia to his own son.

We've actually met her and this situation a little bit earlier. Let me draw your attention back to this. Eudokia had been betrothed to the Vandal Huneric. When, therefore, Valentinian was killed, and when Petronius Maximus now betroths Eudokia to his own son, this of course enraged Huneric and prompted the Vandal sack on Rome in 455. In a sense, we keep looping back on some of these details and, as it were, just taking different vantage points on sort of who did what to whom, when, and under what circumstances.

Leadership in the west now passed these very tense circumstances to a man by the name of Ricimer. Ricimer was a grandson of the Visigoth Wallia. That's not a name to reckon with particularly, but we did bump into it on an earlier day. When the Visigoths left Italy and were marching into Gaul, Alaric had died; they were under the leadership of Alaric's brother Atawulf. In a feud, Atawulf died and Wallia took over fairly briefly as king or chief military officer among the Visigoths. His grandson Ricimer now basically succeeds the key military position in the Western Empire.

In principle, Ricimer's situation would very much have been that of these masters of the soldiers, these barbarian masters of the soldiers, indeed, in recent years, a man like Aetius, there for something like 30 years as dominant in the west. There wasn't anything particularly unusual or distinctive about Ricimer's position, these great *generalissimos* who had been sort of running the Western Roman Empire for a very long period of time indeed. Indeed, we go back all the way to Constantine to Constantius, even to Theodosius I, Theodosius "the Great," and we saw that one of the things that these eastern rulers often did is attempted to influence the west, whoever was augustus or caesar in the west, by controlling great military officers in that part of the empire. My point is that we shouldn't see Ricimer as an unusual kind of figure, as a strange kind of figure, as somebody who really requires explanation.

Ricimer then names a series of relative nonentities—it really is a gallery of people you've never heard of and don't want to hear about—as emperor in the west, until his own death in 472. In some cases, these people reigned a year or two, very, very brief reigns. They aren't particularly interesting people and I'm not going to take time here even to talk about them. The point to which I want to draw your attention is it's interesting that, still, no barbarian claims the imperial office. It never would have entered Ricimer's head to make himself the emperor, nor would it have entered his head to make another barbarian military officer emperor. He continued to find, essentially, Gallic aristocrats actually, and to bring them forward as emperors, as rulers in the Roman world. There was still some sense, maybe almost an atavistic sense, but there was some sense that the Roman world had to be ruled by Romans, even if in this particular instance, the Romans were Gallic aristocrats, Roman citizens, persons of Roman culture to be sure. They were people like, for instance, Sidonius Apollinaris, whose description of Theodoric II, the Visigothic king, I read in an earlier lecture. These were exactly the kinds of people; Sidonius actually was a relative of one of these emperors in this last period of the 5th century. This is the kind of people we're dealing with. The imperial succession in the west is complex, and I'm actually going to come back to it just briefly at the very end.

Let's look at a second issue. The territory of the Western Empire continued to shrink. That's the big point. That's the thing to keep very much in mind. We've seen already, for instance, that Britain was effectively abandoned by 410. The Romans basically pulled their troops out of Britain, left the people in Britain to their own devices, and for all practical purposes, Britain ceased being an effective part of the Roman Empire. We saw, for instance, Stilicho had begun pulling troops out of Britain, basically to put them along the Rhine frontier in 406–407, in that period of time. Northern Gaul, which was increasingly under Frankish domination over the last decades of the 5th century, the very period we're talking about, was effectively abandoned as well. You'll remember perhaps that the capital of the western prefecture had been moved from Trier to Arles in the south of France, so the Roman administration in much of the north of Gaul had just slowly, and almost silently, passed out of being.

As the 5th century wore on—and again we've seen this in earlier lectures, so I'll just remind you—Roman control in Spain became increasingly a dead letter. The Vandals, Alans, and Sueves had crossed the Rhine on the last day of 406, had gone into Spain. Eventually, of course, the Vandals crossed over into Africa. The Visigoths, as part of their treaty with the Romans, which settle them in Gaul between 411 and 418, had to fight shoulder to shoulder with the Romans in Spain against these other peoples in Spain. We've seen that the Visigoths in fact joined the Romans on three or four major campaigns. Gradually, however, what happened is that the Visigoths began establishing their own authority in Spain. We're still, at the moment here, a little before the defeat of the Visigoths by the Franks at Vouillé in 507. In the last decades of the 5th century, the Visigoths are already defeating the Sueves and advancing their own interests in Spain. Broadly speaking, effective day in-day out Roman administration in Spain is gone.

After the Vandal conquest of North Africa, as we have seen, Rome's hold on North Africa was tenuous at best. We have also had occasion to see that the Vandals basically stopped the grain supply to Rome. Broadly speaking, we think what happened is that the Vandals began—they weren't stupid enough to stop selling North African grain—but it seems to have begun going to southern Gaul and to Iberia more than to Rome itself. In any case, the point is that North Africa was no longer a source of food or tax revenues for the Roman state.

Over this period of time, Aetius had more or less been holding things together with his shifting alliance with and against the Huns. Interestingly enough, the very collapse of the Huns cost Aetius his life. This was the moment when Gallia looks around and says, I don't need this guy anymore, we can get rid of him. In lots of ways this was, as I said a few minutes ago, a really stupid step, a really stupid action. The effective territory of the Western Empire has been shrinking, and after the death of Aetius, and certainly after the death of Ricimer in 472, there's no longer really any effective governing presence in the west.

Let's come to a third theme and we can understand in a little bit more detail how it is that the western institutional structure had succumbed. First of all, there were for all practical purposes, no longer any tax revenues from Britain, from northern Gaul, from Spain, or from Africa. In some ways, going all the way back to the regime of Augustus Caesar, but certainly going back to the regime instituted by Diocletian, what we have seen is that the Romans developed a very complex, sophisticated system designed to extract the material resources of the Roman world to pay for a military establishment to defend that world. It goes without saying, doesn't it, that in the last years of the 5th century, the Eastern Roman Empire, which is still doing rather well in terms of collecting taxes and carrying out the various responsibilities that those tax revenues permitted them to carry out, was not going to fund the west. They were not going to send tax revenues to the west. They were not going to kind of help out the west. They had their own problems. They had their own issues to deal with and, as we've had occasion to see, the eastern and the western courts were quite frequently bitter rivals, so there was probably a certain grim satisfaction in Constantinople at the difficulties being experienced by the Western Empire at this period of time.

The territory is shrinking, the land paying taxes is shrinking, and the tax revenues obviously are shrinking dramatically. But, we might say, wasn't it the case that for a long time, the Roman administration could sort of believe that federate, these treated troops, Visigoths, etc., in a sense, having been assigned either land or tax—we saw that that's a little bit of an obscure and complicated subject, exactly how the federate troops inside the empire were financed. We know for example that federates outside the empire were paid a subsidy or a tribute, and they were supposed to defend a stretch of frontier outside the empire. It's when they come inside the empire that the situation gets a little bit complicated. In any case, the Roman administration could effect to believe for a considerable period of time that this new system, this imaginative experiment that had gone a little out of hand, was actually making up the deficit. That's fair enough and maybe. Little by little, it became clear that this system was a fiction. Effective Roman authority was simply not there. It looked like it was there, but there really wasn't much real Roman authority.

We also see some other interesting things. For instance, Italy and Sicily continued to "enjoy" their old tax exemptions. The last two areas in the west where the Romans actually could have extracted some tax had long historically been freed of taxes. We see something else, too. The rural elites—think again about Sidonius whom I've mentioned several times—especially in Gaul, were very largely disaffected from the Roman regime. They didn't want to pay taxes to this regime. This regime was no longer doing anything for them. We find these elites slowly but surely, in effect, throwing in their lot with the barbarians. We notice that traditional urban institutions—and we'll have more to say about this in later lectures when we talk about cities—were weakened. The Roman Senate was weak and was imperiled. Finally, broadly speaking, this Roman state in the second half of the 5th century simply had no military capability. It had no defensive forces; it had no offensive forces.

To return then to the imperial succession very briefly, we left it off when Ricimer died in 472. Now let's take it down to 476. The end when it came was a whimper, not a bang. Ricimer's last appointment, a man by the name of Olybrius, died almost immediately, and Leo from the east sent a man named Julius Nepos to the west. Julius appointed a man by the name Orestes as military commander. He almost immediately rebelled against Julius Nepos and drove him out. Orestes named his own son, a man by the name of Romulus Augustulus. Rome had been founded by Romulus, Augustus was the founder of the empire, and so we have Romulus and Augustulus, the little Augustus. The name is a diminutive. It's quite interesting, isn't it, that the last Roman emperor in the west bears the name of Rome's eponymous founder and of the founder of the empire. Anyway, Romulus Augustulus is named as emperor, but then troops led by a fairly obscure character by the name of Odovacer rebelled against Orestes and took control. Whatever passed for control at that particular period in time, I think you'd agree there doesn't look like there's much control on the scene anywhere, does there? Odovacer deposed Romulus Augustulus on September 4, 476, and he sent the imperial insignia to Constantinople saying that the west no longer needed an emperor.

That is all that happened. If we want an event, if we want a moment, if we want a date, if we want a fact that marks the fall of the Roman Empire, it is the deposition of the nonentity Romulus Augustulus by the equally nonentity character Odovacer, on September 4, 476. As we know, the west would not again have an emperor until Charlemagne was crowned by Pope Leo III in St. Peter's in Rome on Christmas Day in the year 800. That empire would, with some interruptions of course, have a thousand-year history until it was ended by Napoleon in 1806. All the while, let's keep in mind that there is an empire at Constantinople, which always thinks of itself as the Roman Empire, which always thinks of itself not as the heir of Rome so much as the continuation of Rome. For those in the east, there was no break; there was no change in continuity. But, whatever else we may say, after September of 476, there is no longer a Roman imperial regime in the western half of what had been the Roman Empire. There you have the fall of the Roman Empire.

Lecture Sixteen
The Age of Justinian, 527–565

Scope:

The 5th century was difficult for both halves of the Roman Empire. While Roman rule would never be restored in the west, the Eastern Empire raised up the remarkable ruler Justinian, one of the greatest of all Rome's emperors. This lecture focuses on Justinian's relentless efforts to reform Rome's government. One of the most important results of those efforts was the *Corpus Iuris Civilis*, the most significant codification of Roman law and perhaps the most influential collection of law ever assembled. Justinian secured peace with Persia and embarked on a series of campaigns in the west, reconquering North Africa and Italy and establishing a beachhead in Spain. Although these reconquests proved ephemeral, they signify Rome's determination to put right the wrongs of the previous generations. Like his predecessors, Justinian found that religious peace was beyond his grasp. He tried to find theological formulas that would reconcile contending groups. In 532 Justinian faced riots that nearly brought down his regime. In 542 Justinian's realm experienced the worst outbreak of plague in a millennium.

Outline

I. Justinian was unquestionably Rome's greatest ruler after Constantine, but his reign was preceded by two transitional ones.

   A. We met Anastasius in an earlier lecture.
      1. He secured the realm—making peace with Persia and holding his own in the Balkans.
      2. He reformed the small coinage, streamlined tax collection, and left a huge surplus in the treasury.
      3. He could not, however, obtain religious peace.
      4. When Acacius became Patriarch of Constantinople, he and Zeno wanted to find a way to reconcile the Monophysites.

   B. Justin seized the imperial office when Anastasius died.
      1. He was probably illiterate and was married to a barbarian who was a former slave.

2. Conventionally pious, Justin condemned his predecessors and wrote to the pope to end the "Acacian Schism."

3. He promoted many men who had languished under the previous regime, among them his nephew Justinian.

II. Peter Sabbataeus, later styled Justinian, was born in the same Latin-speaking region of Illyricum as Justin. In 527 Justin adopted him and named him coemperor.

    A. Already under Justin, Justinian wrote to the pope about the schism; built a church dedicated to Saints Peter and Paul; learned a lot of theology; served as *magistri militum praesentalis*, which gave him access to the court; and put on spectacular games in 521 (20 lions, 30 leopards, 4,000 lbs. of gold).

        1. He was modest and religious: In Lent he lived on water and wild herbs pickled in salt and vinegar.

        2. He married Theodora, a former actress and prostitute whom he could not legally marry until Justin passed a law permitting it. Until her death in 548, she was his key adviser.

    B. Justinian's long reign was dominated by military affairs, administrative reforms, and religious controversies. And there was a massive revolt and a devastating plague thrown in for good measure.

III. Let us look first at military affairs, where the results are decidedly mixed.

    A. In Persia, Shah Kavad had been ruling since 488, and he began to think about his succession.

        1. In 525 he asked Justin and Justinian to adopt his son Khusrau; they refused, and a war began.

        2. By September of 532, the war had ended on unfavorable terms for Rome: Rome gave up territory and paid 11,000 lbs. of gold.

    B. In Africa the results were more positive.

        1. We have seen that Hilderic was deposed by Gelimer; in 532 he appealed to Justinian.

        2. Virtually all the key advisers at court urged against war. (Remember that the war with Persia had just gone badly and expensively.)

3. Justinian decided to go ahead; he sent Belisarius with 10,000 infantry and 5,000 cavalry. Belisarius won a quick and complete victory.

4. In 534 legislation reintegrated Africa, with the functions of master of the soldiers and praetorian prefect combined in one man.

C. Justinian's war in Italy was a more complicated matter.

1. We have seen how the murder of Amalasuntha provided Justinian with a pretext for intervention.

2. Belisarius recaptured Rome in 536—the first time in 60 years that Rome was under imperial authority—but he was soon driven out.

3. The war took shifting courses, and Justinian sent a second force under Narses.

4. In 539 the Gothic king, Vitiges, persuaded Khusrau to open an eastern front.

5. In 540 Justinian decided to partition Italy, but Belisarius refused.

6. The war followed a tangled course for 11 years, until Narses won a great victory at Busta Gallorum in 551.

7. The "Pragmatic Sanction" of 554 put Italy under largely Greek speakers and military men.

8. The peninsula was devastated.

D. Spain represented a momentary interlude that is nevertheless revealing.

1. Amid factional squabbling, one group invited the Romans to intervene.

2. In 552 Justinian sent an army that established a beachhead in the southeast.

3. The Romans could not advance inland, and the Visigothic factions used the Romans as a tool in their quarrels for a generation, further weakening the already fragile monarchy.

IV. All the while he was engaged in widespread military activities, Justinian was also engaged in reforms of many kinds.

A. Some of Justinian's opponents claimed that the "reforms" of the "emperor who never sleeps" were merely pretexts to raise money for his ill-conceived military schemes.

B. Early in his reign, Justinian streamlined the imperial administration, tried to curtail the sale of offices, limited the public post, and amalgamated the civil and military administrations. (Here was a sharp departure from the regimes of Diocletian and Constantine.)

C. In 528 Justinian appointed a commission to gather previous legal collections, novels, and jurisprudence.

    1. The *Codex Justinianus* was issued in April of 529.

    2. In December of 530, a council of 16 under Tribonian tackled (allegedly) 2,000 law books and 3,000,000 lines of text. The Digest was issued in December 533.

    3. A parallel commission produced the Institutes in November of 533: This changed the shape of legal education in the empire.

    4. All together this was the *Corpus Iuris Civilis*, the most influential law book in human history.

V. Early in his reign, Justinian began legislating on religion and morality.

A. He persecuted Manichaeans and Samaritans, demanded that all pagans present themselves for instruction, forbade the keeping of brothels, limited grounds for divorce, and prosecuted homosexuals.

B. Justinian built or rebuilt 33 churches, most spectacularly Hagia Sophia.

    1. Hagia Sophia was built between 532 and 537 on plans by Anthemius of Tralles and Isidore of Miletus.

    2. The main floor of the church is 250 by 220 feet; the main arches are 70 feet high; and the dome is 180 feet from the floor, with 40-foot windows.

C. In the Eastern Empire there were effectively two churches: one Monophysite and one Melkite.

    1. In c. 543–544 Justinian condemned the "Three Chapters"—some of the works of three writers approved at Chalcedon but especially offensive to Monophysites.

    2. This divided the eastern churches even more and caused a schism in the west when Pope Vigilius at first went along and then demurred.

    3. In 553 Justinian held an ecumenical council that both affirmed Chalcedon and condemned the Three Chapters. This council has always been controversial and did not achieve peace.

VI. Justinian faced two great crises: the Nika revolt and the bubonic plague of 542.

  A. Constantinople was large and fractious, with the Blue and Green factions always poised to make trouble.

    1. In 532 the crowds in the Hippodrome demanded the release of some prisoners. When the government refused, the crowds rioted.

    2. Justinian survived the revolt, but he needed money to pay his Persian subsidy, was in the middle of his legal reforms, and was about to launch his war in Africa. It is remarkable that he survived and thrived.

  B. In 542 the Mediterranean world was devastated by bubonic plague—the first major outbreak since the time of the Peloponnesian Wars.

    1. Constantinople may have lost 230,000 people.

    2. The social, economic, and psychological shocks were enormous.

VII. The last years of Justinian's reign were inauspicious.

  A. Earthquakes shook Constantinople in 554 and 557; the latter brought down Hagia Sophia's dome.

  B. A shortage of bread prompted riots in 556, and a drought in 562 caused more rioting.

  C. In 562 there was a plot to murder Justinian.

  D. Legislation, reform, and military activity were at a standstill.

  E. Justinian had made no provisions for the succession.

  F. The Eastern Empire might itself have collapsed, but instead it drew strength from Justinian's reforms and persevered.

Suggested Reading:

Browning, *Justinian and Theodora*.

Maas, ed., *The Cambridge Companion to the Age of Justinian*.

Questions to Consider:

1. Justinian's reign was marked by successes, failures, and crises. Does he strike you as a great ruler?

2. What do you think of the persistent religious strife in the Eastern Empire? Was it inevitably intractable? Can you imagine a policy, especially perhaps one that was not tried, that might have resolved the controversies?

Lecture Sixteen—Transcript
The Age of Justinian, 527–565

Hello once again and welcome to Lecture Sixteen in this series of lectures on late antiquity. This time we're going to return to the eastern Roman world, in the 6th century in particular, and we're going to look at the reign of Justinian who became emperor in 527 and died in 565.

In lots of ways, Justinian was Rome's greatest ruler after Constantine. To be sure, Theodosius I, Theodosius "the Great" as he's sometimes called, was a very able and effective ruler as we saw. But I think that if we were somehow to kind of weigh up accomplishments, achievements, and so on, we would see that Justinian is really quite a remarkable figure in many ways. But before we come to Justinian, let's just go back to the east, briefly go back earlier in time in the east to Anastasius. You'll recall perhaps that we met Anastasius a couple of lectures earlier when we were talking about the Eastern Empire in the 5th century. Anastasius reigned from 491–518. He sort of came at the end of that group of figures I discussed who came after Theodosius II.

I'd mention that very briefly Anastasius kind of shored up the regime. What exactly did he do? He secured the realm. He got a peace with Persia and he held his own in the Balkans. Those were always the two great objectives of eastern Roman policy. He reformed the small coinage, a modest economic measure, he streamlined tax collection, and he left a huge surplus in the treasury. We're going to see that Justinian spent it all in a big hurry. Anyway, Anastasius left lots of money in the treasury. He couldn't get religious peace. This will be a constant theme in the eastern part of the Roman world, from now really until Muslims conquered most of that world and rendered the religious divisions irrelevant. In any case, for a long time, it's a serious problem.

When Acacius became patriarch of Constantinople in the year 472, he reigned as patriarch until 489, he and Zeno wanted to try to find some way to reconcile the Monophysites. There are substantial numbers of Monophysites in Syria. There are substantial numbers of Monophysites in Egypt. They're in other places as well, very important eastern areas of the empire, and the government wants to find some way to reconcile them. Acacius and Anastasius together issue a document called the *Henotikon*. Actually, Acacius and Zeno and—then Anastasius carries on with this policy—issue a document called the *Henotikon*, the act of union. But all Chalcedonian Christians rejected it. They simply could not get Chalcedonian Diophysite—divine and human natures, two natures in Christ—they couldn't get Chalcedonian Christians to go along with this. Anastasius was a committed Monophysite. Zeno may very well have been much more kind of political. He may have just been looking for some way to kind of cut a deal. Anastasius is himself a committed Monophysite. The schism, the "Acacian Schism" as it's called, when basically the Church of Constantinople is cut off from many other of the churches around the Mediterranean world and from the church in Rome and the bishops of Rome, the pope, the Acacian Schism persisted right down to the death of Anastasius in 518.

When Anastasius died, he was succeeded by a man named Justin, Justin I. Justin reigned only nine years, 518–527. He seized the imperial office actually when Anastasius died. He was probably illiterate. He was married to a barbarian woman who had been a former slave, so this is not a character who comes from a very elegant, a very sophisticated, a very prominent background. He was a man who was conventionally pious. He condemned his predecessors for their Monophysitism, for their tampering with the formulation of Chalcedon, and he wrote to the bishop of Rome. He wrote to the pope to bring an end to the Acacian Schism.

Justin promoted a good many men who had languished under the previous regime. You may recall my mentioning that over the course of the 5th century, certain of the old social elites, the senatorial elite, etc., had actually begun becoming a little bit more prominent, a little bit more visible, in the east Roman Empire than they had been in the 4th century. To a sort of a rough soldier like Justin, these were not the kind of people he liked. Basically, he was promoting other people, people who had been somewhat more obscure, and who had really languished under the previous regime. One of these was his nephew Justinian.

Peter Sabbataeus, as he was born, later styled Justinian, was born in the same Latin-speaking region of Illyricum as Justin himself. They came from just over the edge into the Eastern Empire, but from a Latin-speaking area. You may recall way back when we talked about Stilicho hoping to use the Visigoths to sort of hive Illyricum off from the Eastern Empire to reattach it to the west because it was a Latin-speaking area and there were certain obvious connections. Be that as it may, in 527 Justin adopted Justinian and named him coemperor. Already under Justin, when Justin is ruling, Justinian wrote to the pope about the Acacian Schism that had just been ended. He built a church dedicated to Saints Peter and Paul. These are the two great patron saints of Rome. For a ruler in the east to build a church dedicated to Peter and Paul is sending a very clear message to the bishop of Rome.

Justinian learned a lot of theology. He kind of imagined himself sort of a reasonable expert in the area of theology. He had served under Justin as *magistri militum praesentalis*. What this means basically is that there were masters of the soldiers out there in the provinces leading the field armies of the Roman Empire, but there was always an army present to the emperor; the emperor had an army nearby. So Justinian was the head of the forces that were stationed near the emperor. That position, of course, gave him access to the court. If you were a general with a field army way out in heaven knows where, then you weren't in constant connections with the court. Justinian, as the head of the praesental soldiers, did have regular, indeed daily, access to the court.

In 521, as a way of kind of introducing himself into society, he put on spectacular games. There were 20 lions, 30 leopards; he spent 4,000 pounds of gold on his games. To put that in perspective, remember Constantine issues the gold solidus, stabilizes the currency of the Roman world, currency of account. The solidus is struck at 72 to the pound. Justinian just spent 288,000 solidi, putting on games to introduce himself into society. Let's remember that an ordinary Roman soldier, to be sure he gets food and fodder rations, and that counts for something, but the salary of an ordinary Roman soldier to take but one example was about five or six solidi per year. Justinian just spent the annual income of tens of thousands of men simply to introduce himself to society. You can see where Anastasius's big surplus in the treasury is going.

Justinian himself, before all of that, was actually a rather modest man, and he was a very religious man. We know for instance that during Lent he lived on water and wild herbs that had been pickled in salt and vinegar. He wasn't profligate, he wasn't ostentatious for the most part in his life, and putting on those games was not simply a display of extravagance. It was a well-calculated display to earn him the support, the warmth, the good feelings of the population of Constantinople. Justinian married a woman by the name of Theodora. She's a very colorful character in lots of ways, a former actress and prostitute. Given her earlier career, it was illegal for Justinian to marry her. Justin then passed a law that permitted the marriage. Justinian then went out and married Theodora, and she served as really one of his very most important advisors, down until her death in the year 548.

Justinian's long reign was dominated by military affairs, by administrative reforms, and guess what, by religious controversies. Then, there was a devastating plague and a big rebellion thrown in just for good measure. Obviously, it was a long and very busy reign, so let's go through at least some of the highlights of this reign, this age of Justinian.

Let's begin with military affairs. We've encountered Justinian already in terms of some of his western campaigns. I think you'll be prepared to believe me when I say that the results of Justinian's military policies are decidedly mixed. In Persia in the first place, for example, Shah Kavad had been ruling since about 488. He's now beginning to think about his succession. In 525, he had asked Justin and Justinian to adopt his son Khusrau. Remember my mentioning in an earlier lecture that sometimes the Roman authorities, the Roman emperors, would adopt as sons various rulers, leaders of other peoples and so on, so a fairly traditional move at this particular moment. Justin and Justinian refused, in this case, and war began. War in the east was very often a dangerous and expensive proposition for the Romans and that's precisely the way this one turned out. By September of 532, the war ended on utterly unfavorable terms for Rome. Rome had to pay 11,000 pounds of gold to the Persians, as a result of being defeated in this war.

In North Africa in the war against the Vandals, the results were, in some ways, more positive. We've seen for example that Hilderic had been deposed by Gelimer in 532. It was thought that he was a little bit too pro-Roman, and that this had served as Justinian's pretext for invading Africa. It's interesting that virtually all the key advisors at court urged against this war. Let's remember, the war in Persia had just gone very badly and very expensively. Justinian decided to go ahead nonetheless. In lots of ways, he was a very conservative, traditional Roman. In a sense, he wanted his Western Empire back, so this was part of his motivation. When he sent his great General Belisarius with 10,000 infantry and 5,000 cavalry, Gelimer, interestingly enough, was tied down by a revolt in Sardinia—the Vandals had conquered the islands in the western Mediterranean—which Justinian had very cleverly fomented as a distraction. Belisarius won a very quick and complete victory. We needn't pursue the details very far.

In 534, legislation reintegrated Africa with the function of master of the soldiers, and in effect praetorian prefect, combined in one man. We're going to bump into another couple of examples of this as we go along here, and it points toward the future. You may recall when we go back to the time of Diocletian and Constantine, one of the things that they had done was very sharply, clearly, carefully differentiated civil and military power. One of the things we're now going to see is a blending of civil and military power. We see this for the first time in Africa in the settlement after the defeat of the Vandals. Justinian's war in Italy was in lots of ways a much more complicated manner. We've talked about this when we talked about the Ostrogothic kingdom and the end of the Ostrogothic kingdom. We saw how the murder of Amalasuntha by Theodohad had provided Justinian with a pretext for intervention. You'll notice that he also had looked for a pretext to intervene in North Africa.

The troops come; Belisarius who had been victorious in North Africa now launches his campaign in Italy. Over the next 20 years or so while the Gothic war is being pursued by the authorities in Constantinople, it seems that neither Belisarius nor his successor, his general and leader of this war, a man by the name of Narses, ever quite had adequate resources, adequate manpower, or adequate financing. This may be of course partly a result of Justinian not being able to persuade everybody at court that they should commit resources, it may have been because of that enormous subsidy being paid to the Persians, or it may have been because the African campaign after all had been expensive. There are a lot of things going on. In any case, Belisarius enjoyed some early successes in this war. For instance, in 536 he recaptured the city of Rome. For the first time since 476, the city of Rome was nominally under imperial authority. Belisarius was then very shortly after this driven out of Rome. You may recall my mentioning on an earlier day in an earlier lecture that during the Gothic wars the aqueducts to Rome had been cut. That was one of the ways of course of laying siege to Rome.

You cut the aqueducts, the people in the city don't have adequate water supply.

The war in Italy took shifting courses back and forth and back and forth. Justinian finally sent a second force under the general Narses. In 539, the Gothic king, Vitiges, persuaded Khusrau, the Persian shah, to open an eastern front in the war. The Persians sort of did their part, although they rarely needed much prompting to attack the Romans. They attacked in 540, they attacked in 542, and they attacked in 544. Justinian is trying to deal with Italy, plus now he's got problems in Persia, as well as, it turns out, an Arab revolt along his eastern frontier and also a revolt in Armenia. So Justinian had got problems all over the place. He concluded a five-year truce in the east. In 540, he seems almost as a council of despair to have thought about partitioning Italy. What's interesting is that Belisarius was in Italy and he absolutely refused. There were some at court who thought that actually Belisarius was getting too big for his britches and that maybe he himself indeed actually wanted to take over in the west. I don't think that's probably the case. It does seem that Theodora never really fully trusted Belisarius. Be that as it may, the plan to partition Italy between the Goths and the Romans came to nothing. The war followed a tangled course for 11 more years until Narses won a great victory at Busta Gallorum in 551. By 554, a document called the "Pragmatic Sanction" put Italy basically under largely Greek speakers—a regime for the east was imposed on Italy—and largely military men. Once again as had been the case in North Africa, so too now in Italy, a civil and military administration is blended.

Fundamentally, however, the great fact to take away from the Gothic war is that the Italian peninsula was devastated. In lots of ways, the end of the ancient world in Italy doesn't trace to any of the issues we've talked about in our earlier lectures; it traces to these terribly devastating Gothic wars. Spain represented a momentary interlude, which is nevertheless interesting and revealing. Amidst factional squabbling in Spain, one group invited the Romans to intervene. In 552, Justinian sent an army, which established a kind of a beachhead in the southeast along the Mediterranean coast of Spain. The Romans couldn't advance inland and the Visigothic factions actually used the Romans, the ones settled along the coast, as a kind of a tool in their quarrels for about a generation. I had mentioned this on an earlier day as one of the things that actually weakened the already somewhat fragile Visigothic monarchy. In any case, what's interesting and revealing about it is you'll notice Justinian reconquers North Africa. Justinian launched looked like being a reconquest of Italy. Justinian was indeed going about systematically, step by step, the process of trying to recapture Rome's lost western provinces.

All the while that he was engaged in widespread military activities, Justinian was engaged in reform activities of many kinds. In this he sort of reminds us of Diocletian and Constantine—battles all over the place, but also big and ambitious governmental programs. Some of Justinian's opponents claimed that the "reforms"—as he was called the "emperor who never sleeps" and this was not a compliment—were merely pretexts to raise money for his ill-conceived military schemes. That's not an entirely unfair criticism of Justinian. He basically kept raising more money so that he could spend it on these various military campaigns. Early in his reign, Justinian streamlined the imperial administration, got rid of a certain number of officers, and blended the competencies of certain branches of the government. He tried to curtail the sale of offices and he tried to get rid of that form of venality that had been an old and traditional part of the Roman way of doing things. In many areas, in many aspects, he was amalgamating in the central government as indeed in the local governments in Africa or in Italy, the civil and military administrations. Here, indeed—and I've emphasized this already, but it bears emphasis—there's a sharp departure from the regime of Diocletian and Constantine.

In 528, Justinian appointed a major commission to gather all of the previous legal collections, all of the novels (novels aren't lovely books—the novel is born in the 17th century—novels are *novellae*, new laws) to collect all of the earlier legislation, all of the novels, all of the laws in other words issued between the compilation of Theodosius II in the 430s and Justinian's own day, and finally all of the jurisprudence of the Romans, all of the science of the law—the writing of the jurist consults. In April of 529, the *Codex Justinianus* was issued. This was Justinian's compilation of Roman law that had basically the material that had been in the Theodosian Code, plus all of the new laws, plus all of it sort of revised and streamlined yet again. In December of 530, a council of 16 working under a man named Tribonian—one of the great legists in history—tackled, they said, two thousand law books and three million lines of text. In

December of 533, they issued the Digest. The point of the Digest is this is a book on the theory of Roman law. This is Roman jurisprudence. This is not the individual laws and enactments; this is the theory behind the law, the science of the law, *Iuris Prudencia*.

A parallel commission, meanwhile, produced in November of 533 the Institutes. The Institutes were basically a rationalized, streamlined, abridged form of the *Codex* with a certain amount of jurisprudential material included that was for the purpose of teaching lawyers in law schools, so this was the great textbook for law. It basically changed the shape of legal education in the Roman Empire. Taken all together, then, this body of legal material is what we call the *Corpus Iuris Civilis*, the body of civil law. It is quite simply the most influential law book issued in human history.

Early in his reign, what is more, Justinian began legislating on religion and morality. He persecuted Manichaeans, for example, he persecuted Samaritans. He demanded that all pagans—so there were still pagans around—present themselves for instruction in the Christian faith. He forbade the keeping of brothels. He limited the grounds for divorce in the Roman world, and he prosecuted homosexuals. Justinian was a man of very stern, traditional Roman morality and so he issues a whole variety of laws on various aspects of the moral dimensions of life. Justinian built or rebuilt 33 churches. Most spectacularly, of course, he built his great church of Hagia Sophia, holy wisdom, in Constantinople itself.

Hagia Sophia was built between 532 and 537 on plans drawn from Anthemius of Tralles and Isidore of Miletus. What's interesting here is these were not two of the traditional architects of the city; these were two mathematicians. It's pretty clear that Justinian set out to get something different, something new. Indeed, the great Church of Holy Wisdom has some things in common with churches that had been built before, but it's also rather different in certain respects. It's a centrally planned church. It's actually a church that looks like two great basilicas, two rectangular buildings, laid down together as a Greek cross. The main floor of the church is 250 x 220 feet; it's huge in there. The main arches are 70 feet high. The dome stands 180 feet above the floor and it rests on, appears to rest on, 40 windows, so that in the brilliant morning or evening sunshine, when the light comes through the windows of the dome, the dome itself appears to be floating. It appears that nothing is holding it up. On entering the church for the first time, Justinian is reported to have said, "Solomon, I have outdone you."

Justinian appointed more bishops than anyone before him had ever done, but he couldn't gain consensus. In the eastern parts of his empire, there were effectively two churches: one Monophysite and one Melkite—that is to say they followed the *malkā*, the ruler, the emperor—so the Melkite Church is the official name for the Chalcedonian Imperial Church in the east, as opposed to Monophysite, but there were also Nestorians round about in the east, as well. In 543–544, Justinian, on the advice of some of his advisors, condemned what were called the "Three Chapters." The Three Chapters were the writings of three relatively minor theologians who had been approved explicitly at Chalcedon, but were seen as particularly offensive by the Monophysites. Justinian's really trying to get a good bargain here. What he basically is sort of saying is, look, can't we condemn these three guys, or some of their writings, and wouldn't the Chalcedonians accept that and then the Monophysites would be happy? The point is, of course, that the Chalcedonians were not going to accept this.

This divided the eastern churches even more and it caused a schism with the west, not least because Pope Vigilius, bishop of Rome at the time, first disagreed, then agreed, then disagreed again. He went back and forth on the question of the Three Chapters and whether to accept them or not. If you know Dante's *Inferno*, this got Vigilius put in hell. In 553, Justinian holds a great ecumenical council that both affirmed Chalcedon and condemned the Three Chapters. This council has always been controversial, but in any case, it did not achieve peace in the Roman world. Peace on these contentious religious issues was just always beyond the government's capacity to achieve.

Governmental reforms, religious issues, foreign policy, all the traditional fare of Roman history, Justinian also has a couple of really bad breaks in his reign, or at any rate, two rather cataclysmic events. The first of these is the so-called "Nika revolt," and then the second, the great plague of 542. Constantinople was a large city. It was a fractious city. It was a factious city. The factions in the city were interestingly enough divided along the lines of the cheering sections in the Hippodrome. The most prominent of these were called, at the time, the "Blues" and the "Greens." There were also

"Whites" and "Reds," but we know a little bit less about them. People have tried for years to see, did the Blue faction and the Green faction, did they represent ideological points of view? Did they have particular social backgrounds or origins? Did they represent certain religious policies? It's been very difficult to identify this. What they clearly were are cheering sections. They were fans, if you will, for various of the horse races in the Hippodrome, but they could be incredibly volatile.

In 523, the crowds in the Hippodrome demanded the release of some prisoners. The emperor would very often go to the Hippodrome to go to the races. When he was there, sometimes the crowds would acclaim him and cheer and clap and all that sort of thing, and sometimes they would clamor and demand things of the emperor. That's what happened on this particular occasion. When the government refused, the crowds rioted, rampaging through the city they shouted, *Nika*, victory, hence the Nika revolt. Churches and public buildings were burned down. Some people in the city threatened to elevate a rival emperor. Justinian, it's reported, actually contemplated abdication, but his resolve was steeled by his wife Theodora. She told him that purple makes a good winding sheet. Justinian finally sends troops under Belisarius into the Hippodrome and there were thousands of casualties. This was a replay of something that Theodosius had done in Thessalonica a long time before.

The revolt had a variety of causes. Justinian and Theodora, for example, spent money on wars, and the populace wanted the money spent on them. Old elites were increasingly marginalized and angry. That's a step that Justin had actually begun taking. It was undoing some of the things that had been going on in the 5th century, but in any case, those who were being marginalized and moved to the edge were a little angry. Many of the legal and administrative reforms were unpopular because, as I suggested a few minutes ago, they were basically viewed as contrivances to raise money to fight wars which didn't always turn out very well. Justinian survived the revolt, but he needed money to pay his Persian subsidy. He was in the middle of his legal reforms. He was about to launch his war in Africa. He was just shortly before he was going to launch his war in Italy. It's just before he was about to launch his war in Spain. It's remarkable that he survived and, in certain respects, thrived.

In second place, then, there was the great plague. In 542, the Mediterranean world was devastated by a bubonic plague. It was the first major outbreak of plague in the Mediterranean world since the plague that had run through the Greek world, and indeed much of the wider world, during the time of the Peloponnesian Wars in the 5th century B.C. Some of Justinian's military affairs, it appears, were dictated by a lack of men, by a lack of manpower. It's been estimated that the city of Constantinople may have lost some 230,000 people to this plague, almost a quarter of a million people; that's quite remarkable. The social, the economic, and the psychological shocks of this plague were devastating in the Roman world. When we think of Justinian's reign, we think of all the things that he tried to do, of all this wide range of activities, but then let's remember that he faces this plague with all of its devastating consequences.

The last years of Justinian's reign were in a variety of ways quite inauspicious. Earthquakes, for example, shook Constantinople in 554 and in 557; the latter brought down Hagia Sophia's dome. It had to be rebuilt. There was a shortage of bread in the city, which prompted riots in 556. A drought in 562 caused yet more rioting. In 562, there was indeed even an attempt, a plot, to murder Justinian.

In the last few years, maybe even as much as the last decade, the legislation, the reform, and the military activity that had marked this energetic reign in earlier years had come virtually to a standstill. Justinian, moreover, had made no provisions for the succession and had no male heir himself. In such circumstances, given all of these problems, given all of these difficulties, and given as we saw in the previous lecture, the end of the Western Empire, the Eastern Empire too might very well have collapsed. Instead, in interesting ways, it drew strength from Justinian's reforms, it persevered, and over the course of the 7th and into the early 8th century, as we'll see in a future lecture, it reinvented itself as an empire that we will call Byzantine.

Lecture Seventeen
The Christianization of the Roman World

Scope:

How did an obscure religious sect from a small, insignificant province emerge, grow, and spread all over the Roman world? The question has fascinated people for almost two millennia. In this lecture we will look at the attractiveness of basic Christian teachings, at the slow but steady emergence of a Christian church (a structure no other ancient religion possessed), and at some of the ways in which early Christians defined themselves and differentiated themselves from their pagan and Jewish contemporaries. The lecture will conclude by revisiting the legislation and conversion of Constantine in order to bring those crucial developments into sharper focus and to set the stage for the new faith's success among the Roman elite.

Outline

I. The most remarkable development during Roman imperial times was the triumph of Christianity.

    A. Christianity had serious competitors and had to forge a distinctive identity and effective institutions.

    B. Christianity produced a culture that was in many ways the defining feature of late antiquity.

    C. The process of Christianization is complex: One might contrast "adhesion" and "conversion." Christianization pertains to a whole complex of processes—social, political, ideological, institutional, religious—that captures a broader sense of what was happening at the time.

II. Christianity emerged and spread in a world with old, deeply rooted religious traditions and practices.

    A. Mithraism was an Iranian cult that flourished in the 2nd and 3rd centuries; over 400 cult centers are known.

    B. Gnosticism was a movement whose origins are complicated and contested, and Christian writers treated Gnosticism as either a heresy or a form of paganism.

C. Manichaeanism was widespread and prominent. It may be regarded as a highly developed Gnosticism or as rooted in ancient practices.

D. Judaism was the primal competitor: Perhaps 10 percent of the empire's population in Christ's time was Jewish, and they were actively proselytizing.

    1. The Romans were generally tolerant of Judaism, although less so after 313.

    2. Christian attitudes were derived from Saint Paul, who had taught that Christianity and Judaism could not coexist.

III. Christianity arose in a world with old, deep pagan traditions.

A. *Ta patria* represented the religious rituals of the civic cults that were part of everyone's inheritance.

B. The ordinary events of life were attended by religious rites: birth, death, marriage, war, peace, planting, and harvesting.

C. Civil celebrations and official calendars were infused with religious ideas.

D. Conversion involved, therefore, much more than a change of intellectual allegiance.

IV. There were pagan critiques of Christianity.

A. Pliny dismissed Christianity as a superstitious novelty.

B. Medical and scientific writers dismissed as absurd the Christian (and Jewish) idea of creation *ex nihilo* ("out of nothing").

C. Celsus was Christianity's sharpest and most serious critic.

    1. He said the idea of the incarnation was scandalous and shameful, that the resurrection of the dead was physically impossible, that the claim for one god was extravagant, and that a common criminal who lived recently could not be a god.

    2. Celsus obviously took the trouble to learn a good deal about Christianity, as his mocking refutation shows.

V. Amid their critics and competitors, Christian writers began to forge an identity for Christians.

A. In the 2nd century, the Apologists stepped to the fore.

1. Justin Martyr wrote several apologetic treatises. His *Dialogue with Trypho the Jew* attempted to differentiate between Christianity and Judaism, and in two Apologies he argued that Christian doctrines were compatible with Greek thought. He also taught the Theft Theory.
2. Tertullian was the first Latin apologist.

B. Many other writers could be cited, but they have certain things in common.
   1. Some were obviously concerned to differentiate between Christianity and Judaism.
   2. Some wished to emphasize similarities between Christianity and classical culture, while others rejected those similarities, asserting instead that Christianity was unique.

VI. Christians were also concerned to put their teachings on an authoritative basis.

A. Christians began to find that they had rivals inside the Christian movement. Gradually some were labeled "heretics."

B. Irenaeus of Lyon wrote *Against Heresies* on two foundations.
   1. First he appealed to a definitive "canon" of scripture, the first to do so.
   2. Second he referred to "monarchical bishops," and he identified bishops with their communities.
      a. The New Testament refers to bishops, priests, and deacons.
      b. The emerging church took on the administrative geography of the empire.
      c. The senior priest in a town was the "overseer," the literal meaning of "bishop."
      d. The metropolis (capital or "mother city") of a province got a "metropolitan" bishop (in the Middle Ages, an "archbishop").
      e. Cyprian of Carthage was the first to articulate the idea that the bishops descended from the apostles and retained the authority Christ had assigned to them.

VII. On the eve of the Constantinian revolution, Christianity had two things that no pagan cult ever possessed.

    A. There was an increasingly firm and recognized body of authoritative texts.

    B. There was a sophisticated administrative system.

    C. When Constantine legalized Christianity, embraced the faith, turned to a council of bishops to resolve a heresy, and patronized the church, he gave a powerful impetus to several strong currents that had been flowing for two centuries.

Suggested Reading:

Fox, *Pagans and Christians.*

Wilken, *The Christians as the Romans Saw Them.*

Questions to Consider:

1. In view of all its competitors and rivals, what distinctive features of Christianity permitted the new faith to succeed in the Roman world?

2. Why, in the context of the ancient world, was it important for Christianity to establish a definitive body of teachings and an authority structure to conserve and transmit those teachings?

Lecture Seventeen—Transcript
The Christianization of the Roman World

Hello once again and welcome back to this series of lectures on late antiquity. Today's session, Lecture Seventeen, is the Christianization of the Roman world. In my first couple of lectures I drew your attention to the work of the very famous English historian Edward Gibbon. We talked about his view that the Roman Empire had internal problems, which he labeled immoderate greatness. We spent a good deal of time talking then about the Roman Empire and all of it successes and all of its failures. We saw also that Gibbon said that the Roman world succumbed to external influences: barbarism, and religion. We spent a lot of time in our last sequence of lectures talking about barbarism, the barbarian peoples, and the settlement of the barbarian kingdom. Now we come, in this lecture and in several to follow, to religion—in particular, to Christianity.

I think it's safe to say that the most remarkable development during Roman imperial times during this late antique world that we're studying was the triumph of Christianity. This is simply not a phenomenon that one might have predicted. I've often said if you placed yourself at a certain moment historically and kind of bet on what was going to come next, it would have been very difficult before the 4th century to bet very much, confidently, on Christianity. What we want to do really in this lecture is lay some foundations for exactly how it was and why it was that Christianity proved in the end so very successful in the Roman world.

We're going to pursue some very basic themes. Christianity had some real and serious competitors. This is important. Christianity had to forge for itself a very distinctive identity and it had to forge effective institutions. Christianity produced a culture that was, in many ways, the defining feature of late antiquity. That culture bore important relations with the classical culture that preceded it, and it was its contemporary, and it was also different in various respects. That issue will concern us only a little in this lecture, but we'll come to it in considerable detail in later ones.

I've used the term Christianization. Christianization is a kind of a scholarly coinage and it's meant to serve a certain purpose, to do a certain amount of work. When we talk about religious change, when we talk about the religious interests and allegiances of people, we can talk about "adhesion." That is to say, a person joins a group.

That group could be religious, as for us it will be here, but it could be political. It could be social. It could be a group of many different kinds. One joins a group, but it's very difficult then to capture any sense of people's actual commitments. At the other end of a spectrum is what we might call "conversion." That's really the important subject. That's the one we'd really love to know more about. Alas, conversion is a matter of heart and soul. It is something that is largely beyond the reach of the historian. When we speak of Christianization, we're talking about processes that are at once political and institutional and spiritual and social, perhaps even in certain respects economic. We're talking about the change of the underlying characteristics, foundations, and qualities, whatever you will, of a world. We're going to talk about Christianization, we're going to see people adhere to Christianity, we're going to see people convert to Christianity, but we're thinking more generally about the change of a world.

Let's go back and pursue those themes I enumerated just a second ago. Christianity emerged and spread in a world with old, deeply rooted religious traditions and practices. Christianity did not sort of come and write on a blank slate. That's important to bear in mind. What were some of these competitors that were sort of lively and flourishing in the 2nd, in the 3rd, in the 4th centuries, when Christianity spreads and eventually triumphs in the ancient world?

There was Mithraism in the first place. Mithraism was an Iranian cult. It flourished in particular in the 2nd and 3rd centuries. Archaeologists have discovered over 400 Mithraic cult centers scattered all over the ancient world, from Britain to Mesopotamia. What we see here are small autonomous groups. In other words, there was no Mithraic Church. There wasn't an overall, overarching intuitional structure. Small autonomous groups of males, often soldiers, minor officials, freedmen, slaves—in other words, this does not appear to be a phenomenon that was an elite one—met in very small sites called "Mithrauems" for a common meal. Common meals are a common feature of many religious experiences. There were artistic depictions, which show us this, also literary descriptions, bull-killing rituals. The meaning exactly of these bull-killing rituals is not clear to us. It's possible that Mithraism and its bull-killing rituals were somehow related to widespread ancient cults that centered on the notion of a God who died and was reborn. Obviously there are certain parallels there with Christianity.

In the second place, there was Gnosticism. Gnosticism is a movement whose origins are very complicated and among scholars today, very contested. There are lively discussions of Gnosticism, so I'm on a bit of a fool's errand to try to capture this very, very quickly and simply. In 1945–1946 at Nag Hammadi in Egypt, about 40 Gnostic treatises were found. These revealed a religious worldview and a set of religious ideas that had been largely unknown up until that time, or had been known only from occasional antagonistic remarks by their critics. What do these texts talk about? They talked about a creation of the world, the creation of the whole created order that was believed to be antagonistic to pure spirituality. Spirit and matter are set off sharply against one another. Everyone, it was believed, had a spark of pure spirit that could be liberated through *gnosis*. *Gnosis* is a Greek word that means "knowledge." A very particular kind of knowledge would liberate you from your attachment to the material world and free you for the spiritual world. The Gnostics had a good deal to say about Christ. They claim that he came from the supreme God. He came to bring *gnosis*. He came to bring this knowledge. As a divine being, the Gnostics argued however, Christ never assumed a real human body. He didn't die. This being Christ temporarily inhabited the body of the human Jesus. Christian writers tended to treat Gnosticism as either a heresy, a corrupted form of Christianity, or else they treated it as a form of paganism. On the whole, Christian writers were brutal in the critique of Gnosticism.

In the third place, there was Manichaeanism. Manichaeanism was widespread and prominent. It may be regarded as a very highly developed form of Gnosticism, or it may be regarded as a religious phenomenon that, broadly speaking, is rooted in many ancient practices of different kinds. Compared to Mithraism, Manichaeanism however was a more elite phenomenon, or let me say simply that it attracted members of the elite as well. It had a much broader social purchase on the late antique world. Mani, who lived from about 216–276, had visions. These visions convinced him that he was the paraclete promised by Jesus, the healer or the comforter promised by Jesus. Mani was harassed by the Persians. The official religion of Persia was Zoroastrianism, so Mani fled to India, but then he came back in the middle of the 3rd century to the court of Shāpūr I. We've encountered him as beginning the Persian attacks on the Roman Empire during the crisis of the 3rd century. Shāpūr favored Mani and

Mani had an opportunity to teach and to spread his teachings. Mani's association with the Persian court, by the way, helps us to explain why Diocletian persecuted the Manichaeans so brutally. He really saw these guys as a kind of a fifth column and therefore dangerous to the Roman world.

The basic teachings of the Manichaeans held that there had been a pre-cosmic, a prior-to-creation invasion of the realm of light by the forces of darkness. If this sounds a little like *Star Wars*, we can see where some of those ideas came from. The realm of light was invaded by the forces of darkness, which produced a mingling of good and evil. This is the created world we see around us. There were people called the "elect" who denied all occupations, who denied all possessions, who denied as far as possible all human associations, so that they wouldn't embrace materiality and thus evil or darkness. They were somehow trying to live in the light, in the world of pure spirit. There were also "hearers." These were, in a sense, neophyte Manichaeans who hoped one day to be reborn as members of the elect. Manichaeanism also held, as some other ancient cults had, for a continual transmigration of souls. The idea was that a soul would pass from person to person to person over a period of time, eventually culminating in the salvation of the last person to receive it. Despite fierce Roman persecution, Manichaeanism was only finally rooted out actually by Islam, so it had a very long history in the ancient world.

Judaism, finally, was the primal competitor of Christianity. Perhaps 10 percent of the empire's population in Christ's time, for example, were Jews. The Jews were then, we know, actively proselytizing; they were seeking converts. The Romans had generally been tolerant of Judaism, although curiously, somewhat less so after 313. Constantine makes all religious legal, but Judaism actually then began to suffer certain disabilities under the Roman system. The Jews had been accorded political security despite the fact that they had rebelled against in the Romans in 66, in 115, and in 132. They rebelled three times, but generally they were accorded political security and given some religious privileges by the Romans. They could practice their own faith more or less undisturbed. In 212, a decree of the Emperor Caracalla gave Jews citizenship, as indeed all other people inside the Roman Empire. If Jews were not particularly well-liked or popular, they weren't harassed by the Roman government.

From about the 330s, however, Jews began to experience certain legal restrictions. For instance, they were forbidden to prevent pagans from converting to Christianity. They couldn't own Christian slaves. They couldn't serve as officers in the Roman cohorts. They could not hold honorific offices under the Roman government, high offices that bore particularly elevated titles. The Jews for a while had kind of an autonomous patriarchy under the leader called a "nasi"; this was suppressed in 425. In other words, kind of Jewish religious independence or autonomy was taken away from them. Roman law permitted Jews to exist, as long as they respected Christians. Justinian intervened in the affairs of the Jews in a particularly interesting way, he insisted that they use the Septuagint—that is to say, the Greek version of their own scriptures, of what Christians would call the Old Testament. His idea was that if they read these works in Greek, it might lead them to convert to Christianity.

Christian attitudes, generally speaking, derived from Saint Paul. Saint Paul had, generally speaking, taught that Christianity and Judaism could not coexist, that these were two different things and that they were inevitably opposed to one another. Still, the question arose, it arose acutely for early Christian writers and for others in the ancient world and we'll say more about this in a few minutes, was Christianity the fulfillment of Judaism or was it its total rejection? Prominent Christian writers, for example, issued blistering condemnations of the Jews. Saint Augustine, perhaps the greatest of all the church fathers, had said that Jews existed only to remind Christians of their error. That's a pretty remarkable way to think about Jews and Judaism. Finally, Pope Gregory I—he was pope from 590–604, so we're at the end of the 6th century—said there was to be no coercion of the Jews and no injustices against them. They were to be left as a kind of an eternal reminder of God's favoring of the Christians, and eventually at the end of time they would all be converted.

It's interesting too to think about how Christians appropriated the Hebrew scriptures. What Christians did is read them typologically. What that means quite simply is that instead of reading the Hebrew scriptures, what Christians would call the Old Testament, instead of reading these stories as having validity in their own right as relating to the experience of a particular people as communicating divine truths, the Christians read the Old Testament as types of the New. In other words, everything in the Old Testament had validity to the extent that, and only to the extent that, it prophesied, it predicted, something that was going to happen in the New Testament. Hebrew scriptures were appropriated by Christians.

Let's turn to Christianity's competitors. Thinking a little bit less about formal religious groups and about religion more generally, we can say that Christianity arose in a world with old, deep pagan traditions. These can be captured with the Greek phrase *ta patria*; that means paternal things, paternal stuff. It means your inheritance. It means the culture into which you were born, the culture of which you were a part even if you were a part of it more or less unconsciously. We might think of, for example, all of the civic cults that existed in every city, all of the rituals that people would have experienced in the cities where they lived. We might think of the ordinary events of life that were attended by various kinds of religious rights. I have in mind birth, death, marriage, war, peace, planting, and harvesting. All of these kinds of events and experiences were attended by various religious rituals.

Civil celebrations and the official calendars of the Roman world—of the empire, of the city of Rome, of the great cities around the empire—were infused with religious ideas. It becomes clear, I think, that conversion or Christianization or adhesion, whichever way we choose to view it at the moment, involved much more than a change of intellectual allegiance. There was a lot more involved here than simply saying, I used to believe this and now I'm going to believe that. I used to know this, now I'm going to know that. There was a great deal more involved that sort of reached all the way across the spectrum of human activity.

As Christianity began to rise, began to spread, began to grow, began to flourish in the Roman world, various pagan writers noticed it and issued on certain occasions, rather sharp critiques. For example Pliny, a man who lived between about 61–112, dismissed Christianity as a superstitious novelty. Superstition as the Romans used that term is kind of interesting. I mean one would say gosh, why would people call Christians "superstitious"? Superstition was all of that kind of religion that was not the official religion of the Romans. In other words, if you adhered to the formal pagan cults of the ancient world, that was fine. If you adhered to something else it was a superstition, and Pliny thought this was a novel one. On strictly chronological historical grounds, he was rather correct with his notion that it was novel.

Medical and scientific writers dismissed as absurd the Christian, but also the Jewish, idea of creation *ex nihilo*, creation "out of nothing." Pagan cosmology held that what the gods did is give form and order to the chaos. There was kind of primeval stuff out there and the gods organized it and made sense of it. Christianity said there had been nothing, Judaism had said it too, and God made something. Pagan writers said no, that's impossible. Scientifically that can't happen.

There's a writer named Celsus who wrote in the last years of the 2nd century, perhaps let's say about 175. He was Christianity's most sharp and serious critic. He said, for example, that the idea of the incarnation was scandalous and shameful, that the resurrection of the dead was physically impossible, that the claim for one God was extravagant. It's interesting, we might think polytheism is extravagant; he says no, no, the claim that there is only one God is extravagant. He also said that a common criminal who had lived recently couldn't possibly be a God and didn't deserve the devotion of his followers. What's interesting is that Celsus was not simply retailing Canards. He had obviously taken the time and the trouble to learn a good deal about Christianity. For example, he at one point penned a mocking refutation, which even in its ugliness shows us that he had learned a lot. He said,

> Everywhere in their writings they speak of the tree of life and of the resurrection of the flesh by that tree—I imagine because their master was nailed to a cross and was a carpenter by trade. So if he had been thrown off a cliff, or pushed into a pit, or suffocated by strangling, or if he had been a cobbler or a stonemason or a blacksmith, there would have been a cliff of life, or a pit of resurrection, or a rope of immortality, or a blessed stone, or a holy hide [of leather]. Would not an old woman who sings such a story to lull a little child to sleep have been ashamed to whisper such tales as these?

That's fairly brutal criticism, but you can see that Celsus had actually taken on board a good deal of what the Christians taught.

Amidst their critics and competitors, Christian writers began slowly but surely to forge an identity for themselves, for Christians. In the

2nd century, the Apologists stepped to the fore. *Apologia*, in Greek or in Latin, does not mean, whoops, I'm sorry. It is not an apology in that sense. It is a principled, articulate, defense of a proposition. In this case, of course, the proposition being defended is Christianity. The first of these figures is a man by the name of Justin Martyr, born about 100, died about 165. He wrote several Apologetic treatises. For instance, in his *Dialogue with Trypho the Jew*, he attempted to differentiate between Christianity and Judaism. For many in the Roman world, Christians appeared simply to be a renegade sect of Jews. What Justin tried to do is to demonstrate very clearly, very carefully, how Christians and Jews were different. In two further Apologies, he argued that Christian doctrines, Christian teachings, were compatible with Greek thought. He said that in many ways these ways of thinking, these ways of expressing themselves, overlapped. He taught, interestingly enough, it was fairly widespread really eventually among Christian writers, the Theft Theory. Everything had been revealed by God in the first place, and whatever the Egyptians or the Greeks or whom you pleased knew, they had stolen first from the Jews and subsequently from the Christians. In other words, all knowledge had its origin in God in the first place.

There was a writer named Tertullian in North Africa. He was born about 160, lived until about 225. He was the first Latin apologist. Justin Martyr had written in Greek. Tertullian had a very acid pen, a bit like Celsus in that way. On one occasion he said this:

> What is there in common between a philosopher and a Christian? What between the disciple of Greece and of heaven? The friend and the enemy of error? The Academy with the Church? After Jesus we have no scope for further curiosity, after the gospel no need for further research.

Case closed, from his point of view. You don't have to explore all of these connections between Christianity and classical culture. Elsewhere, seeing no need for rational defenses of Christianity—and this of course again was a response to people like Celsus to others who'd said Christianity is absurd—he said this. He said,

> The son of God is crucified; I am not ashamed because it is shameful; the son of God has died; it is credible because it is absurd; the son of God was buried and rose again; it is certain because it is impossible.

It's a very interesting way of responding to critics, don't you think? Many other writers could be cited here, but they have certain basic things in common, and this is where we could go down a fairly long list of these Apologists. Some were obviously concerned, as I mentioned, to differentiate between Christianity and Judaism. Some wished to emphasize similarities between Christianity and classical culture, while others rejected those similarities, asserting instead that Christianity was unique, definitive, and final. It had superseded all that had come before.

Christians were also concerned to put their own teachings on an authoritative basis. How did Christians know what they knew? How did they believe what they believed? Christians, of course, began to find that they had rivals inside the Christian movement. Gradually, of course, some labeled others as "heretics." But how? What was to be the standard? What was to be the criteria for asserting that one group of people believed rightly and another did not? One of the first crucial steps taken in the way of addressing that question was to try to set down a definitive canon of scripture, those books which would be accepted, those Christian writings, as authoritative. The first person to take a really serious step in this direction is a man by the name of Irenaeus of Lyon. He's born about 130; he died about 200. He wrote a book, *Against Heresies*, and he based himself on two foundations. He, for the first time, appealed to a definitive "canon"; that's a word that means something like a reed, something that is straight up and down, something that is erect, something that is correct. He appealed to a definitive canon of scripture, the first one to do so.

The problem was acute. Not to pursue it too far we could say, if you're Christian, do you accept or reject the Hebrew scriptures? Do you keep or reject what Christians came eventually to call the Old Testament? The documents that would come to become the Old Testament circulated in a couple of different versions. One was a Greek text, the Septuagint translation, in legend translated in 70 days by 70 translators at Alexandria. There was a Greek version of the Old Testament, and then of course there was the original Hebrew version. Do you use the Greek or do you use the Hebrew? I mentioned a little while ago that Justinian had tried to impose on the Jews the reading of the Septuagint because he thought that if they read their own scriptures in Greek it might draw them to Christianity.

Then, of course, where the New Testament is concerned, what came to be called the New Testament, which books should be regarded as authoritative? We had, for example, the problem posed by those Gnostic texts I mentioned a moment ago. There was an enormous amount of Christian literature, of seemingly, of possibly, of potentially Christian literature, circulating in the ancient world. What would be accepted? What would be rejected? What would be kept? What would be set on one side? It eventually took—and we'll talk about this a little bit more in some later lectures—until well into the 4th and 5th centuries for the canon of scripture of the Old Testament and the New to be fixed more or less definitively, and that's an interesting process and it's an interesting story, and we will return to it. For now, I simply wish to flag that Irenaeus of Lyon was the first to acknowledge, to recognize, to see this is a problem and this is a problem we've got to do something about. He for the first time draws a list of those books, those texts, which were to be regarded as authoritative. Interestingly enough, his list conforms very closely to the list that eventually became definitive.

Irenaeus did something else, too. If on the one hand we have a problem of saying, what are the authoritative documents from which our teaching derives, not to say—and we'll have plenty of opportunity to talk about this in later lectures—that once we've fixed a list of books, we're all going to agree on exactly what they say and what they mean. But in the first place, Irenaeus says we've got to get a list of books. In the second place, he thinks hard about the question of who decides. Who makes decisions? Who has authority? Who has power? Who has influence in this growing Christian community? In a way, his adumbration of a fully developed and articulated church is part and parcel of this little bit earlier effort to identify a distinctive Christian identity by way of saying, these are our books and this is what we believe.

In his texts, he referred to "monarchical bishops," *hoi monarchikoi episkopoi*, and he identified bishops with their communities. What's he up to here? The New Testament had referred to bishops, priests, and deacons; *episkopoi, presbyteroi, diakonoi*. As Christianity grew in the Roman world, initially in cities and then only very, very slowly over time in the countryside—and these are themes and issues that we'll talk about in some later lectures as well—the emerging church took on the administrative geography of the Roman Empire. You may recall my mentioning, for example, on an earlier day when we were talking about Diocletian's reform in his grouping of provinces into dioceses. Eventually, of course, Christianity adopts diocese as one of its organizational terms. The Roman Empire was focused on cities. The cities were kind of the institutional nodes in a vast network. That was how Rome governed its empire. It governed through cities. Christianity spread through cities. Here were relatively compact populations to whom one could preach, to whom one could teach, to whom one could gather into the fold rather efficiently. I've emphasized a number of times that maybe 10 percent at a wildly liberal estimate, maybe 15 percent of the population of the ancient world, was urban. The overwhelming majority of people were out in the countryside, but Christianity really takes its rise and begins to spread in cities.

It appears that the senior priest, *presbyteros* in Greek, eventually passes through French and into English as priest. That's where the word comes from. *Presbyteros* in Greek really means "elder," or it can even mean "ambassador." It can mean a bearer of wise information. The senior priest, apparently the eldest, in a given town, was viewed as the "overseer." That's the literal meaning of "bishop," *episcopos* in Greek, one who scopes on, *episcopos*, to literally to scope on, to oversee. Roman provinces were organized under capital cities—that's where the provincial governors were; those were the metropolitan cities of the provinces. They were the "mother cities," the mother *polis* of provinces. The capital cities of the Roman provinces began to have what was called a "metropolitan" bishop. That phrase will seem a little odd to us nowadays. We're more accustomed to the medieval and modern "archbishop," *archi episcopos*, the ruling bishop, but in antiquity, the metropolitan bishop. My point is we can simply observe the emerging Christian church taking on the administrative geography of the Roman world and organizing itself to do its work. Those key officials of course, the bishops, are going to become the great figures of late antiquity intellectually, institutionally, socially, politically, and in a wide variety of other ways too, but that we'll talk about in more detail in some of our later lectures.

There was a writer by the name of Cyprian of Carthage who died in about 258 who was the first to articulate the idea that bishops descended from the apostles; that Christ had given his mandate to teach to the apostles, and those who succeeded to the apostles retained, inherited, this mandate to teach. There was the question.

Who has authority, who is to teach, who is to preach, who is to conserve the faith? The bishops are. By the late 3rd century, we can see a whole series of features of later and more visible Christianity already in place.

Let's sum up by looking at it just a little bit differently. On the eve of the Constantinian Revolution, Christianity had two things that no pagan cult ever possessed: thinking against Christianity's many competitors and rivals. There was an increasingly firm and recognized body of authoritative texts, and there was an increasingly sophisticated administrative system that gradually reached across the empire. Let's remember, when Constantine legalized Christianity, embraced the faith, turned to a council of bishops to resolve the heresy and patronize the church, he gave powerful impetus to several strong currents that had been flowing now for two centuries that were not invented in the early 4th.

Lecture Eighteen
Christianity and the Roman State

Scope:

In earlier lectures we have learned that the increasingly prominent Christian church became progressively enmeshed in the public life of the Roman Empire. In this lecture we will look more closely at how the Roman state shifted from persecution to tolerance to promotion of Christianity. Then we will look at several key pieces of legislation that, taken together, built the church and the faith into the public and private life of the empire. We will conclude by constructing a balance sheet, so to speak, in an attempt to assess whether Christianity and the church gained from Rome's weighty benevolence or lost from Rome's interference.

Outline

I.   We confront a remarkable historical irony: Minor Roman officials in an out-of-the-way province put a petty insurrectionist to death, and his followers triumphed in the Roman world. Two sets of background considerations will be helpful.

   A. Let us first explore the earliest encounters between Christians and Rome.

   1. The story of Jesus, the Pharisees, and the Roman coins (Matthew 22:17–22) provides no hint of trouble.

   2. Jesus's appearance before Pilate, one of very few tales told in all four gospels, is ambiguous and hard to interpret.

   a. The Gospels were written between c. 60–65 A.D. and 100 A.D., so some adjusting of the story may have taken place, not least shifting the blame to the Jews.

   b. There is no clear evidence that Pilate really saw Jesus as a threat.

   c. All accounts agree that after the crucifixion all of Jesus's followers abandoned and denied him. It is hard to see the makings of a mass movement, much less of a threatening one.

3. In his *Annals* Tacitus tells of Pomponia Graecina, a high-ranking woman who was accused of foreign superstition. He also reports violence against the Christian community in Rome in the time of Nero.

4. Suetonius, in his *Life of Claudius*, says that Rome's Jewish community was stirred up by Chrestus, and in his *Life of Nero* he says that punishments were inflicted on Christians for their novel superstitions.

5. Later writers say that Domitian persecuted Christians ferociously.

6. Late in the 1st century, Pliny wrote to Trajan indicating that he was uncertain about how to proceed against Christians, or even if he should do so.

7. Eusebius, in his *History of the Church*, tells of persecutions down to his own day, but it is clear that these were sporadic and not the result of any consistent, coherent policy.

B. If Christianity had checkered and often poor relations with the Roman state down to Constantine, we might ask whether there were factors that contributed to Christianity's spread and success.

1. The *Pax Romana* provided a stable framework.

2. Across the huge Roman Empire, there was a common primary language: Greek.

3. Urban areas were numerous, populous, and relatively open.

4. People on the whole were tolerant of religious views.

II. Across the 4th century, official Roman policy shifted from persecution to acceptance and then to promotion of Christianity.

A. We have discussed Constantine and his important initiatives.

B. The Arian Constantius II and the neopagan Julian complicated matters for a time.

C. The pious and opinionated Theodosius instituted major changes: Legislation between 378 and 380 effectively made Christianity in the form practiced by the bishop of Rome the state religion.

D. It is important to keep in mind that religion was part of the public order in antiquity and not something banished to the private realm.

    1. The emperor's authority was all-encompassing.

    2. Barbarian kings inherited from their Roman predecessors the idea that the church was their special responsibility.

    3. Modern ideas of "separation of church and state" would have made no sense.

III. There can be no question that Christianity and the church benefitted from association with the Roman state. But drawing up a balance sheet is a tricky matter.

    A. We might think of imperial benefactions such as church building.

    B. We might also think of beneficial legislation: For example, clergy were exempted from military service and most taxes, and Sundays were reserved from work.

    C. Bishops became key imperial advisers and confidants.

    D. Emperors also intervened controversially in doctrinal issues.

        1. Constantine was generally praised for calling the Council of Nicaea that condemned Arianism, but he had left the decision to the bishops themselves.

        2. Pulcheria collaborated with Pope Leo I to condemn Monophysitism.

        3. Anastasius and Justinian intervened on their own to try to find a compromise that would reconcile Chalcedonian and Monophysite Christians.

IV. The church borrowed a great deal indirectly from Rome.

    A. The administrative geography and terminology of the Roman state was adapted by the church.

    B. Roman law profoundly influenced the church's emerging canon law (*Ecclesia vivit lege Romana*).

    C. Roman ideas of majesty and hierarchy were generally influential, but especially so in the case of the bishops of Rome.

Suggested Reading:

Barnes, *Constantius and Athanasius*.

Geffcken, *The Last Days of Greco-Roman Paganism*.

Questions to Consider:

1. Taking everything into account, do you think Christianity gained or lost by its relations with the Roman state?

2. What would you regard as the single most significant intervention of the Roman authorities in the affairs of the Christian church?

Lecture Eighteen—Transcript
Christianity and the Roman State

Hello and welcome yet again to this series of lectures on late antiquity. This time, Lecture Eighteen in the series, is Christianity and the Roman state. In the last lecture we spoke in fairly broad terms about the Christianization of the Roman world, the spread of Christianity, the adoption by Christians of a distinctive kind of identity, the articulation by Christians of the basic books of writings on which they would base their teachings, the beginnings of the emergency of an official hierarchy of individuals, bishops in the first instance, who would be responsible for conserving and handing on, transmitting those teachings.

In some of our earlier lectures when we were looking at the Roman Empire, we did meet various emperors who took various actions in respect of the emerging Christian church. What we want to do now actually is gather together these notions, these sort of *disiecta membra*, these sort of separated chunks that we've talked about before, and pull them together and talk about them in one place. And in a certain sense, we're also going to extend our conversation from the last lecture on the Christianization of the Roman world to see particularly what role, what place, the Roman state played in this process of Christianizing the Roman world. What we see is that our subjects are really all quite linked together. There's something ever so slightly arbitrary about isolating one aspect or another aspect or another aspect to talk about in a moment, but you can't say everything simultaneously. We do have to bring a little bit of order to the sequence of discussions here.

We stand before a quite remarkable historical irony. From the Roman point of view, minor Roman officials in an out-of-the-way province of the empire put a petty insurrectionist to death. A few centuries later, his followers triumphed in the Roman world. I've said, on a number of occasions, this is not a movement on which you would have bet anything if you could go back to the middle years of the 1st century A.D. and look around. Yet, we know how it came out. There's always the danger for historians of any time, any place, or any subject to fall into the trap of interpreting things as inevitable in light of what happened. In other words, historians have 20-20 hindsight. In other words, it's easy to predict the past; it's hard to predict the future. What we want to do here is try to run the tape forward. We know Christianity eventually triumphed in the Roman world. I've been trying to suggest in the last lecture, and will again in this one and to some extent in the next couple after that, that the spread, the triumph, the success of Christianity in the Roman world was by no means a foregone conclusion, so what we want to do is see how did this happen. In order to launch our discussion this time of Christianity's relations with the Roman state, I want to look at two basic background issues. First of all, I want to look at the earliest encounter between Christians and Rome, and then we'll turn to some discussion of the broader context of the Roman Empire.

If we look for evidence of the very earliest contacts between Christianity and the Romans or some sense that Christians or Romans were even aware of each other, we could turn to the passage in Matthew's Gospel, it's in chapter 22, where the Pharisees try to trick Jesus. They come before him and they ask if it's all right to pay the tribute to Caesar. Jesus said, hand me a coin. They handed him a coin and he said, "Whose picture is that?" This incident tells us something about how utterly familiar Roman coinage is, it tells us something about how the Romans kind of got their image out, the emperor's image on coins, but it tells us also something about the utter familiarity of people in Palestine and Romans. These people lived cheek by jaw, they were aware of each other, so in other words, it is the utter familiarity of this story that makes it interesting.

The Pharisees hand Jesus a coin, he said, "Whose picture is that?" And they said, "Caesar's." He said, "Render to Caesar what is Caesar's and to God what is God's." Apparently, the point of this story is that Jesus thinks it's perfectly legitimate to pay the tribute to Caesar, but that there will also be ways in which God has claims upon people that are quite different from the claims that Caesar has. Let's move forward a little bit into the Gospel accounts to Jesus's appearance before Pontius Pilate. This tale is significant in a variety of ways. It is one of very few stories told in all four of the Gospels: Matthew, Mark, Luke, and John. There are only a limited number of stories that appear in all four Gospels. Jesus's appearance before Pilate appears, albeit with some slight differences, but it appears in all four texts.

The encounter itself, the way it's described, what was said, the motivations of the various parties, are ambiguous in the extreme, and in lots of ways, actually, very hard to interpret. We know for instance that the Gospels were written between about 60 or 65 A.D., thereabouts, and about 100. We can perhaps see that some adjusting of the story may have taken place. Not least, there appears to be, by the time we have the account of Jesus's appearance before Pilate, a subtle shifting of blame for Jesus's ultimate execution by the Roman authorities from the Romans to the Jews. It's pretty clear that whatever happened, it was in Pilate's authority to make it happen or not happen. There's no clear evidence in these stories that Pilate really saw Jesus as a threat. He makes statements like, I find no fault with this man. Do with him what you will. I mean, Pilate is in some ways sort of flummoxed by this situation. He doesn't really quite understand who this guy is or why he's there at all.

All of the accounts agree that after the crucifixion, Jesus's key followers abandoned him and denied him. What we may have here is some confirmation that Pilate was basically right, that his instincts were right. In other words, that this was not a major insurrectionist, this was not a big problem, there was here no threat to Rome, there was no threat to good order in the government. Pilate behaved, I think we can say, pretty much the way any sort of minor provincial bureaucrat would behave. What does that mean? He didn't want any trouble. He wants peace, he wants order, he wants harmony. Whatever pleases the largest number of people the most, for the longest period of time, that's what you want. It's not a great matter of principle; that's my point. It's hard to see then, in other words, that there was here a major encounter of some kind between emerging Christianity, or at any rate Christianity's leader, and the Roman state.

Our next insights, not exactly chronological because in a sense we kind of move back and forth across the course of the 1st century by when particular authors wrote and by the dates of the events about which they wrote, so we could order our discussion one way by authors, we could order it another way by date of events. I'm basically going to proceed by some authors here. The Roman historian Tacitus, you may recall we talked about him and his *Germania*, his book about the Germans, but he also wrote two major historical works, the *Histories* and the *Annals*. In his *Annals*, in Book 8, chapter 32—Tacitus himself lived from about 56 to about 118—he tells of a woman named Pomponia Graecina, a high-ranking woman who was accused before the authorities of foreign superstition.

It has sometimes been thought, it has sometimes been assumed, that this foreign superstition was actually Christianity. That's not crystal clear and Tacitus doesn't say so, but it is possible. It's interesting further that if the foreign superstition to which Pomponia Graecina felt some allegiance or in which she had some interest, if this were actually Christianity, this would be the first time an elite Roman of any kind, let alone an elite Roman woman, had shown an interest in Christianity. Later on, various women are going to be very important in the spread of Christianity. We'll have something to say about them in some later lectures. You may recall in an earlier lecture we talked about the enormous influence of the women of the Theodosian House in the 5th-century Roman east, but this is very early mid-1st century for a story like that to be told. In Book 15, chapter 44, Tacitus reports about violence against the Christian community in the city of Rome in the time of the Emperor Nero. Later Christian writers all agreed that Nero was a great persecutor of Christians. Some of you may have seen the old famous movie *Quo Vadis*, for example, which is about the Neronian persecutions. Supposedly, Nero put to death Peter and Paul, for example, in Rome.

Another Roman writer whose name was Suetonius lived from about 70 A.D. until about 130. He wrote the *Lives of the Twelve Caesars*. He began narrating biographies, basically, of the caesars beginning with Julius Caesar, so he wrote the *Lives of the Twelve Caesars*. In his *Life of Claudius*—Claudius reigned from 41–54—Suetonius says that Rome's Jewish community was stirred up by a man named Chrestus. Chrestus, or *Chrestos* in Greek, simply means "the anointed one." Almost certainly, this is a story that has something to do with Jesus Christ, but it's interesting that either Suetonius didn't know very much about the situation or wasn't particularly interested in the details, but he says that a Chrestus stirred up Rome's Jewish community. Chrestus, Christ, had never been in Rome, so it must have been followers of Chrestus, the teachings of Chrestus, something like this. We again don't know the details very fully. This may also be the first faint hints of the kind of thing that I talked about in the last lecture when among the early Apologists there was felt a need to differentiate between Christianity and Judaism.

In his *Life of Nero*—Nero reigned from 54–68—Suetonius says that punishments were inflicted on Christians for their novel superstitions. Two points: One, this confirms what Tacitus had said, that the Christians suffered under Nero. Later Christian writers tell us the same thing, but here we have two Roman writers who independently tell us that Christians suffered under Nero. The second interesting point here is one that again loops back to a point that I made in the last lecture. Remember when we talked about Pliny and his comment that Christianity was a novel superstition? Here, almost contemporaneously, we have Suetonius telling us that Christianity is a novel superstition. There's a perception that it's something relatively new and that it's outside the bounds, it's outside the norms, of the traditional religious experiences of people in the Roman world.

Later writers say with considerable emphasis that the Emperor Domitian, who reigned from 81–96, persecuted Christians ferociously. There's agreement among later Christian writers about that. Domitian was succeeded by Nerva and then by the Emperor Trajan. The Emperor Trajan sent someone he knew very well, a Roman blue blood, Pliny—a man I've referred to a couple of times here—out to govern in the province of Athenia. Pliny wrote a substantial correspondence, a lot of it survives. It's an enormously valuable source full of all sorts of interesting information about the Roman world in his time, but the information that concerns us at the moment is that Pliny was encountering Christians, so we're at the very beginning of the 2nd century. Pliny was encountering Christians in some of the cities in the province over which he had responsibility, and he wasn't quite sure what to do with them. He didn't know, for instance, if being a Christian was against the law. He didn't know if under certain circumstances he should go out and round up Christians and prosecute them, or whether they should be more or less left in peace.

Trajan wrote back a fairly moderate response. If Christians come to your attention, then you have to deal with them. If they don't come to your attention, leave them alone. But, the key point here is that whatever we may make of the persecutions under Domitian, they had not evidently established a firm, definitive, clear Roman policy with respect to Christians or Christianity. Just a few years later, Trajan and Pliny are a little unsure. They're a little confused about exactly how they are to proceed. There is some sense that these Christians are sort of not the best sort of folk and that there may be problems here, but there was no hard and fast policy.

Jumping over a whole series of other figures, who could attract our attention but won't here, we come to the Christian historian Eusebius, really the founder of church history. Eusebius is born about 260, and died in about 340. He knew Constantine; he wrote a biography of Constantine. He was, at certain points, a fairly influential advisor to Constantine. Between about 303 and 323, he wrote his *History of the Church*, the first history of Christianity. Among many themes, one of his themes is the role of bishops in towns, but among the various themes on which Eusebius lays considerable stress, persecution ranks very high. He told of persecutions from the 1st century right down to his own day. It was very clear that he tended to regard the Roman authorities as consistently hostile to Christianity and that Christians had, in many different places, suffered—sometimes suffered grievously under the impact of Roman official hostility. It's important here particularly to bear in mind that Eusebius would have had very much in mind the experience of the great persecution of Diocletian, which had happened actually—which had begun and which was initiated—at just about the same time he'd begun writing his history of the Christian church.

The interesting thing that we can do with Eusebius's account is in a way read it against itself. If we actually go back through his account and we kind of line up his discussion of persecutions, one of the things we discover is that once again there was not a longstanding, consistent, coherent, uniformly applied Roman policy with respect to Christianity. Occasionally, yes, Christians were persecuted, but it tended to be local, it tended to be sporadic, and in many instances we don't even actually know exactly why a persecution broke out in this town or in that town or in another town.

I don't want to leave the impression that the Roman state was benign with respect to Christianity. That is certainly not the case, but it is important to keep in mind that the Roman state did not uniformly consistently persecute Christianity from the 1st century until Constantine made Christianity legal. That's one broad set of background reflections: a dawning awareness on the part of the Romans and of the Christians that each exists and that there may be points of friction between them.

A second background issue that we might look at for a minute is to say if Christianity had these kind of checkered and often poor relations with the Roman state down to the time of Constantine, were there any sort of broad background factors in the Roman world that might have contributed in some way to Christianity's spread and success, and can we attribute at all to the Romans some role in creating these background conditions? Not, mind you, that the Romans created these conditions to help Christianity spread, but is there anything about the way that the Romans treated their world that was of some benefit or advantage to Christianity? I can think of several things.

The *Pax Romana*, the "Roman Peace," this remarkably successful Roman imperial regime from the time of Augustus Caesar until the early years of the 3rd century, indeed until the inception of the 3rd-century crisis, provided a remarkably large and stable framework. There was ordered peace across the Roman world. People, goods, ideas could travel very freely, very widely, very easily. That's one issue. You can't quantity that issue; you can't weigh it up and say that's 22 percent of the reason why Christianity was successful, but there's clearly something there. Across this huge Roman Empire there was a common primary language, Greek. One might compare that, let's say, to the role of French in the 18th or 19th centuries, to the role of English in recent decades in the world. After all, all of our early Christian texts are written in Greek.

Urban areas were numerous, were populous, and were relatively open. There were lots of cities, particularly in the eastern Mediterranean, and that's where Christianity arose. People on the whole in the ancient world were tolerant of religious views. They were polytheists; they believed in many gods. They had, as I indicated in the previous lecture, a lot of different kinds of religious allegiances, so there was not a predisposition to be hostile to something new. Yes, it's true that some Roman writers flagged the novel superstition of the Christians, but on the whole, new ideas were not intrinsically a bad thing.

This brings us then to the 4th century, and across the 4th century, official Roman policy shifted from persecution or prosecution— Christians felt persecuted, the Romans felt that in certain circumstances they prosecuted as people were breaking the law— Roman policy shifted from that to acceptance and even to promotion of Christianity. This is really quite a remarkable change. We've talked about Constantine and his important initiatives. I indicated when we talked about his making Christianity legal, his promotion of the Christian church, his benefactions to the Christian church, and eventually, of course, his own embrace of the Christian religion, that it's very difficult for us to go back and assign specific motives to Constantine. We know what he did and what he did had immense consequences; that's clear. About this, there isn't any controversy.

We also know for instance that the Arian Constantius II, Constantine's son, and then the neopagan Julian from 361–363, complicated matters for a time. But Constantius did not set Christianity off on what would be a definitively and permanently heretical path; Julian obviously did not eradicate Christianity. In some ways actually, Julian's actions led more or less to the eradication of paganism. We saw that the pious and, to be sure, rather opinionated Theodosius instituted major changes in legislation between 378 and 380. He effectively made Christianity, you recall, in the form practiced by the bishop of Rome, the state religion of the Roman Empire.

In thinking about what Theodosius did, or even thinking about the legislation of Constantine, it's important to keep in mind that religion was part of the public order in antiquity. It was not something that was banished to the private realm. It was very much a part of public life. It was part of people's interaction with the world around them. In this world, also, the authority of emperors was imagined as all-encompassing. To be sure, Christianity's relations with the Roman state were going to bring forward—and we'll talk about this in this lecture, we'll talk about it in the next lecture, we'll encounter it again in some future lectures—some acute problems about where responsibility lay: what could emperors do, what could bishops do. But in general, what we can say is that emperors regarded their authority as comprehensive, and therefore their ability to rule on behalf of, in respect of, to the benefit of, the church, seemed to them perfectly natural. It's also interesting in this regard to say that barbarian kings inherited from their Roman predecessors the idea that the church was their special responsibility. They should protect it, they should guide it, they should help it, and they should benefit it in various ways. But, there's an old motto in Roman law, *protectio trahit subjectionem*—protection drags subjection in its wake. Protection can be a very positive and beneficial sort of thing; it can be a very negative or dangerous sort of thing.

It's also important finally, on this particular head to say, that modern ideas of the "separation of church and state" would have made no sense whatsoever to people in late antiquity. They would have understood what a state was, but they wouldn't have understood what a church was, as an independent autonomous entity separate from a state, separate from the lives of public people living out their lives under particular institutional frameworks within given geographical areas, be that a city, a province, a diocese, a prefecture, or what have you. We have to be very careful to avoid anachronism. We may look back at late antiquity and say this is an outrageous violation of the boundary between church and state. No one then would have understood there to have been such a boundary.

Looking back, I think we can say that there's no question that Christianity and the Roman state benefited from their association with each other. Christianity certainly benefited the more, but drawing up a sort of balance sheet is really a quite tricky matter. For instance, we might think of imperial benefactions such as church building—Constantine for example, dedicating Saint Peter's, Saint Paul Outside the Walls, the latter in basilica in Rome. This all happens a century or more before, for instance, the bishops of Rome, the popes—to whom we'll turn in our next lecture—before they began building churches in Rome. We may say, building lovely churches is not such a bad thing. When Constantine goes to Constantinople, he builds churches there. In an earlier lecture, we talked about Justinian, for example, and his magnificent church of Hagia Sophia in Constantinople. We might look at this and say, building churches like this was a positive thing. Moreover—and we'll come to this in a little bit more detail in a later lecture—these churches were beautifully, beautifully decorated. This provided employment for artists, it provided scope for magnificent Christian imagery, and it gave a powerful spur indeed to the development of Christian art (again, we'll talk about the Christian arts in some later lectures) but this enormous amount of patronage, simply of cash support if you will, for the physical entities of the church. This is very much a positive, and no one had the kind of resources the imperial regime did. If we're drawing up a balance sheet, maybe we put a positive mark, maybe we put a black mark, in the column in the black.

We might also think of beneficial legislation with respect to the clergy. The clergy, for example, were exempted from military service. Clergy were exempted from most taxes. We might think, I could go down a very long list, but Sundays were reserved from work; it was made a day of rest. We might look at this and say, this is beneficial, this is advantageous, this is helpful, these are good things, and perhaps that's true. But is there not a danger that what is given can be taken away, that it is hard to draw a line and say, you may benefit us thus far, but not further? Beyond a certain point, we won't regard your benefactions as beneficial. It's very hard to say. I've given just a couple of examples here. The Theodosian Code— 438, issued by Theodosius II, we've talked about this on a couple of earlier occasions—contains hundreds of rulings on ecclesiastical matters. They're scattered in some ways throughout the code, but Book 16 is made up entirely of ecclesiastical legislation. It is pretty impressive and very much food for thought to look at the enormous array of areas in which the Roman state legislated for the church, on behalf of the church, with respect to the church. This is really quite a remarkable development and phenomenon, and clearly something that cannot have existed before Constantine. In about a century, an enormous amount of legislation was passed. Is that a plus or a minus? I'll let you think about that.

Bishops became key imperial advisors and confidantes. Constantine had people like Hosius of Cordova and Eusebius around him. Over time, bishops became more and more and more important and prominent as advisors, but you remember we told the story about the encounters between Theodosius, himself a very pious and dedicated Catholic, and Bishop Ambrose at Milan. I daresay, Theodosius may have had days when he wasn't entirely sure that his relations with Ambrose were an entirely good thing. There was something very costly in terms of prestige, in terms of authority, in Theodosius's submitting to the strictures of the bishop of Milan. The fact that the emperors drew the emerging Christian elite into their scheme of things, into their system, into their court, perhaps that's a positive, but there were going to be disagreements and that was going to be more complex and difficult.

Constantine was generally praised for calling the Council of Nicaea that condemned Arianism, but he had left the decision to the bishops themselves. He said it wasn't appropriate for him to sit with them in deciding these grave matters. He said on one occasion, he was bishop for those outside the church. He didn't mean for all the pagans and Manichaeans and so forth, he meant he was bishop for those who aren't members of the clergy. He wasn't actually a bishop, and could not sit with the bishops in council.

Press forward a century. Arianism had been the great problem that Nicaea in Constantine's time. As we've seen, Monophysitism had become the great issue. Here we find a happy collaboration between Pulcheria—the sister and key advisor to Theodosius II, eventually the wife of the Emperor Marcian who succeeded Theodosius—and Pope Leo I in Rome collaborated quite effectively to condemn Monophysitism. Here we see, again, an effective collaboration. But you may recall my discussing in the last few lectures the Emperor Anastasius, a convinced Monophysite, and the Emperor Justinian trying to find a compromise formula and all of their efforts to try to find some formulation that would reconcile Chalcedonian with Monophysite and actually to a much lesser degree with Nestorian Christians too, but the big issue here was really the Monophysites. Here, the churchmen who were Chalcedonian felt the heavy hand of imperial influence to be an utter intrusion. Those who were perhaps Monophysite felt, look, the emperor's coming in on our side and trying to help us out. These were volatile explosive issues.

We know too that the church borrowed a lot directly and indirectly from Rome. I've emphasized in earlier lectures, and so won't repeat here in any detail, that the church simply borrowed the administrative geography and terminology of the Roman state. Is this a plus or a minus? It's interesting, isn't it? Roman law profoundly influenced the church's emerging canon law. Indeed, there was a motto in the Middle Ages, *Ecclesia vivit lege Romana*—the church lives by Roman law. A whole legal system was contributed to the church and shaped the jurisprudence of the church itself. Roman ideas of majesty and hierarchy—think of the ecclesiastical hierarchy, think of individuals appearing speaking before their people, wearing distinctive clothing, addressed by distinctive titles—all of this was taken over from the Roman hierarchy by the church and invested in particular in the person of the bishops and never more so than in the bishops of Rome, to whom we shall turn in our next lecture.

Lecture Nineteen
The Rise of the Roman Church

Scope:

One of the most remarkable and durable achievements of late antiquity was the papacy's rise to prominence and then to leadership in the Christian world. On what bases did the bishops of Rome, the popes, rest their claims to authority? How did they exercise authority? How did the popes interact with other church leaders and with the emperors? Who were some of the more interesting and significant popes?

Outline

I. The eventual prominence of the bishops of Rome is almost as surprising as the rise of Christianity itself.

    A. By what steps did Rome's bishops achieve preeminence?

    B. On what bases did Rome's bishops claim to possess and exercise authority?

    C. What, in fact, could Rome's bishops do and not do?

II. Everything begins with Saint Peter.

    A. The fundamental text is Matthew 16:16–19. This "Petrine text" would be drawn upon for centuries (down to today).

        1. Attention to Peter is unparalleled.

            a. He was called first and is always named first.

            b. He invited Jesus to walk on water.

            c. Jesus got into Peter's boat on the shore.

            d. Peter alone spoke at the Transfiguration.

            e. He asked Jesus, "Lord, if my brother betrays me …"

            f. He asked for an explanation of the thief in the night.

            g. He asked John to ask Jesus who would betray him.

            h. He speaks on behalf of all the apostles.

            i. The angel at Jesus's tomb tells the women to report to Peter.

            j. The Lord's appearance to Peter is mentioned by Paul.

            k. The *Acts of the Apostles* lays stress on Peter's leadership.

2. There are serious questions here: Was Peter's leadership symbolic? Did it die with him? Could it be transmitted?

B. From the 2nd century, the Roman community maintained a powerful sense of the memory and cult of Peter.

    1. The place of his martyrdom and burial was preserved.

    2. Places and relics associated with Peter were venerated.

III. To whom, or to what, might Peter's "office" be transmitted?

A. The Pauline and Catholic Epistles suggest a larger sense of community.

B. The First Letter of Clement to Corinth expresses the idea that various Christian communities have responsibility for each other.

C. When Ignatius of Antioch was on his way to Rome to be martyred, he wrote to six churches.

D. When Polycarp was praying before his martyrdom, he referred to "the whole Catholic Church throughout the world."

E. Cyprian of Carthage said that the unity of the church had to be preserved at all costs.

F. Clearly the church was not conceived as local, but what was it, and who had authority within it?

G. There was a sense of the church as a larger whole: The idea of apostolic succession had taken hold, and there was some sense that Peter's authority had been transmitted to the bishops of Rome.

IV. The actions and expressions of several early Roman bishops are revealing.

A. The pontificate of Stephen I is revealing.

    1. During Decius's persecution, some Spanish bishops had lapsed; one went to Rome to obtain rehabilitation. Other Spanish bishops appealed to Cyprian, who was angry but "excused" Stephen on grounds of ignorance.

    2. Stephen refused to be in communion with bishops who rebaptized persons who had lapsed during the persecution.

    3. Stephen was the first pope to try to impose his views in serious, contested circumstances.

B. Julius I refused to side with Arianizing bishops who deposed others and said, portentously, that he should have been consulted in the first place.

C. The Council of Serdica established that episcopal trials could be reviewed by Rome.

D. In 385 Siricius issued the first extant "decretal," and he said that decretals become instantly the law of the church.

V. The 5th century was decisive in the elaboration of claims to papal authority.

   A. Innocent I said that no decision was valid unless it had been submitted to Rome for judgment.

   B. Pope Leo I "the Great" was the real architect of the "Petrine theory" of papal authority.

      1. We have 143 of his letters and 97 of his sermons, so we know his views in unusual detail.

      2. He gained wide authority over the churches of the Western Empire, aided by legislation of Valentinian III.

      3. He imposed his will on Chalcedon.

      4. He claimed again and again that the pope is the Vicar of Peter—that the authority Peter possessed is still possessed by his successors.

   C. Pope Gelasius I made audacious claims.

      1. While Anastasius was struggling to find a compromise formula, Gelasius wrote to him to object to his interference in a dogmatic controversy.

      2. His famous letter said that the world was governed by the "power" (*potestas*) of kings and the "authority" (*auctoritas*) of priests. Kings rule mortal bodies, whereas priests rule immortal souls; therefore, the authority of priests is greater than the power of kings.

      3. Gelasius lacked the means to put his ideas into force, but they are revealing—and remarkable—just the same.

VI. Conciliar and imperial decisions were important as well.

   A. At Nicaea Constantine's key adviser, Hosius of Cordova, signed first, but later forged copies put the signatures of the pope's representatives first.

B. At the Council of Constantinople I, the bishop of Constantinople was said to rank after the bishop of Rome because "New Rome" was second only to "Old Rome."

C. At Thessalonica—as we have seen—Theodosius said all had to believe as the bishop of Rome believed.

D. At Chalcedon the decree of the Council of Constantinople I was affirmed, but Leo I objected strenuously.

E. Valentinian III said that the authority of the pope was based on Saint Peter, the majesty of Rome, and the holy council. Whatever the pope decrees has the force of law.

F. Nevertheless, Rome's bishops always asserted that their authority rested on the Petrine text and apostolic succession.

VII. By the end of the 5th century, the papacy had gained enormous influence and prestige.

A. There was certain logic in operation: Christ founded one church and assigned its leadership to Peter; by apostolic succession each apostle transmitted his authority to his successors. The bishops of Rome are Peter's successors, and as his vicars they inherit his full authority.

B. Papal authority was neither full nor universally accepted.
  1. The popes lacked coercive mechanisms.
  2. There was no consensus on whether the bishop of Rome had a primacy of honor or of authority.
  3. Papal relations with rulers were ambiguous in the extreme.

C. The rise of the papacy is one of the great, original, distinctive achievements of late antiquity.

Suggested Reading:

Grisar, *A History of Rome and the Popes*, vol. 1.

Schimmelpfennig, *The Papacy*, chaps. 1 and 2.

Questions to Consider:

1. What were the fundamental bases of the bishop of Rome's claims to leadership in the church?

2. What were the most decisive steps in the papacy's rise of leadership in the late antique church?

Lecture Nineteen—Transcript
The Rise of the Roman Church

Hello and welcome once again to our series of lectures on late antiquity. This time, Lecture Nineteen, is the rise of the Roman Church. In our last couple of lectures, we've talked about the Christianization of the Roman world in some general terms. We talked in general terms about Christianity's interactions with, both positive and negative, the Roman state. I've been stressing that, in many respects, the emergence of Christianity is something that we can describe, in certain respects it's something we can explain, and in certain respects it is something that is really quite surprising.

We come now to one particular theme in the context of Christianization of the Roman world, the relations between Christianity and the Roman state, and the spread and success and eventual triumph of Christianity, and that is the prominence of the bishops of Rome. I daresay that in many ways, the eventual prominence of the bishops of Rome is almost as surprising as that of the rise of Christianity itself. I've mentioned in earlier lectures that what gradually emerges in the ancient world is a Catholic form of Christianity, a universal set of teachings accepted by all. We've seen, for example, that already in the 2nd the 3rd centuries, Christians were concerned about their authoritative documents, about the persons who would have authority to teach and to transmit those documents. We're going to have occasion in some later lectures to look in some more detail about the content of Christian teaching, and of how Christians defined what was acceptable teaching, orthodox teaching, Catholic teaching, and what was not.

Nowadays it's easy to look back and to think that one inevitably would couple Catholic Church and bishop of Rome. Yet, in antiquity it was not so obvious that that coupling would be achieved or become permanent and durable. That's our job in this lecture, to explain how the bishops of Rome rose to prominence and what that prominence meant. In particular, I'm going to pursue a series of themes. By what steps did Rome's bishops achieve preeminence? How did that happen? On what basis did Rome's bishops claim to possess and exercise authority? That is, in certain respects, a little different story than how did it happen. In a sense, we'll say how did it happen, and then we'll say why did it happen, or what was the theory on the basis of which it happened. Finally, we'll come at the end to the question of what actually could Rome's bishops do and not do? What powers did they have and what powers were denied them? What possibilities did they have to act in this Christian world of late antiquity?

Everything begins with Saint Peter. The fundamental text is in the Gospel of Matthew 16:16–19. This "Petrine text"—it comes eventually to be called the "Petrine text" because of the text about Peter, but it's the theoretical basis for the authority of those who descend from Peter. Again, we'll have more to say about each of those aspects of this issue as we move along here. The Petrine text would be drawn upon for centuries, right down to today. It is still the valid basis for the authority of the bishop of Rome in the Catholic Church. If we look at the Gospels and the other New Testament materials, attention to Peter is absolutely unparalleled. He was called "first among the apostles." He is always named first when the apostles are named. It was he who invited Jesus to walk on the water. Jesus got into Peter's boat on the shore. Peter alone spoke at the scene of the transfiguration. Peter speaks often to Jesus. He said, "Lord, if my brother betrays me," and so on. Peter asked for an explanation of the thief in the night. Peter asked John to ask Jesus who would betray him. Peter speaks on behalf of all of the apostles. The angel at Jesus's tomb tells the women to report to Peter. The Lord's appearance to Peter is mentioned by Paul, and Paul and Peter were rivals in certain respects. The *Acts of the Apostles* lay stress on Peter's leadership. There's nothing else like this in the New Testament.

That's all very clear. Here's what's not so clear. Was Peter's leadership symbolic? Was Peter's leadership personal? Did it die with him? Could it be transmitted? Could anybody inherit this leadership that Peter seems to have had? It goes without saying, so I'll say it anyway, Peter didn't have a Vatican, he didn't have a newspaper, he didn't have a radio station, he didn't have a "popemobile," he didn't have a great big bureaucracy, he didn't have a museum, so we have to be very careful. We're not trying to draw a straight line between Peter and now. Although, in a sense, we could certainly draw, as it were, a dotted line from Peter until now. We want to keep this in manageable proportions when we think about Peter. But this stress upon Peter in the Christian scriptures is really quite striking.

From the 2nd century we know that the Roman community maintained a very powerful sense of the memory and the cult of Peter. The place of his martyrdom, directly under the altar of today's Saint Peter's Basilica, the place of his martyrdom and burial was preserved. We know that it was there in the 2nd century and that people came there to reverence the site. We know that places around Rome and relics associated with Peter were venerated. For example, the chains with which he was bound when he was in prison are today in the Church of San Pietro in Vincoli, in Rome. Saint Peter in chains in Rome, the chains are there. Whether they're actually Peter's chains or not I'm not prepared to say, but those chains have been in Rome for a very long time. The bandages that were on his legs under those chains were venerated in antiquity. A stone where Peter knelt and into which his knees impressed small indentations was venerated, and rainwater that collected there was gathered and taken away by people. There was a very powerful sense—and I could go on and on actually with examples like this—in Rome of connectedness to Peter. Peter, of course, began in Palestine as one of the apostles, eventually was in Antioch, and then went to Rome. Rome becomes significant only because Peter went there. Peter could have gone anywhere. As it happens he went to Rome, and so it was there that his cult, that his memory and so on, was venerated in particular.

There is Peter, prominent in the Christian scriptures. There is Rome, which venerates Peter with a particular reverence, with a particular devotion. But did Peter have an office, and could that office be transmitted? Or, maybe just to formulate that question slightly differently, to whom might such an office be transmitted or in what context, in what framework?

The Pauline and Catholic Epistles, the letter material, the epistolary material of the New Testament, suggests in various places a larger sense of community. In other words, Christians are beginning to have a feeling that they're connected to other Christians. Paul, for example, writing back and forth to other Christian communities suggests that these are not utterly independent autonomous groups that have no interest in or connection with each other. There is a letter from the early 2nd century written by Bishop Clement of Rome; traditionally he's bishop in Rome from 91–101. Clement wrote to Corinth to express the idea that various Christian communities have some responsibility for each other. It's rather interesting. There were controversies in Corinth; that will come as no surprise to anybody who has read Saint Paul's letters to the Corinthians. There are continuing struggles in Corinth, Clement writes. Is he writing as a pastoral matter? Is this a fraternal gesture or does he imagine himself somehow to have authority and responsibility for a quarrelling, struggling, fellow Christian community, and therefore he intervenes in some official way? I wouldn't want to press that very far, but I wouldn't want to ignore that possibility.

When Ignatius of Antioch—lived from about 35–107—is on his way to Rome to be martyred, he wrote letters to six churches to inform them of what was about to happen. When Polycarp, the bishop of Smyrna, who lived from about 69–155, was praying before his martyrdom, he referred to "the whole Catholic Church throughout the world." He has a sense of a much larger ecclesial entity out there. Cyprian of Carthage—we met him in an earlier lecture because he's the first really to articulate the notion, the idea, the doctrine of apostolic succession, that bishops today inherit their position from the apostles who were their predecessors. Cyprian said that the unity of the church had to be preserved at all costs. In other words, he saw in his own time various movements and various tendencies that threatened to fracture the unity of the church, and he thought the unity of the church was something utterly crucial.

We're building here a little bit of a framework, a little bit of a context. There is apparently a sense of a large Christian community. Maybe it's the whole Catholic Church throughout the world; maybe it's simply the church whose unity must be preserved. If Peter had an office and if it could be transmitted, clearly it's going to be transmitted in the context of this church.

It's perfectly clear that the church was not conceived as local, but was it then and who had authority within it? Clement of Rome, whom I mentioned just a moment ago, said that the apostles appointed men, I quote him now, "so that other approved men should succeed to their ministry." In other words, he suggests that the apostles carefully chose individuals who would succeed to them. Jesus chose the apostles; the apostles choose others. Irenaeus suggested the succession of bishops in all the churches. I mentioned in the last lecture, I think, that Eusebius, the historian of the church, also laid great stress on the succession of bishops in all the churches. Indeed very interesting, wherever he could find information,

Eusebius lists the bishops in order who presided in the various churches around the Mediterranean world.

Cyprian of Carthage, we've referred to him several times now, says that in controversies they dare to appeal to the throne of Peter and to the chief church whence priestly unity takes its source. They dare— Cyprian was sometimes a little upset because people would appeal to the bishop of Rome over his head or appeal to the bishop of Rome for a decision that he wasn't entirely happy with, but he acknowledges that people are applying and appealing to the bishop of Rome. There was a sense of a church as a larger whole. There is a sense of apostolic succession, that the church is led now by bishops, and that those bishops are in some sense the successors, one after another after another after another, of the original apostles.

This rather now begs the question, doesn't it? If the Christian scriptures make utterly clear Peter's leadership among the original apostles, is it then clear that that one who succeeds to Peter retains, inherits, possesses Peter's leadership within the bishops now at any given moment in time, working out historically? The actions and expressions of several fairly early Roman bishops are revealing. I keep using the phrase bishop of Rome; the official title of this officer is the bishop of Rome. All the duties, rights, responsibilities, privileges, burdens, etc., prerogatives, what have you, attach to the fact that this individual is the bishop of Rome. *Papa, pope*, is a term of endearment; it means "father." It is not the title. This is not like president, prime minister, or pope. No, it's president, prime minister, bishop of Rome, if you see what I mean.

The pontificate, *pontifex* in Latin, is one of the words from antiquity that gives us one of the words like pontiff that is used for the bishop of Rome. We refer to the period of time when a pontiff rules as his pontificate, so we can see how some of this language emerges. The pontificate of Stephen I, 254–257, was brief. It's also true that a great many of the early popes were murdered. Actually they were, but they were martyred. The pontificate of Stephen is revealing. During Decius's persecution, 250–251 A.D., some Spanish bishops had lapsed. They had kind of gone over to the authorities, had collaborated with the authorities. One of these lapsed bishops went to Rome to seek rehabilitation. The pope, the bishop of Rome, was sympathetic to him. Other Spanish bishops who were much more rigorous on this particular issue appealed to Cyprian in Carthage, a man of immense prestige and immense influence. Cyprian was not prepared really to criticize Stephen; he wasn't prepared at the same time to give Stephen a free pass. He basically took the view that Stephen had made a mistake. He should not have rehabilitated this bishop, but he "excused him" on the grounds of ignorance. In other words, he said Stephen didn't really understand the whole situation. If he did he might have made a different decision, but he's made his decision and that's that. We can see certain issues intention here, can't we?

Stephen refused to be in communion with bishops who rebaptized persons who had lapsed during the persecutions. He's now making a theological, which is also a political, which is also an institutional decision, about what he'll do and what he won't do. We know, Cyprian tells us so, the examples of Stephen's pontificate tell us so, that people were beginning to appeal to Rome for decisions. That's clear. People were appealing to the bishop of Rome and asking him to adjudicate various kinds of controversies. But then it's also clear that not all were prepared to accept the decisions rendered in Rome. Stephen was the first of the popes to try in a really serious way to impose his views in serious contested circumstances. If we were really exploring all of these issues in much greater detail, we could back up a few decades to the time of Pope Victor I, who tried to settle, in the ancient world, the date for Easter. Easter, of course, for Christians is a movable feast. It doesn't fall on the same day every year. Christmas is December 25. Easter falls on a different day every year. There were various calendars in use. Some thought you should use the Jewish calendar for figuring the date of Easter; some thought you should avoid the Jewish calendar for figuring the date of Easter. Pope Victor tried to settle a date for Easter and had absolutely no success. We can look at some small cases like that and say, we do see these bishops of Rome actually fairly early on trying to make binding decisions all around the place. But I think it's in Stephen's time, as I've been indicating, that we see issues of larger consequence, issues with more importance for larger numbers of contemporaries, and from Stephen's time on, we see these pretty consistently.

We skip up into the early 4th century. Pope Julius I, 337–352, refused to side with the Arianizing bishops who had deposed certain others. Let's bear in mind now, the emperor is Constantius II, Constantine's son, who is an Arian. A considerable number of bishops trimmed their sails to the prevailing winds. That is to say they embraced Arianism, or at any rate they played footsy with Arianism, and they sometimes tried to depose other bishops who were not Arians. Julius refused to have anything to do with these bishops. Then he said rather portentously, that he should have been consulted in the first place. Not that he's going to decide about a thorny issue as it's playing out, but before the issue even emerged, someone should have checked with him. During his very pontificate, the Council of Serdica, in the Balkans in 341, established that episcopal trials could be reviewed in Rome. In other words, decisions made by local bishops could be reviewed by the bishop of Rome. Mind you, that decision was not made in Rome; it was made at Serdica.

Let's just pause there too. There's another term we ought to clear up, episcopal. I'm not referring to the modern Episcopal Church. I'm referring to the fact that language plays all sorts of silly games. In modern English, we use the word bishop; yes, that's related to the Greek *episcopes*, to the Latin *episcopes*, all right, fair enough, but it actually comes to us through the German, *bischof.* We don't have an adjective in English, *bishopal*. We really should, but we don't. For some peculiar reason, we use a noun, bishop, that comes to us via German, and we use an adjective—episcopal—that comes to us via Greek and Latin. When we're talking about episcopal, we're talking about things to do with bishops, an adjective that attaches to bishops because we don't have the word *bishopal*. I hope that will clarify that little piece of terminology.

In 385, Pope Siricius issued the first extent decretal. A "decretal" is a decree made by the bishop of Rome in his own name, on his own behalf, on his own authority. He said that decretals become instantly the law of the church. Where had the law previously been made? It was made in church councils. He now says not that the church councils don't issue valid law. Of course they do, but that decretals issued by the bishops of Rome, and only by the bishops of Rome, not by the bishop of any place else, become instantly the law of the church. We also know that collections of decretals, collections of these decrees made by the popes, by the bishops of Rome, began to be assembled and circulated. We have substantial collections of this material. People out and around the Christian world began to see the decisions of the bishops of Rome as authoritative.

The 5th century was especially decisive in the elaboration of claims to papal authority. What we've been seeing is an emerging church, an emerging idea of apostolic succession, an emerging focus of that notion of apostolic succession, particularly on the bishops of Rome who succeeded to the Apostle Peter, and we're also seeing again those bishops of Rome acting in certain concrete specific ways. Now what we're going to do is see them spell out the theory.

Innocent I, pope from 402–417, said that no decision was valid unless it had been submitted to Rome for judgment. In a way, this reaches back all the way to the time of Serdica, if you will. This reaches back to the implications of the actions of Pope Stephen about whom we spoke a second ago. Pope Leo I, Leo "the Great," one of only two popes ever to be called "the Great"—the other is Gregory whom we'll meet a little bit later in this course—Leo is pope 440–461. He is the real architect of the "Petrine theory" of papal authorities. Now we come back to our Petrine text. Remarkably, 143 of his letters and 97 of his sermons are extant. For no bishop of Rome before his time do we have this kind of material surviving that enables us really to form a pretty comprehensive and clear sense of his views on things. We know his views unusually fully. We find very little in what we know of Leo and what Leo said that strikes us in any meaningful sense surprising. What we never find earlier is the kind of comprehensiveness, clarity, order, or precision that we find in the writings and the teachings of Leo "the Great." He actually gained, for example, very wide authorities over the churches in the Western Empire. He was aided very much in this by the legislation of Emperor Valentinian III. Valentinian passed legislation supporting, as it were, the bishops of Rome, not unlike the legislation passed by Theodosius between 378 and 380, supporting Christianity generally and the bishop of Rome.

We saw that Leo effectively imposed his will on the Council of Chalcedon. That is to say, he steeled the bishops at Chalcedon against any tendency to compromise with the Monophysites. But he claimed again and again and again that the pope is the Vicar of Peter, that the bishop of Rome, the pope, possesses fully now all the authority which Peter possessed. The authority of Peter is still possessed by Peter's successors and by them alone. Here we have an interesting little fact about papal history. Every pope succeeds Peter. For example, in the year 2005, Benedict XVI was not elected to succeed Pope John Paul II. Benedict XVI was elected to succeed

Peter. John Paul II succeeded Peter. Paul VI succeeded Peter, and so on, back through more than 200 bishops of Rome.

Pope Gelasius I, who was pope from 492–496, again a brief pontificate, made some pretty audacious claims. Let's think back to our discussion earlier of the Emperor Anastasius. We saw that his immediate predecessor Zeno had issued a document, the *Henotikon*, the act of union, his attempt to find a compromised formula that would reconcile Monophysites and Chalcedonians. Zeno was unable to achieve agreement with his decision. Anastasius becomes emperor. Anastasius is basically a committed Monophysite. With Zeno it's a lot harder to say, but Anastasius is clearly a committed Monophysite. He also wants a compromised formula. In a sense, what he attempts to do is hearken back to the *Henotikon* of Zeno. He really wants to see if he can work with that.

Gelasius writes a very interesting letter, which is extant, it survives, to Anastasius to object to his interference in a dogmatic controversy. First of all, Gelasius we may say constructs his brief rather narrowly. He doesn't talk about all imperial benefactions for the church and different issues that we've talked about in this and in earlier lectures. He says doctrine, dogma, the teachings of the church, are no part of the emperor's writ; you must keep your hands off the teachings of the church. Why is this the case? Here's where Gelasius makes a quite remarkable statement. His famous letter says that the world is governed by the "power" of kings and the "authority" of priests. These people understood the power of language. To say that kings— and he uses the word king, but we might have expected emperors— possess mere *potestas*, power, police power, brute force, coercion, whereas priests possess *auctoritas*, authority, legitimacy, was extraordinarily loaded language. There had been no question that at the imperial court, the people would have heard these words exactly as Gelasius meant them to be heard. But how did he get to that point?

Gelasius basically says something rather interesting. He says, on the whole, kings do their thing and priests do theirs. Their areas of responsibility and competence day in and day out are distinct and they shouldn't come into conflict. But if they come into conflict, the authority of priests must take precedence over the power of kings because priests are concerned with men's souls that are immortal and emperors or kings with men's bodies that are mortal. What a remarkable claim, indeed. Think back four and three-quarter centuries earlier, a minor Roman official killed the founder, sort of executed or permitted the execution of the founder of Christianity. Now a bishop of the city of Rome has articulated a plausible claim for why priests in general, and the bishop of Rome in particular, is more important not than Pontius Pilate, but than the emperor of the Roman world. But it's not quite as simple as all that. Gelasius lacked the means to put his ideas into force. He couldn't coerce the imperial court. He couldn't sort of tell the emperor what to do. His claims are remarkable, but we have to keep in mind the practical reality of the thing.

Conciliar and imperial decisions were important, too. We've referred to these a little bit already in this and in earlier lectures, so let me just review a few points and make one or two new ones as we move forward. At Nicaea, Constantine's key advisor had been a man named Hosius of Cordova. In the official acts of Nicaea, Hosius signed first. You think of all those grand signatures on our Declaration of Independence or something, the bishops who attended the council all sign; Hosius signed first. There are later medieval copies of the documents of Nicaea in which the names of the popes' representatives are placed first. They're clearly forged copies, but it's interesting that later on, somebody adjusted and stuck the name of the popes' representatives first.

At the Council of Constantinople I, that met in 381, the bishop of Constantinople was said to rank after the bishop of Rome because "New Rome" was second only to "Old Rome." Here a council sort of ranked Rome and its bishop. At Thessalonica in 380, as we've seen, Theodosius said that all had to believe as the bishop of Rome believed. At the Council of Chalcedon, we've met this a number a number of times, affirmed Diophysite, divine and human nature teaching, against Monophysite, divine only nature. But there are a lot of canons issued at Chalcedon. Canon 28 really reaffirmed the decree of Constantinople. One, namely that Constantinople stood second to Rome in ecclesiastical as in secular matters. Leo I objected strenuously. Leo had said that the power of the bishop of Rome, the authority of the bishop of Rome, has absolutely nothing to do with church councils, it has nothing to do with imperial decisions, it has nothing to do with the fact that the bishop is in Rome, however interesting, important, and significant Rome may be, it has to do with Peter, period. End of discussion.

The Emperor Valentinian III had once said, and basically here he was speaking the simple truth, that the authority of the pope was based on Saint Peter, on the majesty of Rome, and on the Holy Council. He further said, whatever the pope decrees has the force of law. That is perfectly true. That is an accurate historical description, but let's bear in mind that Pope Leo I said no, no, no, no. It's not a matter of historical contingency; it's a matter of the word of God as expressed to Peter and recorded in the scriptures.

By the end of the 5th century, then, Rome's bishops had been asserting their authority rests on the Petrine texts, it rests on apostolic succession. These are by now fairly old teachings. The papacy had gained enormous influence and prestige. There was a certain logic in operation here and I hope you've been able to kind of follow me. Christ had founded a single church. Leadership had been assigned to Peter. By apostolic succession, bishops succeeded to the apostles, Peter had been the leader of the apostles, and Peter's successor is now Peter's vicar, is now the leader of the church as a whole.

That's the logic. It's clear. It's elegant. It basically remains, to this day, the ecclesiology, that's a big fancy name for the area of theology that thinks about how churches are organized. The ecclesiology of the Catholic Church to this day rests essentially on these basic late antique formulations. But we have to admit that papal authority was neither full nor universally accepted. The popes lacked coercive mechanisms. They didn't have tools at their disposal to make people do things. There was very little consensus on whether the bishop of Rome had a primacy of honor, kind of prestige, or a primacy of authority. Papal relations with rulers were ambiguous and were going to remain ambiguous for decades, indeed centuries into the future. All of that having been said, the rise of the papacy is one of the great original distinctive achievements of the late antique world.

Lecture Twenty
The Call of the Desert—Monasticism

Scope:

The Egyptian desert may not seem a promising launching pad for a vast movement whose consequences are with us still. Yet in the years around 300 A.D., a few leaders with a new vision of what the Christian life might entail attracted followers—eventually thousands and thousands of them. These were the monks, those who, ironically, lived alone together. Instead of engaging the world, as the church and its leaders did, monks fled the world. In seclusion and in prayer, while denying themselves all bodily comforts, monks—and eventually nuns, too—heard the call of the Gospel in a radical new way. This lecture will focus on the "Desert Fathers" and their first followers in other parts of the Mediterranean world.

Outline

I. The emergence of Christian monasticism in Egypt is one of late antiquity's most dynamic and characteristic achievements. But how do we explain it?

   A. Asceticism is not uniquely Christian.
      1. Philosophical sects (e.g., Pythagorean brotherhoods) appeared in antiquity.
      2. Jewish communities such as the Essenes and the Qumrān groups displayed ascetic tendencies.

   B. Some think that solitaries fled persecutions—or perhaps tax collectors.

   C. Some see a conscious effort to live the *vita apostolica*: a life of communal renunciation and prayer.

   D. Some believe that Christianity got "too easy" after Constantine.

   E. Some look to the theology of Origen and his promotion of Adam's personal state before the Fall.

   F. Perhaps there was a fundamental dichotomy in Christianity's posture vis-à-vis the world: Embrace and change it, or flee it.

G. Even if any one of these explanations captures a portion of the truth, monasticism as it developed was something unique.

II. Central to monasticism was asceticism. What does this mean?

A. Ascesis/asceticism derives from the Greek *askēsis,* which means "exercise" or "training." It implies therefore a disciplined, methodical way of life.

B. Usually the discipline is defined negatively: A person gives up food, strong drink, sex, companionship, etc.

C. Ascetics would have defined it positively as a disciplined means of transforming one's life and relationship with God.

D. *Anachoresis*—radical isolation—could be understood literally or metaphorically. Likewise the "desert" metaphors so prominent in monasticism can be understood as pertaining to a physical place or to the radical emptying of the self.

III. However isolated and disciplined they may have been, monks were not, as a rule, illiterate. Moreover, their way of life attracted a great deal of attention. Consequently the phenomenon is well attested.

A. An anonymous author wrote *History of the Monks of Egypt* in the 390s.

B. Palladius spent several years in Egypt and wrote his *Lausiac History* as the story of the "friends of God."

C. In the 4ᵗʰ and 5ᵗʰ centuries, someone began collecting the *Apophthegmata Patrum* ("Sayings of the Desert Fathers"—and mothers), and these alphabetical collections were reworked many times and translated into several languages.

D. As we shall see, there were many monastic "rules."

E. Some particularly famous monks received biographies.

F. Ecclesiastical historians and church legislation took occasional notice of monks.

IV. Traditionally the Egyptian Anthony is seen as the great founding father of monasticism.

A. Around 270 he gave away all his possessions and adopted an ascetic life.

B. For a time he studied with an old ascetic, so he cannot have been the true first.

C. After a while Anthony went into the desert—literally.

D. Anthony attracted large numbers of men and women at Nitria, west of the Nile delta, and at Scetis, 40 miles to the south. A later writer said there were 5,000 monks in all—an impressively large but suspiciously "round" number.

E. Most of what is known about Anthony comes from seven letters (now generally regarded as authentic) and from Athanasius's *Life of Saint Anthony*.

    1. Athanasius was the long-serving and controversial patriarch of Alexandria.

    2. His *Life of Saint Anthony* undoubtedly contains many authentic details but was in part written to settle many of Athanasius's accounts and to establish Anthony as a firmly anti-Arian figure.

    3. The Greek text was quickly translated into Latin and circulated widely, popularizing the monastic life.

V. The earliest monastic experience therefore relates to the desert: *heremos* in Greek.

A. Hence the earliest form of monasticism is called "eremitic" (compare "hermit") and stresses the solitary life.

B. Anthony was famous but by no means unique. There were many *appa* (later, more familiarly, *abba*—compare *abbot*—and also *amma*—mothers; that is, female leaders, more commonly called *abbesses* in the monastic tradition) in Egypt attracting followers and teaching them.

C. Palladius describes the communities at Nitria in his work.

VI. Traditionally Pachomius is regarded as the founder of a new strain of monastic life.

A. Pachomius was a pagan who had been a Roman soldier. He left the army, became a Christian, studied with a hermit, began to attract followers, and then created a monastery at Tabennisi.

B. There are several "lives" of Pachomius surviving in different languages; he wrote some letters and possibly "Instructions"; and a later Latin version of his rule may owe a lot to him but is probably not by him, although the tradition has always attributed it to him.

C. Pachomius played a key role in forging the organized monastic life, but no source details why he felt called upon to do so.

    1. Some have suggested that he brought to monasticism the regimentation of the army barracks.

    2. Some suggest that the individualism of the eremitic communities was not to his taste.

D. He required monks to pray together at least twice daily, to eat together, to worship together, and to do assigned work to make the community (not each member) self-sufficient.

E. There were probably some 10,000 monks living at Tabennisi in the 4th century, gathered in a series of loosely associated communities.

F. The form of monasticism created by Pachomius is called "cenobitic," from the Greek *koinos bios*, meaning "common life."

G. With Pachomius we see the great paradox of monastic life, for a monastery is a place where many monks live alone together.

VII. Although monasticism emerged in Egypt, it soon spread all over the late antique world.

Suggested Reading:

Chitty, *The Desert a City*.

Dunn, *The Emergence of Monasticism*, chaps. 1–4.

Questions to Consider:

1. Bearing in mind the various "background" factors that may help to explain monasticism, what nevertheless seems different or distinctive about Christian monasticism?

2. How did Anthony and Pachomius differ? What did they have in common?

Lecture Twenty—Transcript
The Call of the Desert—Monasticism

Welcome once again to our series of lectures on late antiquity. This time, Lecture Twenty, is the call of the desert, the Christian monasticism. In our last few lectures, we've been talking about the rise, the spread, the success of Christianity in the Roman world, Christianity's relations with the Roman state, the emergence of the bishops of Rome; in lots of ways, we might say, very public, visible manifestations of Christianity. Now we're going to look at something very different. Now we're going to look, in a way, at those who opted out. Though, in this lecture and also in some ways in the next one, we're going to see another of these wonderful ironies of late antiquity that is precisely the ways in which those who opted out profoundly influenced the society from which they had departed.

What we're talking about here is the rise of a phenomenon, Christian monasticism—and we'll talk about this terminology here as we go along—that is one of late antiquity's most dynamic, characteristic, original, and significant accomplishments. But what exactly is it and how do we explain it? We might say, for example, in the first place that asceticism is by no stretch of the imagination uniquely Christian. Philosophical sects in antiquity—for instance, Pythagorean brotherhoods—had already appeared. There were groups of individuals who went off separately from the wider society around them in order so that they might pursue their studies, their reflections, on their own without distraction. There were Jewish communities, for example, those such as the Essenes or the Qumrān communities, who seem to have been responsible for, for instance, the Dead Sea Scrolls. These kinds of groups displayed aesthetic tendencies, a tendency to separate from the world around them.

There are some who suggest that solitaries were individuals who, in the late antique world, or perhaps even beginning in the 3rd century just as the late antique world was dawning, fled persecution and perhaps fled tax collectors. You'll recall that until the time of Constantine, Christians had been persecuted in various areas, and some have said people fled persecution. Others have said, as the Roman burden of taxation grew greater and greater, there may have been people who simply opted out of the Roman system. They went to get away from paying higher and higher and higher taxes.

Some see a conscious effort to live the *vita apostolica*, to live the apostolic life. The ideal of capturing the apostolic life has been a constant theme in the long history of Christianity. Suffice it to say that in many places, among many groups of people, what the apostolic community actually was, how one might recapture it and bring it back to life in a given time and place, and why one would want to do that, these have been very controversial matters over a long period of time. If we attempt to capture this in perhaps its simplest terms, what we could say is that the *vita apostolica* was understood as a life of communal—very important—communal renunciation. The world out there was going to be given up and exchanged for a life of prayer. That would be the notion of the apostolic life in simplest terms. Its source was evidently, of course, the *Acts of the Apostles*. It was a question of how people read that book of the New Testament, the *Acts of the Apostles*.

Some believe that they can detect in the writings of certain, particularly early 4th century, let's say the first half of the 4th century, Christians, the idea that after Constantine made Christianity legal, Christianity got "too easy"; that back in the days when Christianity was persecuted and prosecuted, when Christians were hounded and harassed, that that was the great courageous early day of Christianity, and once Christianity was made legal, it just really wasn't so hard anymore, and therefore people fled to find a more rigorous and disciplined form of life for themselves.

Some have looked at the theology of Origen, one of the church fathers. In some later lectures, we'll bump into Origen a number of times again. For now, we'll say he lived from about 185–254. Origen, among other things, promoted the idea that Adam had led a particular form of life, a particularly pure form of life, before the Fall, before he ate the fruit from the forbidden tree. Accordingly, human existence was best ordered when it tried somehow to recapture that pre-Lapsarian, that pre-Fall state; Adam, in paradise before the Fall.

Some have suggested that there was a fundamental dichotomy or perhaps we might say a powerful creative tension in Christianity's posture vis-à-vis the world around it from the very beginning. We turn, for instance, to the so-called "Great Commission" at the end of Matthew's Gospel, go forth and teach all nations. Here the idea is that Christians have been commanded by their Lord to go out, to grab the world by the scruff of its neck, to shake it, and to make it something different and better than it used to be.

We can look at the writings of Saint Paul. Paul was a great teacher. He wrote to and was written to by other great teachers. Clearly, in certain ways, Paul was out there acting actively in the world. But there is a very powerful strain in Paul that views the world as dangerous, that views the world as tempting, that views the world as distracting, and that suggests at the end of the day that what one is best doing is avoiding that world, fleeing that world. We think, for example, of Paul's famous remark about marriage, "better to marry than to burn." It's much better, of course, if you can avoid, for instance, all sexual attraction and all physical attraction to persons, to other human beings, but humans are weak, so perhaps they have to do this. Grasp the world as it is, change it, and make it better, make it different; leave the world alone. It's a bad place; it's a dangerous place. There is a suggestion that there has always been this dichotomy or this powerful and creative tension in Christianity from the very beginning.

Even if any of these explanations captures a portion of the truth, one important thing to say about Christian monasticism is that as it developed in late antiquity, it was something utterly unique. There's been a tendency for large numbers of scholars to look at monasticism and say gee, this is kind of familiar with, it's kind of similar to a whole lot of other things we've seen before. Maybe this explains it, this explains it, this explains, that explains it. That's a perfectly legitimate enterprise for scholars to undertake. At the same time, it can be pretty powerfully reductionist. It can miss all that was unique, all that was central to Christian monasticism as it arose. What I've been describing up until now is simply a way of saying, gee, there are ways that we can look at this phenomenon and say that it does bear certain similarities to, it does seem related to, a lot of other phenomena that existed, maybe we can find various explanations for it, and that's fine. But I do want to insist that at the end monasticism is something new, it's something different, and it's something quite distinctive.

Central to monasticism was asceticism. I mentioned a few minutes ago that we have groups like the Pythagorean brotherhoods, that we have groups like the Essenes of the Qumrān community, we could point to Buddhists, for example, so asceticism isn't uniquely or distinctively Christian. But what exactly is asceticism then, and then as we move along here, we'll say what does it have to do with monasticism? Ascesis, asceticism, derives from the Greek *askēsis*, which means "exercise" or "training." It implies, therefore, a disciplined methodical way of life; that's important. This is not like stopping off at the gym to exercise for an hour on the way home from work. This is a whole way of life. This is what asceticism is. The word means a sort of exercise, training, practice—yes, it has those basic meanings—but we have to let our minds be a little more generous in defining this term so that it attaches to a way of life.

The discipline, the training, the practice is sometimes, and perhaps often indeed, defined negatively. That is to say, a person gives up. What's given up? It's food, strong drink, sex, companionship, and so on. One can dress a very long list of things that one gives up as a part of asceticism, as a part of this disciplined methodical practice of life. Fair enough, that is certainly a way of characterizing asceticism and ascetics. But it's also true that if we could interrogate ascetics— actually there are still ascetics now, so it's not at all difficult to do— we would see that they would define asceticism positively. That is, they wouldn't lay stress on all the things they're giving up; they would lay stress on a disciplined means of transforming one's life and of therefore entering into a particular kind of relationship with God. That may seem like splitting hairs, but it is important to say that an ascetic doesn't simply say, poor me, I've just given up all these things. No, an ascetic would say joyfully, I have embraced a different kind of life and I am now more fully open to the presence and power of God.

Asceticism has, as one of its key components, another Greek word, *anachoresis*. What this means is "radical isolation." *Chora* in Greek means the "country" or the "countryside," so *anachora* basically is the implication; the figural meaning here is out in the country. Moving from the literal to the metaphorical and back to the literal, we have a notion of going out in the country, actually of radical isolation. There is a powerful sense that the ascetic is someone who, in addition to whatever else he or she—very important—may have given up, has separated from all that is familiar.

This concept is actually a little bit more complicated than I just implied. In a great deal of early monastic literature we find "desert" metaphors very, very prominent. In a lot of ways, this isn't surprising at all. The particular phenomenon that we call "Christian monasticism" emerges in Egypt. In Egypt it is not very hard to get to the desert. You live in a town, the desert's just right out there, so there's desert all around you. Desert would have been a constant companion of life. It's like, what are there, dozens or something of words for snow in Eskimo, so Egyptians thought naturally in terms of desert images. That's fair enough, but the notion of these desert images prominent in monasticism could imply either a physical place, I shall go into the desert. In our next lecture, we're going to find monks from Mesopotamia to Ireland. There are no deserts in Ireland, but Irish monks talked about the desert. It's a notion of physical separation. I'm going out there. I'm going away from all of you. But another way of thinking about desert, a more metaphorical way, was the radical emptying of the self. In other words, the desert could be out there, a physical place, or the desert could be in here, a place in my own heart, in my own soul, in my own being, where if I have sufficiently detached myself from that world out there, I can attach myself to the inner life of the experience of God.

It's also important to say that however isolated and disciplined they may have been, monks were not, as a rule, illiterate. Thank heavens, because their way of life attracted a great deal of attention, and a great many of them wrote a great deal. Consequently, the phenomenon of monasticism is very well attested in antiquity, so we may have people separating themselves from all kinds of things physically, literally, or metaphorically. The point is they left an awful lot of records behind, and other people left an awful lot of records behind about them.

Let's just take a few minutes here and talk about how we actually know about this phenomenon that we call "Christian monasticism." An anonymous author wrote a *History of the Monks of Egypt* in about the 390s. A man by the name of Palladius who lived from about 364–420, perhaps as late as 430, spent several years in Egypt visiting monasteries, living with communities in those monasteries, and later on he wrote his *Lausiac History*, as a story of the people he called the "friends of God." His *Lausiac History* is a wonderful and very revealing document in all sorts of ways. In the 4th and 5th centuries, someone began collecting what we know as the *Apophthegmata Patrum*, the "Sayings of the Desert Fathers." Interestingly enough, they arrayed these sayings alphabetically. They're not arrayed chronologically, they're not arrayed geographically by the various communities in Egypt to which these fathers belong, and I should add that there are also sayings of some of the Egyptian *Ammas*—that is to say, women ascetics in Egypt. They arrayed these collections alphabetically. They're short aphorisms, but we can read them and think about them, and we learn something about the kinds of teachings—sometimes the rather oracular teachings—of apparently some of these great figures out in the Egyptian desert, sort of at whose feet other people went to study and to learn.

Eventually there were a great many monastic "rules." A monastic rule, *regula* in Latin, is basically a set of prescriptions governing the daily or the weekly routines of a community of people living together. Generally speaking, we don't think of rules as pertaining to isolated solitaries. They apply to communities. We'll have more to say about solitaries and communities in just a few minutes. The point is that a large number of rules were written, and these rules survive and tell us some very interesting things about the arrangement of these monastic communities. In a few minutes I'm going to talk about one rule connected with a particular figure in Egypt. In our next lecture, we'll actually encounter a whole bunch of rules and talk a little about what they have in common and how they differ and how they spread. Suffice it for now to say simply that a great many monastic rules survive and that they're extremely precious sources for the life of monastic communities.

You may also just think of the irony of this falling Roman Empire when presumably law and ordered ways of life have vanished off the face of the earth. This is when the great compilations of Roman law are made. This is when the great collections of canon law are produced, and this is when communities of ascetics, for crying out loud, are writing rulebooks. This was not a rule absent law and rules; this was a world awash in law and rules.

Back to our subject. Some particularly famous monks received biographies. We're going to talk about Anthony and Pachomius in just a moment, but they're not alone. They're not distinctive in having received biographies. These biographies have all the great strengths and weaknesses of the ancient genre of biography. That is, they are intended to reveal character, intended to reveal essential qualities, rather more than the grotty details that we historians would love to have. Sometimes they're a little short on facts and a little long on ideas and we're not always quite sure what to make of those ideas. Still, we're very glad to have these texts.

Let's look at ecclesiastical historians; Eusebius we've mentioned a number of times. We could talk about Theodoret and Sozomen and Socrates and a whole series of ecclesiastical historians who wrote histories of the church or histories of particular churches. As the 4th century wore on and turned into the 5th and into the 6th, many of these ecclesiastical historians took occasional notice of monks or monastic communities and wrote about them. Similarly, ecclesiastical legislation, the canon law, the councils of the church, began slowly but surely to notice monks, to legislate about them, and to incorporate them into their ways of organizing and imagining the organization of the church as a whole. I hope that will suffice to give some sense of the very rich array of materials that survive from late antiquity and that permit us to know something about this monastic phenomenon.

Let's come a little closer to it. Traditionally, the Egyptian Anthony, whose traditional dates are 251–356—he lived to be 105; is that possible? It's a little hard to know how seriously we should take the dates. But anyway, traditionally, Anthony is seen as monasticism's great founding father. Here's the story. Round about 270, he gave away all his possessions and embraced an ascetic life. He's portrayed in certain ways as an innovator, and yet at the same time, his biography—we'll have a little more to say about that biography in a second—portrays him as having studied with an old ascetic. The text actually tell us, in spite of itself, that Anthony couldn't have been the first because he went out and studied with an old ascetic in the desert. After a while, Anthony went into the desert, quite literally, and he began to attract large numbers of men and women. They assembled around him east of the Nile, east of the Nile Delta, and then a little bit later further to the east. There's a lot of people out there. This is the beginnings of, as it were, the monastic phenomenon.

Most of what we know about Anthony comes from seven letters, which are now generally regarded as authentic. I'm not an expert on these matters and some of these materials are in any case written in Coptic, a language that I don't know. Scholarly views have gone back and forth and back and forth on whether or not Anthony's letters are authentic. It seems to me that right now the consensus view is that they are, so that's the view I will adopt here. We have seven letters, and then we have a *Life of Saint Anthony* written by Athanasius, the very long-serving and very controversial patriarch of Alexandria in the 4th century.

The *Life* undoubtedly contains a great many authentic details, no question about that, and we're very glad to have it. But it's also clear on very careful reading that something else is going on in that *Life*. Arias, the founder of Arianism, had after all been an Egyptian. He taught in Alexandria. Arianism took its rise in Egypt. Athanasius was militantly, violently anti-Arian. In writing his *Life of Saint Anthony*, it's very clear that among other things, he has appropriated Anthony as a great firm anti-Arian figure. What that does suggest to us is just how prestigious Anthony and his memory had already become that it would occur to Athanasius to appropriate him for the anti-Arian cause, but it does mean that there may be perspective and slant in Athanasius's *Life of Saint Anthony* that is not quite what we would expect if we had a wider array of sources.

The Greek text of Athanasius's *Life of Saint Anthony* was very quickly translated into Latin. It circulated very widely and it was, we might say, a late antique bestseller, and a text that did a lot to promote the monastic life, awareness of the monastic life, and indeed, even the popularity of the monastic life. The earliest monastic experience, therefore, relates to the desert, *heremos* in Greek; that's the Greek word for desert. Hence, the earliest form of monasticism is called "eremitic." Compare our word "hermit." It stresses the solitary life.

Anthony was famous, no question about that, but he was by no means unique. After all, we're told that there were 5,000 of these folks out these in the desert. Later on, there were many *appa*. That word *appa* gradually morphed into *abba*, a word that means "father." Compare the English *abbot*, the head of a monastic community. There were also many *amma* in the Egyptian desert. Curiously enough, we never got the word *ammot*, we got the word *abbess*, so the woman who leads a community of women is a "fatheress." Go figure—language just plays all sorts of rather silly games with us, doesn't it? In any case, these *abba* and *amma* attracted considerable numbers of followers out in the desert, producing of course a very interesting and curious dichotomy inside the history of monasticism itself. What is a monk? A *monachos* means "one alone." What is a *monasterion*? It's a monastery. A monastery of course is a place where a whole lot of monks go to live "alone together." Language again sort of plays tricks on us.

Our friend Palladius—we mentioned him a moment ago in his *Lausiac History*—describes the communities at Nitria this way. He says,

> On the mountain live some 5,000 men with different modes of life, each living in accordance with his own powers and wishes so that it is allowed to live alone or with a number of others. There are seven bakeries in the mountain which serve the needs of these and of the anchorites of the great desert, 600 in all. ... In the mountain of Nitria there is a great church ... next to the church a guest house where they receive the stranger who has arrived until he goes away of his own accord, without limit of time, even if he remains two or three years. ... In this mountain also live doctors and confectioners and they use wine and wine is on sale. ... [And] these men work with their hands at making linen so that all are self-supporting.

We might just add here that other sources also talk about basket makers. Here is a kind of a wonderful picture of these communities of eremitic monks. It's not yet fully organized communally, but clearly groups of people are living together with some sense of responsibility for one another.

Traditionally it is Pachomius, who lives from about 290–346, who's regarded as the founder of a new strain of monastic life. Pachomius was born into a pagan family and he had been a Roman soldier. When he left the Roman army and became a Christian, he studied with a hermit for a period of time, and then he began to attract followers. This seems to be a very common pattern with the great figures of monasticism about whom we have knowledge. How many people would have fit this model is utterly impossible to say, but the idea is that somebody studies with a hermit, opts out of society, goes off by himself, and then attracts followers. I suppose there's kind of an inevitable curiosity that we all have, isn't there, about someone who leaves us. It's sort of, what is she doing out there? We're not content to just leave them be out there by themselves; we think we have to go find out what they're doing.

In any case, in a place called Tabennisi, or outside a place called Tabennisi, Pachomius founds an individual monastery, and then there's a whole bunch of other monastic communities that begin to form round about Tabennisi. There are several "lives" of Pachomius surviving in several different languages. He seems to have written some letters. It's also possible that he wrote a work called the "Instructions." There is a later Latin version of this text that calls it a rule and that attributes it wholly to Pachomius. There has been sometimes a tendency to say, in the context of the history of monasticism, that Pachomius wrote the first rule. That's not wrong exactly, but we really don't know the relationship between that Latin text and Pachomius's "Instructions." We don't know if all the material in the Latin text is authentically Pachomian.

Pachomius played, in any case, a key role in forging organized monastic life. It's interesting that no source details precisely why he felt called upon to do so. He does clearly advance beyond the kinds of communities that existed at Nitria and a place called Scetis, about 40 miles to the south. From the passage from Palladius that I read a moment ago, you can see that if they have to make linen or they have to make baskets, there's a sense that they've got to kind of look out for each other. There is a great church on the mountain, so they obviously are going to worship together. There are also those anchorites who go out in the great desert. There are some people who aren't really quite part of this community. I don't want to suggest that eremitic folk are unorganized or disorganized, but Pachomius is going to give the whole situation a slightly different spin. Some have suggested, for instance, that he may have brought to monasticism the regimentation of the army barracks, that had he been a Roman soldier, he thought, we got to get organized. Some have suggested that the individualism of the eremitic communities was really not to his taste, that he was just a person who, generally speaking, preferred a more ordered form of life. It appears that what Pachomius did is required the monks to pray together at least twice a day. He required them to eat together. He required them to worship together, and he required them to do assigned work. The aim here is that he's going to make the community self-sufficient, not each member of the community. There will be a much greater corporate sense.

Various credible sources suggest to us that there may have been some 10,000 monks living at Tabennisi in the 4th century, gathered in a series of loosely associated communities. This is a lot of people living alone, together. The form of monasticism, created by Pachomius, is called "cenobitic," from the Greek *koinos bios*, meaning a "common life." We have eremitic and cenobitic.

With Pachomius, we see the great paradox of monastic life, this sense of a monastery where many people live alone together. Monasticism took its rise in Egypt, but as we're going to see in our next lecture, it very soon spread very widely all over the late antique world and became, to be sure, one of that world's most familiar elements.

Lecture Twenty-One
Monasticism—Solitaries and Communities

Scope:

Within a century of monasticism's origins, monks and nuns could be found in large numbers in every corner of the Roman Empire. This lecture will begin by exploring how and why the monastic movement spread. We will also note the many different forms of monastic life that eventually emerged. In the east the more solitary form of monasticism generally prevailed, whereas in the west the communal form triumphed. The lecture will emphasize the greatest of the eastern monastic founders, Saint Basil, and the greatest of the western figures, Saint Benedict. We will also explore women's contribution to monasticism.

Outline

I. Monasticism proved to be an immensely popular and powerful phenomenon in late antiquity, by no means reserved to Egypt.

    A. Several factors contributed to monasticism's spread around the Mediterranean world and beyond.

        1. Monastic literature, such as the histories, biographies, and collections of sayings mentioned in the previous lecture, was widely circulated.

        2. Visitors to Egypt were numerous and often brought forms of Egyptian monasticism back to their homelands.

    B. There was no single form of monasticism in Egypt, so various forms of monasticism emerged in other areas. Broadly, one can say that in the east the eremitic pattern prevailed, and in the west the cenobitic.

II. Monasticism passed from Egypt to Palestine early and easily.

    A. Hilarion of Gaza came from a pagan family but was converted to Christianity in Alexandria.

        1. He spent some time in the desert with disciples of Anthony.

        2. By 306 he had settled in Gaza, where he practiced an extreme form of asceticism.

        3. Eventually he went traveling because he disliked acquiring followers.

B. A more organized form of monastic life centers on the semilegendary figure of Chariton, who came from Anatolia and settled in caves outside Jerusalem. The group of caves where Chariton and his followers settled came to be called a *lavra*, a word meaning "street" or "alley."

C. The great monastic figures of Palestine were Euthymius and Sabas.

    1. Euthymius established a great *lavra* near Jerusalem, as did Sabas—Mar Saba, founded in 478.

    2. The *lavra* was a particular eastern adaptation of the eremitic and cenobitic forms of monasticism.

    3. Monks lived in individual cells but they worshiped together occasionally and followed the guidance of a common abbot.

D. In the east, Syria presented a third pattern: extraordinarily rigorous asceticism.

    1. One monk wore chains so heavy he could only crawl, and another lived in a room with so low a ceiling that he always stooped.

    2. There were "dendrites," monks who lived in trees.

    3. The greatest figure was Symeon, who began as an anchorite, became a cenobite, but was expelled by his community for excesses.

III. The great monastic founder in the east was Saint Basil, who was also prominent as one of the greatest church fathers.

A. Basil was far from the first ascetic in the east, but he was the first serious organizer.

B. In 357–358 he visited Egypt, spending time at Nitria and Scetis but he was most influenced by Pachomian communities.

C. He lived a solitary life for a while but decided that a common life was better.

D. He wrote "longer" and "shorter" rules, which were not detailed, coherent plans for a community but teaching manuals in question-and-answer format.

E. Basil's rule became normative in the Orthodox churches.

IV. Monasticism spread to the west in the later decades of the 4th century.

  A. Saint Martin of Tours was a former Roman soldier who established a hermitage at Ligugé, later becoming a disciple of Saint Hilary of Poitiers, an influential anti-Arian theologian.

   1. *Life*, the biography of Saint Martin by Sulpicius Severus, was immensely influential and popularized Martin's ascetic life.

   2. Martin became bishop of Tours in 371 but was always sharply different from the elegant gentlemen bishops of Gaul.

  B. John Cassian was born in the Balkans, traveled widely, lived in Egypt, and settled in southern Gaul.

   1. He wrote *Institutes* and *Conferences*, the former collections of rule-like documents and the latter short treatises of advice on aspects of the monastic life.

   2. Cassian's preferences were eremitic, and he was not influential in this respect, but his *Conferences* were widely read and studied.

  C. Saint Honoratus was a high-born Roman who, after his conversion, traveled to Syria, Palestine, and Egypt and then settled at Lérins, an island off the coast of Cannes.

   1. There Honoratus established a famous monastery that implemented the teachings of Cassian.

   2. The monastery became so famous and prestigious that many Gallic bishops were trained there and people came from far away—even Ireland.

V. Although eremitic monasticism appeared to be prospering in the west, it would be cenobitic monasticism that triumphed.

  A. Already Saint Augustine wrote a rule—the first western rule—that was moderate and well organized, striking a balance between human weakness and religious rigor.

  B. But the future belonged to Saint Benedict of Nursia.

   1. He came from a middling family, studied in Rome, but then went to Subiaco and finally on to Monte Cassino.

   2. Between 520 and 540, he prepared his *Rule*, an amazingly learned document based on the Bible and earlier rules.

3. Arrayed in 73 chapters, the *Rule* stressed order, balance, and moderation.
   a. Its central vows—hence aims—were obedience, stability, and conversion.
   b. The *Rule* created strong community bonds through lengthy daily rounds of prayer, practical guidance for all contingencies, and work.
4. Some see Benedict as a conscious alternative to Cassian, Lérins, and Egypt.
5. It is somewhat ironic that Benedict's became the western rule.
   a. Benedict and his *Rule* were promoted by Pope Gregory I in Book 1 of his *Dialogues*.
   b. Benedict's *Rule* was eventually embraced by the Anglo-Saxons, who sent many missionaries to the continent.

VI. Thus far, our story has been about men. To what extent was monasticism attractive to women?
   A. Christianity's attitude toward women was ambivalent.
      1. All regular ecclesiastical offices were barred to women (except for deaconesses, who were declining in significance).
      2. Monasticism offered holiness, prestige, and influence outside the institutional church.
   B. Some men went into the desert precisely to escape sexual temptation, but there was also a belief that rigorous asceticism could render men impervious to temptation and permit women to transcend gender: They either became "male" or lived the idea that gender was illusory and temporary.
   C. Pachomian communities may have begun as a way to accommodate the women of families whose men had become ascetics.
   D. In Rome and elsewhere, widows and young virgins vowed themselves to consecrated lives of chastity and renunciation.
      1. Some visited Egypt and Palestine.
      2. Some wanted to deepen their study and required male teachers; hence, in Rome, Saint Jerome acquired a group of aristocratic women pupils.

3. Some women settled with Jerome in Bethlehem, and others settled elsewhere in the Holy Land.

E. Gradually, various male apprehensions led to the "cloistering" of women.
   1. There were always (prejudicial) fears that women would tempt men and that, therefore, there could not be mixed communities.
   2. Some men were scandalized by wandering female ascetics.
   3. Saint Caesarius of Arles wrote a rule for nuns that effectively shut them up in a convent, and this became the prevailing norm in the West.

VII. Between 300 and 600, monasticism had produced communities of men and of women spreading from Ireland to Mesopotamia, had produced legislators and theologians, had produced spiritual writings of great beauty and influence, and had given the church many bishops.

Suggested Reading:

Caner, *Wandering, Begging Monks.*

Elm, *Virgins of God.*

Questions to Consider:

1. Compare eremitic and cenobitic forms of monasticism as lived experiences.

2. What accounts for the attraction of monasticism to women? How did women's experiences differ from those of men?

Lecture Twenty-One—Transcript
Monasticism—Solitaries and Communities

Hello and welcome back once again to this series of lectures on late antiquity. Last time, we talked about the origins of monasticism in Egypt. This time, in Lecture Twenty-One, we'll talk about solitaries and communities; we'll talk about the spread of the monastic phenomenon. As I indicated last time, monasticism turned out to be an immensely powerful and popular phenomenon in late antiquity, and it wasn't by any means reserved to Egypt. We focused on Egypt last time and we talked about a variety of issues that might have led to the creation of a movement, of a phenomenon like monasticism. Today what we want to talk about is, where did this movement go and why did it go, and by whose agency did it move?

We can say that there were several factors that contributed to monasticism's spread around the Mediterranean world and eventually even beyond that. Some of these I talked about last time. Monastic literature such as the histories and the biographies and collections of "Sayings of the Desert Fathers"; I mentioned these last time. I mentioned also, but I want to emphasize now and we'll see a few examples of this as we go along here in this lecture, that there were large numbers of visitors to Egypt. This phenomenon that was emerging in Egypt, people heard about it, people were interested in it, people were puzzled by it, people were attracted by it, and they went for varying periods of time and with very different motivations, they went to Egypt to see what they could learn. Sometimes they stayed there, but very often they brought something of what they had learned in Egypt back to their homelands.

We saw that there was no single form of monasticism in Egypt. We saw, broadly speaking, that there were two patterns, the eremitic and the cenobitic; so also then when monasticism left Egypt we can say that it took on a variety of different forms. We can generalize very broadly and say that in the east the eremitic—remember *heremos* is Greek for desert, so eremitic, think hermit, the very solitary pattern—in the east, the solitary pattern tended to be more prominent. In the west, the cenobitic—*koinos bios*—common life, the communal form of monasticism eventually became a good deal more prominent. As I say, those are broad generalizations that are basically valid, although one could certainly find exceptions to each one of them.

Let's move beyond Egypt then. Monasticism passed from Egypt to Palestine very early and very easily. Palestine is immediately next to Egypt; one has a fairly short traverse to make in order to go from Palestine to Egypt or vice versa. The first figure that we meet who seems to have been of some prominence is a man by the name Hilarion of Gaza. Of course, Gaza is immediately between Palestine and Egypt. Hilarion came from a pagan family, like Pachomius in that right, but he was converted to Christianity in the city of Alexandria. He spent some time out in the desert, in particular with disciples of Anthony. By about 306, it appears he had settled in Gaza where he undertook a very, very extreme form of asceticism. Remember, asceticism is sort of a rigorous practice or discipline. Eventually he began to go travelling—why? He disliked acquiring followers. We notice the ironic phenomenon in Egypt that individuals would go out into the desert to be alone and they would acquire followers, and so one eventually began to have large numbers of people living alone together. What happened with Hilarion is he began to attract followers and so he sort of went wandering off.

A somewhat more organized form of monastic life then in the general region of Palestine centers on the semilegendary figure of Chariton. We just don't know very much about him. He appears to have come from Anatolia, for example, what we would call Turkey today. He seems to have settled in some caves outside Jerusalem. There are caves all over the place out there. The group of caves where Chariton and his followers settled came to be called a *lavra*. That's a word that means a "street" or an "alley." Very often these *lavra* communities had a whole series of individual monastic dwellings sort of arrayed along a road or arrayed along a street, hence the name that they acquired. I'll have a little bit more to say about the *lavra* formally in just a couple of minutes, but it appears that it arises with this figure of Chariton.

The great monastic figures of Palestine were Euthymius and Sabas, basically Euthymius a 5th-century figure, Sabas living on into the early years of the 6th century. Euthymius established a great *lavra* near Jerusalem, as did Sabas, called Mar Saba. Mar Saba is still there, impressive ruins to this day that one can go and see. The *lavra* again was a particular eastern adaptation of the eremitic and the cenobitic forms of monasticism. It wasn't quite the one or the other. Monks lived in individual cells, but they worshipped together occasionally, they followed the guidance of a common abbot, and they might undertake common work, for example, to support the community as a whole. Very often when we look at plans, for example, of a *lavra* type monastery, we do see a whole series of these cells sort of strung out down a road, up the side of a mountain, around a mountain, around a lake, along a river, wherever it might be, hence the notion of a street or a road that connected all of these together.

In the east, Syria presented a third pattern, and here we find extraordinarily rigorous asceticism. Some of the most famous and familiar stories told about the early monks, sometimes some of the most humorous and entertaining stories told about the early monks, are actually about monks who lived and worked in Syria. We hear of one monk, for example, who wore chains. He wore so many chains wrapped around himself that were so heavy that he could only crawl. He couldn't actually walk. He couldn't stand up. We hear of another one who deliberately lived in a room where the roof was so low that he could only stoop; he couldn't stand up straight. There were monks called "dendrites"—*dendron* in Greek means "tree"—who lived in trees.

The greatest, the most famous—actually the most puzzling of these figures—is a man by the name of Symeon Stylites. He was not the only one of the Stylite monks. Stylite means "people who lived on columns." Symeon began as an anchorite, so he began living a solitary life, a life of great asceticism. Then, he became a cenobite. He joined a community. He was soon expelled by his community because he was too rigorous in his ascetic practices. The community said look, he's never going to sort of get with the program, he's not going to be like the rest of us, so he was thrown out. He lived for a time in a cistern. He used to refuse food all the time, much to the consternation of his friends and associates.

He especially, for example, refused food during Lent. There's something kind of interesting there. During the Lenten season, even to this day, Christians are sometimes given to giving up things, to give up food or some favorite practice or whatever it might be. The idea of giving things up during Lent is, in an interesting kind of way, the idea that all people should take unto themselves something of the ascetic practices that monks take on as a way of life. What Symeon Stylites would do is instead of reducing his intake of food during

Lent, he just gave it up, and then that bothered some of his contemporaries. Eventually he climbed up on a column. The first one we understand was about 10 feet high. At the end of his life he lived on one that was about 60 feet high. He lived all together some 37 years perched on the top of columns. He regularly preached from the top of these columns, and people came from all over the place to see him. They used to take away dust from the foot of his columns and carry it all around the Mediterranean world. The Stylite phenomenon became really quite a prominent one in late antiquity.

The great monastic founder in the east, the one who is looked back to in the Orthodox Church as the great founding father of monasticism, although from what I've just been saying it'd be perfectly obvious he was by no means the first and certainly not the only great ascetic figure in the east, was Saint Basil. We're going to meet Basil again in some later lectures because he was also one of the greatest of the church fathers, one of the great intellectuals of early Christian history. He's very far from the first ascetic in the east, but he's the first serious organizer. In 357–358, he visited Egypt. He spent some time at Nitria and Scetis, the great communities that emerged early in the 4th century in Egypt. He was most influenced, however, by the Pachomian communities, by the cenobitic communities, by the communities living a common life. The rigorous ascetic practices of the eremitic communities had some attraction for him, but he was drawn to the idea of a more organized life. What's interesting is that he himself lived a solitary life for a period of time, and he decided that for the great majority of people, a common life was better. A common life would work more effectively.

Basil we know wrote two works that are called *The Longer* [*Rules*] and *The Shorter Rules.* You may recall last time we talk about Pachomius's rule that exists in all kinds of different versions, probably none of which actually goes back to Pachomius himself. Basil didn't actually write rules. What he wrote was a couple of works, one longer than the other, for the long one and the short one, that are kind of question-and-answer format teaching manuals that respond to a lot of practical questions about how one might live this ascetic life. My point is that he didn't actually sit down and write from front to back a comprehensive rule governing the lives of monks. Nevertheless, these teaching devices, his "longer" and "shorter" rules came to be normative in the Orthodox churches, as they indeed remain to this day.

Monasticism spread to the east; it struck deep roots. Eventually it formed one kind, the *lavra* form, which blended the eremitic and cenobitic, and then another great form in the more cenobitic types of communities that descend from Saint Basil. What then about the west? Monasticism spread to the west in the later decades of the 4th century, and we could go back and talk again about the monastic literature and visitors to Egypt and so on and all of that would be true. Who are some of the key early figures? Saint Martin of Tours, who died in about 397. I don't try to claim to know exactly when he was born. There are very real complications with the chronology of his life. Martin was a Roman soldier who left the service and then established a hermitage near Ligugé in the center of France. He became a disciple of Saint Hilary of Poitiers. Hilary lived from about 315 until 367 or 368. Hilary was a very influential anti-Arian theologian. We've talked plenty about Arianism, so we have a sense then of what it was that Hilary was combating.

In Martin's case, it was in some sense the events of his life, but more particularly his *Life*, his biography, as written by a man named Sulpicius Severus that was immensely influential and popularized his ascetic life. This was a text that was copied again and again and again and again, on into the Middle Ages. It was very, very widely read; it was very influential. It's interesting that Martin became bishop of Tours, one of the great old sees, the great diocese of France, in 371, but he was always sharply different than the elegant gentlemen bishops of Gaul. We've talked about how in the great cities of Gaul during this late antique period we find sometimes the great aristocratic families that had formally provided lay officers to the state, began to provide episcopal officers to the church. In Gaul, many of these people were really sort of great aristocratic gentlemen in lots of ways. Martin was kind of uncouth and unkempt and lived in a cave outside of town, and he simply didn't behave like one of these great gentlemen. They didn't like him very much, nor did he like them very much, but the very fact that there was this controversy over Martin's behavior and appearance and so on, and that Sulpicius recorded it, tells us something about the tensions that were emerging between one kind of clerical life and another.

A second figure to whom we ought to pay at least a little attention is John Cassian. Cassian was born probably 360, died about 435. He was born in the Balkans. He traveled very widely, he lived for a period of time in Egypt, and he eventually settled in the south of

Gaul. This is not uncommon for a number of these Christian figures in the world of late antiquity, that they had sort of traveled around from one place to another and sat at the feet of various masters and learned different kinds of things. Cassian wrote two works that we know of. He wrote his *Institutes* and his *Conferences*. Cassian's *Institutes* is, broadly speaking, a collection of rule-like documents. He gathered up a lot of these earlier question-and-answer documents or partial rules or prescriptions or guidelines that various people had composed; he collected a lot of these. The *Conferences* were greatly more influential over the long haul. This was a series of short sort of advice treatises on various aspects of the monastic life. Cassian's own preferences were eremitic. What's interesting is that he was not influential in this respect. His book came to be very widely read in cenobitic circles, which wound up being the dominant circles in the west. Indeed, Saint Benedict, to whom we'll come in a few minutes, only mentioned a couple of books by name in his rule that his monks should read. One of them was Cassian's *Conferences* and yet, as I said, Cassian's own preferences were eremitic, not cenobitic.

A third figure we might mention briefly is Saint Honoratus. He died 429 or 430, thereabouts. Honoratus was a high-born Roman who after his conversion—not his conversion to Christianity, his conversion to the eremitic life, his *conversatio morum*, his "change of way of life"—traveled to Syria, to Palestine, and to Egypt. He traveled and visited some of the great monastic centers of the Mediterranean world, and then he settled on the island of Lérins, an island just off the coast of Cannes in the south of France. Honoratus established there a very famous monastery that, broadly speaking, we can say implemented the teachings of John Cassian. The monastery became so famous and so prestigious that many Gallic bishops were trained there. That's one interesting thing about this monastic community established at Lérins, and indeed we ought to emphasize then about its eremitic orientation. Large numbers of people came there and studied and went off and became bishops and therefore brought something of the monastic spirit, something of the ascetic spirit, something of the spirit of renunciation, this rigorous Christian life. They brought it back to their ordinarily ecclesiastical work. We also know that a number of people came to Lérins from very far away, indeed even from Ireland. For instance, in the biographies of Saint Patrick, it's impossible that this is true, but it's alleged that Saint Patrick had actually studied at Lérins in the south of France.

If we were to look at these early figures—if we were to look at Martin, if we were to look at Cassian, if we were to look at Honoratus—we would assume that the eremitic form of monasticism is going to be the one that took root in the west and that became most prominent there and most dominant there. As I've said many, many times in this course of lectures, if history could stop and we could say, now bet on which phenomenon is going to win, you'd all bet on eremitic monasticism, and you'd all lose your bet, but it would be the only sensible bet to make at that point in time. Something happened; what was that? As is often the case, there was something that was ever so slightly accidental or what one thinks of Huxley's great remark that "Luck is the residue of design." Who was the designer? It was a man by the name of Benedict. We'll come to him in just a second because it was as a result of him that cenobitic monasticism triumphed in the west.

Already Saint Augustine—we've mentioned him before, we're going to have a lot more to say about him in some future lectures, born 354, died 430—wrote a rule, the first western rule that was reasonably comprehensive, that was moderate and that was well organized; it sort of struck a balance. This is very characteristic of Augustine's theology as a whole. It struck a balance between human weakness, a genuine appreciation for human weakness, and for religious rigor. He has very high expectations, but he has a sense of whom he is asking those expectations. But the future belonged, as I suggested a moment ago, to Benedict, to Benedict of Nursia.

There are people who have suggested that Benedict maybe never existed at all, that he was basically a literary invention of later times, but it is curious that the great founder of western monasticism is called *Benedictus*, "blessed." I mean that's almost too good to be true. It's curious that he has a sister, Scholastica. Contemporary sources don't acknowledge his sister Scholastica. Did he actually have a sister? Maybe he did, it's very hard to say. The story is that he came from a middling family and that he studied in Rome. We are of course moving through the 5th century in Rome. We're moving across the period of time when the western imperial administration has ended. The Western Empire has ended; there's no longer an emperor in the west, but there is still, as we've seen, an administration in the city of Rome. There's still an urban prefect. The government was still a pretty good place to get a job. So it appears that Benedict's family had sort of destined him for a job of some kind in the imperial administration he'd been studying, probably studying law in the city of Rome. At some point, he became disgusted with his studies, he became impatient with his studies, and he retired to Subiaco, just outside of Rome, where he sort of lived in caves and lived by himself and he began to practice very much an ascetic life.

He was fairly quickly recognized by some local monks as a very holy man, and they asked him to come and organize them to sort of be their father, to be their abbot. He reluctantly agreed, the story goes, and tried to organize them, but—and this is ironic because Benedict is later seen as the great organizer of moderate monasticism—these monks felt that Benedict was so rigorous and so ascetic and so tough on them that they actually plotted to kill him, so he thought, well, this isn't going to work. He left and he went away about 80 miles south of Rome to Monte Cassino where he founded a monastic community. There remains, of course, a monastic community at Monte Cassino to this very day, although you would barely need more than the fingers on your two hands to count the number of monks who live there now.

Anyway, sometime between about 520 and 540, we don't know for sure, he prepared his rule, the *Regula Benedicti*, the *Rule of Benedict*. In some ways it's an amazingly learned document. It is drawn very heavily on the Bible. It's drawn on a series of earlier monastic rules, so obviously Benedict had read deeply in the monastic literature of his time. There are occasional references to a few of the writings of some of the church fathers.

The church fathers will be the subject of the next series of lectures that we have here, so I won't track that down just at the moment here. The point that I'm making is that this was not something that just sort of came off the top of the head of some wild and woolly ascetic living out in the wilderness. This was a book that was arrayed very, very carefully on the basis of a close reading of a whole series of important books, but particularly the Bible. About three-quarters of the *Rule of Benedict* is drawn from the Bible.

The *Rule* is arrayed in 73 chapters. Broadly speaking, we can say that it stresses order, balance, and moderation. Benedict says he's creating a little school for the Lord's service, and that's important to bear in mind. That's what Benedict thought he was doing; he was creating a school for the Lord's service. He says he wishes to ordain nothing harsh or burdensome. I suspect most of us sitting down today and reading the *Rule of Benedict* would find it to be both harsh and burdensome, but his point of course is that he is reacting against, from his point of view, excessive asceticism of the monastic life of his day, compared to an ordinary lay life. No, of course, that would have been much less harsh and burdensome.

The central vows of Benedict's *Rule* are—mark my words carefully because this is going to seem a little surprising to people who kind of know anything about Roman Catholic religious orders and so on— the vows were obedience, stability, and conversion. You expected me to say poverty, chastity, and obedience, didn't you? Those are Jesuit vows, they're priestly vows, they take their rise really much, much later in Christian history. Let's go back and look at Benedict's.

Obedience: The great structuring principle of his *Rule* is the absolute obedience owed by monks to their abbot, by sons to their father. That's the central notion. Then there's stability. Stability could have lots of possible meanings; what does it mean here? What it means here is *stabilitas loci*, "stability of place." You enter a monastery, you stay there. You don't come and go, you don't kind of make up your mind periodically, you don't change your mind, you come and you stay—the notion of stability.

Then there's conversion—you say, conversion? Good heavens! What's this got to do with anything? Aren't these guys already Christians? Of course they are; this is *conversatio morum*, it's a conversion, a change of your way of life, of your manner of living. Obedience, stability, and conversion are the central core issues that inform the *Rule of Benedict*.

The *Rule* also does lots to build a sense of community through very strong bonds, for instance, of daily prayer. The psalmist had said seven times daily do I praise thee, and the Benedictine monk, seven times a day, goes to chapel with all the other members of his community and prays. The *Rule* is full of practical guidance on all manner of things: food, clothing, what time of day to do things, and so on. One may say, it's too busybody and it sort of regulates everything, but the point is it doesn't leave much to chance. Some have seen Benedict as a conscious alternative to Cassian, to Lérins, and to Egypt, and there is something in that. It is, as I have suggested, a rule that is cenobitic at its very core. It's somewhat ironic that Benedict's became the western rule, however. He wrote this rule from Monte Cassino. There's no evidence that he ever thought that his rule was going to become the Benedictine rule. How did that happen?

A generation or two after Benedict's death, Pope Gregory I wrote a book called the *Dialogues* in four books. It was basically about the saints of Italy. Book 2 of the book of the *Dialogues* is a biography of Benedict. That book became enormously influential and Benedict's life became very widely known. Among other places that it had become very widely known was in England. Pope Gregory I sent missionaries to England. The English Church had a particular fondness for Gregory, and when they read Gregory's *Dialogues* and they read about Benedict, the English got a particular fondness for Benedict's form of monasticism. A number of Anglo-Saxon English missionaries in the 7th and 8th centuries went back from England over to the continent of Europe. One of the things they took with them very often was Benedictine monasticism.

These Anglo-Saxons influenced not least Charlemagne and his son Louis the Pious, both of whom legislated that the Benedictine rule was the rule that had to be observed in all monasteries. There's a very curious history as to how Benedictine monasticism emerged and why Benedict's form of monasticism became dominant in the west. Partly to be sure, we should lay some stress on the excellence of the rule itself, but partly he had a little help in some rather unforeseen ways. You could see why I was suggesting earlier that one would have supposed that the eremitic form would take precedence in the west, but in fact it was the cenobitic that did.

Our story up until now has been very largely about men. To what extent was monasticism attractive to women? We can say here that Christianity's attitude toward women was very ambivalent from the very beginning. Paul had said in Galatians, there is neither male nor female, neither bond nor free; but in Timothy I, we read that women should learn in silence and in all subjection. Are they all equal or are they not? All regular ecclesiastical offices, we know, were barred to women, except deaconesses.

Deaconesses were declining in significance across the course of late antiquity. Why is that? What were deaconesses in late antiquity? Normally a deacon was either a servant of the church—*diakonein* in Greek means "to serve"—or it was a person in training on the way to becoming a priest. When Christianity first began to spread in the

Roman world, the largest number of people converted, of course, were adults. Among these adults, of course, were women. These women were going to have to be baptized. To preserve modesty, deaconesses assisted women at the time of their baptism. As more and more and more of the population of the Mediterranean world, of the late antique world was Christian, most of those being brought for baptism were infants. Where infants were concerned, modestly was rather less of an issue, and the need for deaconesses began to decline. My point is that there really were not offices in the formal, structural, institutional church that were particularly available to women.

Monasticism offered women some interesting things. It offered them a kind of holiness. Great nuns, great female monastics, came to be famous. We'll have something more to say about this in just a second; they came to be very well-known. Holiness was, as we've seen, becoming increasingly a kind of a badge in late antiquity—a mark of honor in some of the respects that other marks of honor had adorned the people of classical antiquity and late antiquity.

Here was a road to holiness, or maybe we could use a slightly different word and say prestige that women had otherwise not particularly had. Here was an opportunity for influence outside the institutional church. Communities of women quite regularly were organized by women.

One can think, for instance, of the arguments made in our own time about the continuing value of women's colleges. Every question answered in the classroom is answered by a woman. All of the leaders of all the organizations are women. Women in female monastic communities, here was a situation where women governed other women, women lived under the rule of other women, and women lived with women; they weren't living under the thumb of men.

That's the ideal. Some men, of course, went into the desert precisely to escape sexual temptation, but there was also a belief, a very interesting kind of belief, that very rigorous asceticism would render men impervious to temptation, and would permit women to transcend gender. The idea was they would either become "male," or that gender would be something illusory, contemporary. In one very interesting way, men writing about women basically said that the less they are women, the more they have right to claim upon our attention as holy figures. There were many *ammas* in Egypt, for example—

abbas, fathers, *ammas*, mothers. The sayings of some of these were collected. For example, we have the sayings of at least three of them in the collection of the "Sayings of the Desert Fathers," and mothers you see, that I mentioned last time. One saying of Amma Sarah is revealing.

> Two old men came to visit her. When they arrived one said to the other, "Let us humiliate this old woman." They said to her "Be careful not to become conceited thinking to yourself 'look how anchorites are coming to see me, a mere women.'" Anu Amma Sarah said to them "According to nature I am a woman, but not according to my thoughts."

There's a very interesting sense here that she was quite up to the task of responding to these men who had come to trick her.

About one-third of Palladius's *Lausiac History*, which I mentioned in the last lecture, is about women. Pachomian communities, for example, may have begun as a way to accommodate the womenfolk of families whose menfolk had gone off to become ascetics. In other words, it was the idea of living a common life. Some had gone off to live an eremitic life, so a common life was formed for others.

In Rome and elsewhere, we hear of widows and young virgins who vowed themselves to consecrated lives of chastity and renunciation. We know some of these visited Egypt, some of them visited Palestine; they traveled very widely. Some wanted to deepen their study. They required male teachers. There weren't female teachers available. In Rome, for example, Saint Jerome acquired a group of aristocratic women pupils. Some of these women settled with Jerome when he went off to Bethlehem.

Gradually, various male apprehensions led to the "cloistering" of women to close up. There were always prejudicial fears—I think they were prejudicial—that women could tempt men, and therefore there should no longer be mixed communities. Interestingly enough the notion was that women would tempt men, not that men would tempt women. Some men were scandalized by the notion of wandering female ascetics. Saint Caesarius of Arles who lived from 470 to about 542 wrote a rule for nuns that effectively shut them up in a convent. This became the prevailing norm in the west for the next 1,500 years.

My point quite simply then, in conclusion, is that between about 300 and 600, monasticism produced communities of men and of women that spread from Ireland to Mesopotamia. It produced legislators and theologians, it produced spiritual writers of great beauty and influence, and it gave the church many bishops. This is one of the remarkable phenomena of this late antique world.

Lecture Twenty-Two
The Church Fathers—Talking About God

Scope:

As Christianity gained freedom, and then stature, in the Roman world, serious intellectuals began to enter the church in significant numbers. We call these thinkers the "church fathers," and their writings have remained influential to this day. Among the Greek fathers, Saint Gregory of Nyssa, Saint Gregory of Nazianzus, and Saint John Chrysostom will be discussed in the next lecture. In this lecture we will look at prominent Greek writers to see how they passed the Bible through the crucible of Greek philosophy to create a vocabulary and structures of thought for the Christian faith. They invented Christian theology, a word that in the simplest sense means "God-talk."

Outline

I. Before turning to the greatest of the late antique Christian writers, let's remember that we have spoken of the Apologists and of monastic authors.

    A. The church fathers (from Latin *patres*) created the Patristic period.

        1. This period runs from the end of the Apologists in the mid-2nd century to John of Damascus in the mid-8th century.

        2. The greatest figures wrote between 350 and 450, with important contributions down to c. 600.

        3. It is legitimate to see this as the last great age of ancient literature, but the period is not usually seen this way, especially by classicists.

    B. We have already seen that the post-biblical period posed the acute problem of deciding what scriptures would be accepted as authentic.

    C. Once the "source" problem had been solved to most people's satisfaction, huge questions remained as to what the scriptures meant.

        1. Christianity arose among Aramaic speakers who wrote and proselytized in Greek and then later in Latin.

2. Christianity could not help but absorb Greek thought with the Greek language.
3. Greek lacked certain ways of expressing things: For instance, the verb "to be" had no present participle, no way to say "being," and Christian writers had to "invent" *ousios*.
4. In Latin, Tertullian invented the words for "Trinity," "sacrament," and "person."

II. Technical problems were not all that was at stake. Fundamental issues were involved.

A. God had become incarnate—had been "enfleshed" ("*et Verbum caro factum est*")—so how does one talk about or understand this crucial issue?

B. The Bible spoke of God in various triadic formulations: How was one to understand them?

C. How do these named beings relate to one another? Are they distinct? If so, how is monotheism preserved? Are they merely different manifestations of, ways of putting into words, one God? Was each of these "beings" divine in the same way? Did Christ only seem to be human? Did a particular human being only seem to be divine? If the divinity of these three beings, or persons, were somehow different, how did they relate to one another?

III. The first time these issues arose in a serious way was with Arius, who said that Christ was "unlike" the Father, that he was a created being—"the firstborn of all creation"—and that there was a time "when Christ was not."

A. In his *Incarnation of the Word of God*, Athanasius became the first proponent of the Nicene theory that Christ had a true body and also that he was "one in being with the father" (*homoousious*). Late antiquity paid less attention to the Holy Spirit.

B. In Alexandria the tendency was to argue that Christ was the *logos*, the "wisdom of God"—hence in a way the same substance as the Father: *logos* and *sarx* (word and body) are fused in one being, Jesus Christ.
1. There was a dangerous tendency here to downplay the humanity of Christ.
2. The Council of Constantinople addressed this "balance."

C. Yet the Alexandrian school moved forward on logic of its own to put the emphasis on Christ's divinity.

    1. Eutyches argued that Christ had only one, divine nature. He was the "founder" of Monophysitism.

    2. Monophysitism was vigorously opposed by Pope Leo and the Council of Chalcedon but survived in much of the east.

D. If Alexandrian "Christology" is to be regarded as "high," then "low" Christology emerged in Antioch, where Christ's humanity was emphasized.

E. People were struggling to come to terms with Trinitarian and Christological issues.

    1. Greek and Latin Catholics have always embraced the formulations of Chalcedon, but most of the east has not.

    2. At bottom we are back to thesis, nature, essence; hypostasis (individuality/person or nature), *ousia* (nature, substance, being) and *prosopon* (subject, person, personality).

F. Talking about God is really, really hard.

Suggested Reading:

Hanson, *The Search for the Christian Doctrine of God.*

Kelly, *Early Christian Doctrines.*

Questions to Consider:

1. What advantages and disadvantages did the absorption of Greek thought and terminology provide to Christianity?

2. Why do Trinitarian and Christological issues make monotheism so difficult to define?

Lecture Twenty-Two—Transcript
The Church Fathers—Talking About God

Hello and welcome once more to our series of lectures on late antiquity. In the last couple of lectures we talked about the monastic world, one very important new phenomena in late antiquity. In this one and the next couple, this one being Lecture Twenty-Two, we're going to talk about Christian intellectuals, writers, and cultures in some very broad terms. This time we're going to talk about the church fathers, and talking about God. Let me just remind of you of one or two pieces of background that will help to put this into perspective. We've already talked about earlier Christian writers. We talked, for example, you may recall, about the Apologists, writers in the 2nd and early 3rd centuries, a group of writers who had attempted to differentiate between Christianity and Judaism, who had attempted to differentiate between Christianity and classical culture, and who had tried to provide Christians with some practical guidelines on how to live in a pagan world. We've also—and we saw this particularly in our last two lectures—talked about monastic literature, a wide array of materials that began to arise in connection with or in response to the monastic phenomenon that we talked about.

It will be familiar to everyone, I'm sure, that the ancient world had produced large numbers of gifted writers in Greek and in Latin over a very long period of time. As gradually the church began to attract into its fold larger and larger numbers of serious authentic intellectuals, it was not surprising that they were going to turn their attention to some of the great problems that interested the church itself. Resting to be sure on this apologetic foundation that we've talked about in earlier lectures, when these great intellectuals began to address themselves to some fundamental problems, they sort of made of themselves a group of people we now call the "church fathers," from the Latin *patres*; hence we speak of their period as the Patristic period.

You may very well say, was there a Matrisic period? Were there *matres ecclesia*, were there mothers of the church? The answer is no. Generally speaking, one thinks of various pagan writers, Origen for example had said that, "The Pagans would think us fools if we permitted women to teach." That was a tradition of course that reached back also to Saint Paul. Generally speaking, one could say women didn't teach in the secular world of Rome and they did not teach in the Christian world of Rome. We don't find a serious Christian woman intellectual until the 10th century, Hrotswit of Gandersheim, for example. Then, from the 12th century with Hildegard of Bingen and lots of others, we begin to have a large number of them right down to the present day. But in the late antique period, when I talk about the church fathers, I am not blundering and ignoring and leaving out all the great women writers; there weren't any. There simply weren't any. It isn't as if I have suppressed a significant body of evidence. We talk then about the Patristic period, the age of the church fathers.

We can say that the period runs from the end of the Apologists' writings, mid-2nd century, maybe late 2nd, perhaps we could even say early 3rd century, something like that, down to the writings of John of Damascus, the last of the Greek fathers in the mid-8th century. It's a very long period from one point of view. You might ask, how would we differentiate Patristic writing from Apologetic writing. Broadly speaking, Apologetic writing addressed the three issues that I enumerated just a moment ago, whereas Patristic writing began to address systematically, coherently, and in very rigorous terms specific Christian issues. Rather than setting Christianity off from all that it was not, people began to turn to say, what is Christianity actually? In a certain sense, that's how we can kind of define where that dividing line is. We could say in a way that the Patristic period comes to an end when a whole variety of fundamental points could more or less be taken for granted. Not to say that everyone agreed about all of them all the time—it would be absurd to suggest that—but a wide array of things could finally come to be taken pretty much for granted. Having said all of that, the period from about 350–450 is the great Patristic age; this is the height of the Patristic age. Most of the figures we talk about in this lecture and the next couple of lectures actually lived and wrote in that period. There are some fairly significant contributions down to about 600 A.D. We mentioned a moment ago John of Damascus who lived into the 8th century. Down to about 600, there are some fairly significant figures, and we will come back and have a little something to say in this lecture, but more particularly in the next couple of lectures about some of those figures. But what I really want to draw your attention to is the period from about 350–450. There's nothing sacred about those two dates, but that gives you a notion of kind of where we are, a little orientation chronologically.

You'll notice then, in other words, that we're really talking here about the period not long after Constantine grants legal recognition to Christianity. Almost immediately, Christians can function as a licit religion, as a legal religion, as a public religion in the Roman world. On the one hand, they begin to quarrel with each other. We've had occasion to talk about the Arians as one particular example of this and I'll be coming back to Arians here in just a few minutes. Not only did the Christians come to quarrelling with one another, they also began to realize, look, we have some really hard problems that we have to define. We have really got to address ourselves to some very basic and tough issues.

If you were to go to a library and stand in front of all the writings of the church fathers, you'd be impressed. It's an enormous corpus of material. We could look at this as the last great age of ancient literature. Interestingly enough, because it's Christian writing, it's never been viewed that way by classicists. Generally speaking, the Greek and Latin style and techniques and so on of these authors have never been appreciated in the same way as those of the classical period. It has largely been a prejudice against writers who merely wrote about Christian subjects as opposed to writers who wrote about the gods and the goddesses and the heroes of Greece and Rome and so on. There's a very interesting prejudice, even though most of those people who peopled the classics enterprise in the last three centuries were themselves Christian, but there was still this kind of curious prejudice against all of this material.

It's also true, for example, that the most prolific author in all of Latin letters was Saint Augustine. It has been said of him, and not said as a compliment, he was not the greatest writer of Latin, he was perhaps the greatest man who ever wrote Latin. There is kind of a backward compliment in that remark, isn't there?

We've already noticed for instance that the post-biblical period posed, in a fairly acute way, the problem of what scriptures should be accepted as authentic. We talked about the canonical problems. How do we decide what are the basic texts? You may recall we actually talked about this in connection with the subject of what texts would be accepted as authentic, partly in connection with the spread of Christianity through the ancient world, and partly in connection with how did the church establish the authority to go about its business. On what basis could the church act in the world? What were the sources for its authority? Those were some of the early and crucial issues. In many ways, those issues are still being addressed as the ones we're going to turn to right now are being addressed. We don't really want to view these things as a series of successive stages coming one after another; these things were happening more or less contemporaneously.

One can pose the issue, I think, this way. Once the "source" problem had been solved, in other words, to most people's satisfaction, we're going to accept these books as authentic and inspired, not those books. Now the problem arose, what on earth do these books say? You might say, it's perfectly clear what they say. Any fool can read the scriptures and they make perfect sense. It would be only a fool who would say such a thing. Christianity, after all, rose among Aramaic speakers who wrote and proselytized in Greek, and their writings were later translated into Latin and then into all the languages of the globe. Right away it'll make sense to you that there has to have been some slippage, some change, some problems, and some interesting issues going on here. We can also say that there is what we call "Harnack's Conundrum." What's this all about? Adolf von Harnack, 1851–1930, was one of the great historians of Christian thought in the modern world. Harnack's Conundrum is basically this. He said that it was inevitable that Christianity would absorb Greek thought with the Greek language, but that it was a very bad thing indeed for Christianity to have absorbed Greek thought. In other words, the conundrum is, by using Greek, which was the language you had to use if you were going to get the message out, you were going to take on board all of the baggage that came with Greek. Taking on all the baggage that came with Greek was inevitably going to have an effect—a good effect, a bad effect? Harnack thought it was bad. Others have thought it was neutral. Some have thought maybe it was actually beneficial. Be that as it may, what I'm suggesting is that the Greek language was not a neutral vessel in which Christianity could simply travel. It was laden with concepts, with ideas, with issues, with problems.

I'm going to use a couple of examples here in just a second that probably most people, most alert, educated, articulate people, are not familiar with, but I can give you one that most people are quite familiar with: The opening of John's Gospel, *"En arche en o logos,"*

"In the beginning was the Word, and the Word was with God, and the Word was God." That's perfectly clear, isn't it? It's perfectly obvious what *logos* means in that sentence, *logos*. In the beginning was the word, *logos*, and the word was with God, *logos*, and the word was God, *logos*. If you know a good deal about Greek thought, you can see a couple of things. You can see what John is doing. What he's doing is putting his message in terms people can understand, terms with which they were familiar. It also shows that he was relatively familiar with a certain Platonic way of talking, with a certain way that people educated in Plato's tradition knew how to talk. That's the kind of point that I'm trying to make. It would be very easy to go through the scriptures and find all kinds of examples of really hard words that almost defy simple understanding.

Greek, however, interestingly enough to flip the thing around, lacked certain ways of expressing things that Christianity needed. For instance, the Greek verb "to be," for whatever reason, *einai*, had no present participle. There was no way to say "being" in Greek. If you're going to talk about a supreme being, if you're going to talk about the being, the way of being, of God, you've got to have that word. It was Christian writers who "invented" the word *ousios*. *Ousios* appears nowhere in the scriptures, but it's absolutely essential to have that word to explain a great deal of what the scriptures say. We're going to have a few more examples of this as we go along here in the next few minutes. The New Testament is originally written in Greek. We've had occasion to see also that there is the Septuagint version, the version allegedly done by 70 translators in 70 days at Alexandra, the Greek version of the Hebrew scriptures or the Old Testament, so there's a Greek Old Testament that's traveling. But the Christian scriptures of course are written in Greek in the first instance. Slowly but surely as the scriptures are better and better known in the western Mediterranean, in the part of the world where people know Latin more than they know Greek, there began to be various Latin translations. Not surprisingly, there also began to be Latin theology.

For example, the first of the great writers—we generally reckon him an Apologist more than one of the church fathers—Tertullian, is the first of the great writers in Latin. It is Tertullian who invented the word "Trinity." Tertullian invented the word "sacrament." He applied the word sacrament to the mysteries of Christianity to those rights and rituals of the church that we think of today as sacraments.

They're called "mysteries" in Greek, *mysteria*; he used the word "sacrament." It's very interesting because the Latin word *sacramentum* means "oath"; it's the ordinary word in legal Latin for oath. So Tertullian really stretched its meaning to give it—I didn't say distort, he stretched its meaning—to give it an application here, but also the word *persona*, "person." We have to talk about three persons in one God: Father, Son, and Holy Spirit. The word persona does not appear in the scriptures. It doesn't appear in *prosopon*—which would be its Greek form—either.

But there's more at stake here than merely technical problems. In other words, there are some really nasty issues of technical problems. What words are going to be used to explain what concepts? That's serious business. But there are also fundamental issues involved, so it's not simply learned people being playful and engaging in the kinds of silly games that learned people engage in. There were some really serious problems here. We have to remember that, on the one hand, this is still a world when Christians are trying to take their message to the Mediterranean world, and as we saw when we talked in earlier lectures about the spread of Christianity in the Roman world and so on, this was not a world that was ignorant, this was not a *tabula rasa*, a blank slate, on which Christians could come along and write whatever they wished. These were people who had many rites and rituals in their daily lives that were religious and that had certain valence, had certain meaning to them. They were also people who knew a lot, who had read a lot, who had heard a lot, who understood a lot, so there was a strong matter of having to be able to explain things to people. That's very, very important. Then, inside the Christian community, there was a very powerful need to say, what is it actually that we believe and how do we decide when what we believe stops and what we don't believe takes over? What is the difference between orthodoxy, the right up and down rule, and heresy, those who choose a different way?

We can take, for example, an issue such as the fact God had become incarnated, he had been "enfleshed," the words of the creed, "*et verbum caro factum est*," the word was made flesh. How does one talk about or understand this crucial teaching? This is a very complex matter, this business of incarnation. Not surprisingly, you may recall we talked a little bit about the pagan writer Celsus, who had said, this is absurd. This is simply absurd. You can have men, you can have God, that's fine, but this business of a God-man—no, no, you can't do that, he said. This is a very complex matter. Do you remember we also quoted Tertullian as saying, "I believe because it's impossible." In other words, there are things I can't understand, yet I believe them, I take them on faith. Faith can mean in Greek or Latin—*pistis* in Greek—granting intellectual ascent to things, the body of doctrines to which I grant intellectualism, but faith also, and we use the word this way fairly often I suppose in our ordinarily daily discourse. It means "confidence" or "trust." I put my faith in you. There are two very different issues here. They're closely related; they're like two sides of a coin.

How does something like the issue of God being enfleshed come up and how does one try to understand what it seems the scriptures tell us? Let me give you just a few examples of places where the Bible speaks of God in various triadic formulations, threes. We have, for example, in Matthew 28:19, the end, the Great Commission, the end of Matthew's Gospel, "Go therefore and make disciples of all nations baptizing them in the name of the Father, and of the Son, and of the Holy Spirit." There we have our triad. There we have our three, our Father, Son, and Holy Spirit, our three persons. The word person isn't used there, the word trinity isn't used there, and the relationship among these persons is not explained there. We might say, isn't it kind of taken for granted? What exactly is taken for granted? That's not so clear.

We might look at the second chapter of the Acts of the Apostles.

> They ask Peter and the other apostles, "What we to do, brothers?" Peter answered, "You must reform and be baptized, each one of you, in the name of Jesus Christ, that your sins may be forgiven; then you will receive the gift of the Holy Spirit. It was to you and to your children that the promise was made, and all those still far off whom the Lord God calls.

There's our three again. There's a triad again, used in quite different ways. From one point of view you can say, we can kind of see what these guys are talking about. Yes, we can, but is it perfectly clear?

We have the wonderful passage of Corinthians II; persons who are Catholic, persons who are Episcopalian, persons who are Anglican, some who are Lutheran, hear this at the beginning of worship every week: "The grace of the Lord Jesus Christ, and the love of God, and the fellowship of the Holy Spirit be with you all." There's our three again.

How do these named beings relate to each other? Are they distinct? If so, how is monotheism preserved? Are they merely different manifestations of ways of putting into words one God? Was each of these "beings" divine in the same way? Did Christ only seem to be human? Did a particular human being only seem to be divine? If the divinity of these three beings or persons were somehow different, how did they relate to one another? How is one to understand these triadic formulations? I gave you but three examples; there are many more. I think you would see they actually raise a whole series of interesting and complex problems. Anyone who I think has ever tried to explain the trinity to anybody else will have some sense of what it is I'm grappling with here, or what they were grappling with in their time, the church fathers that is.

The first time that these issues arose in a really serious way was with Arius. We've bumped into Arius and the Arians lots of times, but let's just pause for a second and put a little focus on what he actually did teach. He was trying to preserve absolutely strict monotheism. He said that Christ was "unlike" the Father, that he was a created being—"the firstborn of all creation," Arius said. Arius also said that there was a time "when Christ was not." He made him ever so slightly subordinate to the Father. One calls Arians' kind of theology subordinationism, and subordinationism has appeared in various forms over the long history of Christianity. But it's important to see that what Arius is really trying to do is he's looking at those triadic formulations that I just read a moment ago. He's reading the same words that I just read you, and he's trying somehow to preserve strict monotheism, and therefore he makes Jesus ever so slightly subordinate to his father. In his book the *Incarnation of the Word*, Athanasius became the first proponent of the Nicene theory that Christ had a true body and also that he was "one in being with the father." He had a true body; he was a true human being. He didn't appear, he wasn't a phantasm, but he was one in being with the father. He was *homoousious*. Once again, anyone accustomed to reciting the creed will immediately recognize that phrase, one in being with the father. In some ways, that's what the whole Nicene Creed was about, that phrase.

The word *homoousious* appears nowhere in the scriptures. I don't think any serious Christian would argue that there is anything unorthodox about *homoousious*, but it is not scriptural, it's not biblical, but you need it to explain a biblical concept. Here is a kind of a good example of Harnack's Conundrum. It's also interesting that late antiquity, on the whole, paid a good deal less attention to the Holy Spirit. Generally speaking in late antiquity, the great problems, the great Trinitarian problems, turned on the relation of Jesus and the Father, rather more than thinking about the place of the Holy Spirit in all of this, and the great Christological problems—to which we'll be turning in just a couple of seconds—turned on the nature of the human and the divine in Christ. It's not to say that the church fathers utterly ignored the Holy Spirit, but we can say that they didn't put anything like the same degree of stress on the Holy Spirit that they did on the first two persons of the Trinity, the Father and the Son.

In Alexandria, there was a longstanding tendency to argue—and again their reading is very much prompted by the opening of John's Gospel—that Christ was the *logos*, the "wisdom of God." Hence, in a way, he was the same substance as the Father. For them, *logos* and *sarx*—*sarx* is the Greek word for body, *logos*, the word for wisdom of God—*logos* and *sarx* are fused in a single being, Jesus Christ. They're fused more or less indissolubly. They're fused in such a way that there was, among Alexandrian theologians a tendency, viewed as dangerous by most other theologians, to downplay the humanity of Christ—not to deny it, but to downplay it, to lay much greater stress on the divinity of Christ, on Christ as the *logos* of God.

It was the Council of Constantinople in 381 that for the first time addressed this "balance" or, from the standpoint of that council, this imbalance that in their view Alexandria had sort of gotten things a little bit out of balance. They placed a little bit too much stress on the divinity of Christ. The formulations at the Council of Constantinople in 381 owed most to a group of three church fathers whom we call the "Cappadocian Fathers." They came from Cappadocia, a region in Anatolia in antiquity, in what we would call Turkey today. These were Basil—we met him in our last lecture as a great monastic founder—Gregory of Nyssa, and Gregory of Nazianzus. These are Basil, 330–379, Gregory of Nazianzus lived 329–390—that kind of brackets the period—and Gregory of Nyssa lived until 395.

These three theologians were prepared to speak of Christ being of like being with the father. They were trying to preserve his full humanity. They were trying to preserve his full divinity. They were trying to differentiate between two persons. They were trying to insist that Christ had to be fully human in order to reconcile and save fellow humans, and they were trying perhaps, in some way, to reconcile the teachings of those in Alexandria and others. There's a kind of a funny story here that I'll tell very briefly. You may have heard the expression that that doesn't make an iota's difference. Iota first of all is a mispronunciation of the Greek vowel *Iota* [pronounced "yota"]—not Yoda from *Star Wars*, "yota." We should talk about a "yota's" difference, but anyway, that would be a lesson for a different day. The *Iota* is *homoousious, homoiousias*. It's the *Iota* in that word of like substance of one substance; that's where the *Iota* comes from. That old saying, there's not an "yota's" difference between this and that. That all goes back to the Cappadocian Fathers, but I don't think they actually knew that they were giving us that amusing little saying.

The Alexandrian school moved forward, on a logic of its own, to put continually the emphasis on Christ's divinity. Eutyches, the great theologian of Alexandria, argued that Christ had only one divine nature, so he just really eventually pushed the point to its logical conclusion. There's only one divine nature. He becomes the "founder" of Monophysitism, quite literally "one nature-ism." Orthodox Christianity, in all its forms, Catholic, Orthodox, or Protestant, is diophysite, "two nature-ism." Monophysitism was vigorously opposed by Pope Leo and the Council of Chalcedon. It survived, however, in a great deal of the east. I've mentioned that before; we're going to encounter that fact again in some future lectures. A great deal of the east was monophysite, and this had very important political and, even as we'll see later on, military consequences for the Eastern Roman Empire.

If Alexandrian "Christology" is regarded as "high," in other words places great stress on the divinity of Christ, then Antioch's Christology we might say is "low." It placed great stress on Christ's humanity. One sometimes hears high and low Christology used among theologians today and, generally speaking, this sort of is a pastoral thing and a theological thing. It emphasizes whether the goal of human existence is to strive to be as much like the divinity of God as possible, or to lay great stress on the suffering servant, a Christ who comes as a man to live among men, to work with them, to help them, to suffer and die for them. In certain ways, this high and low notion is something that reaches back to the battles between Alexandria and Antioch in antiquity. The valance in antiquity is a little bit different that it is now, but one can see the similarities.

In Antioch, the Patriarch Nestorius, 380–451, appeared to split the two natures of Christ by arguing that Mary was *Christotokos*, could not have been *Theotokos*. She was the bearer of Christ, not the bearer of God. She did not bear God. Christ became God in some sense by adoption, but the point is that much greater stress here then is laid on Christ's human nature than on his divine nature. What one can see is that people were struggling really hard to come to terms with Trinitarian and Christological issues. These are really difficult kinds of problems. We may say, again, if we go back to Harnack's Conundrum, does anybody actually need to know all of this? Does any of this really matter? That's an interesting question and it's one I daresay that most people would have to answer for themselves. Is it true that a great deal of language is created by the church fathers, that does not exist in the scriptures? Yes. Is it perfectly clear that everything said in the scriptures is utterly transparent and requires no understanding, no explanation?

For instance, we have words like thesis, nature, essence, yes. That's an old Greek word—hypostasis. If you were to go into any Christian church today and ask people what their view on the hypostatic union was, I daresay most of them would look at you rather baffled! At the same time, with only a few Christian sects accepted, they all believe in the hypostatic union. They just don't know that they believe in the hypostatic union, the union of hypostases. Hypostasis is yet another of those Greek words for person, but person in the particular sense of the divine in human and Christ. It was at the Council of Chalcedon in 451 that the doctrine that has come to be called the "Doctrine of the Hypostatic Union" is formulated definitively for what have ever since been Orthodox Christianity. Mind you, Nestorians don't accept it. Monophysites don't accept it. There are people who have always rejected the Chalcedonian formulation, but that has been the way of explaining how various *prosopa* are enhypostasized in a single metaphysical being, namely God, the second person of the Trinity, Jesus Christ.

Prosopon, subject, person, *persona*, personality, quality, characteristics, each of these is a very difficult word, a word with a very old, long, deep, rich tradition in Greek philosophy, and words that are taken on board in Christianity. The point with which I want to leave you quite simply is that talking about God—and that is what theology is, the word theology in its simplest acceptation means talking about God, or "God-talk"—talking about God is really hard, and the church fathers were among the first to teach us that lesson.

Lecture Twenty-Three
Patristic Portraits

Scope:

One of the minor Latin church fathers, Vincentius of Lérins, reputedly said that if anyone tells you he has read everything Saint Augustine wrote, you know that person is a liar. Indeed, Augustine was the most prolific author in ancient Latin letters, pagan or Christian. In his long and colorful life, he became one of the most influential thinkers in the history of Christianity. This lecture will focus on Augustine, but it will include discussion of some of the Greek fathers encountered in the previous lecture, as well as towering Latin fathers such as Ambrose and Jerome.

Outline

I. The church fathers addressed many more issues than just the complicated matter of talking about God.

   A. Origen, born in Alexandria of Christian parents, was tremendously influential, particularly in setting biblical scholarship on paths it would follow for centuries.

   1. Origen produced the Hexapla Old Testament (Hebrew, Greek transliteration of the Hebrew, and four different Greek translations).

   2. Origen developed the "Threefold Method of Biblical Interpretation: Literal, Moral, and Allegorical."

   3. Origen did not invent but did anchor the typological reading of the Old Testament: Everything in the Old Testament foreshadows what is in the New Testament.

   B. We mentioned the Cappadocian Fathers in the previous lecture. Here we need to note that these prolific writers addressed a wide array of issues.

   1. They wrote biblical commentaries, saints' lives, liturgies, poems, and letters. More than 300 of Basil's letters survive, as do more than 250 of Gregory of Nazianzus's letters.

   2. The letter collections reveal international communications among the great fathers.

C. John Chrysostom ("the Golden Tongued") had a pagan upbringing and was taught by the great scholar Libanius. He was baptized at 18.

    1. He wished to be a monk but had to take care of his aged mother, so he rose instead through the clerical ranks in Antioch and then became bishop of Constantinople in 398.

    2. He was a spectacularly gifted speaker and writer who wrote biblical commentaries, treatises on virginity and the priesthood, more than 240 letters, and a liturgy second only to Basil's in influence.

    3. John opposed the wholesale allegorization of the scriptures that characterized the Alexandrian school and stressed the literal meaning, thus promoting the Antiochene school.

    4. John was especially concerned about moral reform, and he was often tactless in criticizing people's behavior, especially that of the women around Empress Eudoxia.

D. Turning to the Latin west, we come first to Saint Ambrose of Milan. He was born at Trier, the son of the praetorian prefect of Gaul, and served for a time as a lawyer and governor in northwestern Italy, with his seat at Milan. He was chosen bishop spontaneously by the people in 374, even though he was only a catechumen.

    1. Ambrose mediated Origen's allegorical methods to the Latin west.

    2. Among his biblical commentaries, his *Hexaëmeron*, treating the six days of creation, was influential for centuries.

    3. His book *On the Duties of Christian Ministers* Christianized Cicero's influential *De officiis* and created a Christian ideal of public service.

    4. He wrote beautiful poems and hymns, and his influence made hymns a regular part of the liturgy in the western church.

E. Saint Jerome was born in northeastern Italy, studied in Rome, traveled in Gaul, became an ascetic, and joined for a time a rigorous community in Syria before visiting Constantinople and then returning to Rome, where he became secretary to Pope Damasus.

1. We noted in an earlier lecture that Jerome became tutor and mentor to a group of aristocratic widows and virgins.
2. Damasus prompted Jerome to work on what became the Vulgate (the Latin Bible).
3. Jerome wrote theological treatises, biblical commentaries, and dozens of letters. His Latin style was long admired and imitated.
4. He translated into Latin works of various Greek fathers.
5. Jerome was the greatest scholar of all the church fathers.

II. The towering figure among the church fathers, and one of the most original and influential figures in the entire history of Christian thought, was Saint Augustine.

A. Augustine was born at Tagaste in North Africa of modest but ambitious parents who sacrificed a great deal to get him a good education, at first locally and then at Carthage.
1. Augustine became a professor of rhetoric, first at Carthage, then at Rome, and later at Milan.
2. In Milan he fell under the influence of Ambrose, and in 386 he embraced Christianity.

B. Augustine was the most prolific author in all of Latin letters, classical or Christian.

C. Shortly after returning to Africa, Augustine wrote his *Confessions*, a lengthy prayer addressed to God in which Augustine charted his intellectual and spiritual growth.

D. Three examples of how Augustine addressed specific issues will reveal something about his thought and methods.
1. Having spent some years as a Manichee, he eventually wrote to refute them, and this led him to reflect on the problem of good and evil.
   a. Is the world torn between two primordial forces, good and evil?
   b. Is evil authentic and "something" that actually has an impact?
   c. No, Augustine said. God created everything good. Evil is therefore the absence of good, a deprivation of the good. It has no reality in and of itself.
   d. As a moral matter, the existence of evil is attributable to sin and free will.

2. Augustine wrote against the Donatists, and this led him to reflect on the church and sacraments.

3. In replying to Pelagius, Augustine had to think about divine grace and original sin.

    a. Pelagians believed that people could take the first steps toward their salvation on their own initiative.

    b. On the contrary, Augustine said, humans are burdened from birth by the stain of Adam and can act only with the help of God's grace.

    c. But, Augustine said, humans are endowed with free will and can choose to call upon God for help.

E. The pagan world and classical learning attracted Augustine's attention many times, but his *On Christian Teaching* is especially revealing.

    1. Augustine proposes in this work to lay out a set of rules for understanding the scriptures.

    2. Augustine argues that the Bible is full of difficult and obscure language, contains tropes and metaphors, and exhibits many levels of meaning.

    3. To understand the Bible, therefore, one needs prodigious learning.

    4. But why does this matter? For Augustine the Bible charts the sure path to salvation. Classical education, therefore, is preparatory and no longer has any intrinsic value of its own. He uses the metaphor of "spoiling the Egyptians."

F. Augustine's greatest work was *City of God*, a massive theology of history.

    1. When the Goths sacked Rome in 410, people were shocked and outraged.

    2. Augustine took a different view: States had come and gone repeatedly through time; what happened to Rome was part of an old pattern.

    3. The danger, as Augustine saw it, was to depend too much on Rome itself or even to equate Rome with the church and to see Christian Rome as somehow part of God's providential purposes.

    4. For Augustine, humans lived at some indeterminable point on a line that stretched from Creation to the Last Judgment. All events are ephemeral and inconsequential.

III. Let us take our leave of Augustine by remarking on the astonishing fact that he had rendered classical culture instrumental and Rome itself irrelevant.

Suggested Reading:

Brown, *Augustine of Hippo*.

Kelly, *Golden Mouth*.

———, *Jerome*.

McLynn, *Ambrose of Milan*.

Questions to Consider:

1. What intellectual interests and approaches did the church fathers share?

2. What is most striking to you about the emergence of these Christian intellectuals?

Lecture Twenty-Three—Transcript
Patristic Portraits

Hello and welcome once more to these lectures on late antiquity. This time, the 23rd in the sequence, I call "Patristic Portraits." The church fathers addressed many more issues than just the complicated matter of talking about God, as we'll see as we go along here, and there were many more figures involved than just, for instance, the Cappadocian Fathers, on whom we placed some stress in the last lecture. One of the minor western fathers, Vincentius of Lérins, once said, "If someone tells you he has read everything that Augustine wrote, you know that person is a liar." This lecture will focus on the writings of Aurelius Augustinus, the greatest of the Latin fathers, perhaps the greatest of the church fathers as a whole, but we'll talk about a few other figures too, both Latin and Greek, to see what kinds of contributions they make, and in a few instances, how they actually influenced and moved Augustine along in his career and in his thinking.

The figure with whom we should really start is Origen of Alexandria. He's born about 185, died in 254. He was born of Christian parents. He wound up being a tremendously influential man, particularly in setting biblical scholarship on paths that it would follow for centuries. It is interesting because only a relatively small amount of Origen's actual writings survive. He's quoted constantly by later writers, and so it's been possible for scholars to kind of go back and reconstruct some of what Origen wrote, but for the most part, his own words have eluded us. Origen produced the Hexapla Old Testament, the six-form Old Testament. It was a book arrayed in six columns. The first column, the one on the left, was in Hebrew. Then, there was a Greek transliteration of the Hebrew, not a translation, a transliteration, the Hebrew letters turned into Greek letters. Then, there were four different Greek translations. This was a study Bible. This was meant for scholars to look at to study the various versions of the text. Origen developed what came to be called the "Three-fold Method of Biblical Interpretation: Literal, Moral, Allegorical." Literal: What do the words on the page say? Moral: How are these words talking to me right now? Of what use are these to me right now? How they do teach or instruct me? Allegorical: What is the deeper spiritual meaning concealed behind the literal words on the page?

Origen didn't invent but he did anchor the typological reading of the Old Testament. We've mentioned this in some of our earlier lectures. The typological reading of the Old Testament of the Hebrew scriptures is that basically those scriptures have no independent validity. The point is that everything in the Old Testament foreshadows something in the New. You read everything in the Old Testament as a type of something that will appear in the New, typological reading.

We mentioned the Cappadocian Fathers in the last lecture. Here, let me just take note of a few additional things that these very prolific writers addressed. I stressed last time how they contributed in such fundamental ways to talking about God. They talked about a lot of other things, too. They wrote biblical commentaries. One of the great projects of the church fathers as a whole, and almost every significant church father wrote at least some commentaries on some books of the bible; the Cappadocian Fathers were no different. They wrote saints lives, lives of famous exemplary early Christians. They wrote liturgies, service manuals for the church. They wrote poems; they wrote letters. More than 300 of Basil's letters survive, for example; more than 250 of Gregory of Nazianzus's letters survive. Those letters deserve another comment: One of the things they reveal to us—oh, they reveal all kinds of interesting ideas about teachings and ideas and opinions and impressions and so forth—they reveal international connections and communications among the great fathers of the church. These were not isolated ivory tower intellectuals sort of sitting off in utter isolation one from the other. No, they were very much in touch with each other, they knew what the big issues of the day were, and they talked about these issues with each other. It's a great benefit for us today to be able to read their letters and to hear them talking about these issues.

John Chrysostom, "the Golden Tongued," 354–407, had a pagan upbringing. He was taught in Antioch by the great teacher and scholar Libanius. One of the last great pagan intellectual figures of the Roman world. Nevertheless, John was baptized at about the age of 18. He seems to have wanted to become a monk, but he had to take care of an aged mother, so he pretty much had to stay at home and he wound up sorting rising through the clerical ranks in Antioch. He eventually became bishop of Constantinople in 398. He was, as his nickname Chrysostom, "the Golden Tongued," indicates to us, a spectacularly gifted speaker. He was also really quite a gifted writer.

He wrote biblical commentaries, he wrote a treatise on virginity, he wrote a treatise on the priesthood, he wrote more than 240 letters, so another prolific writer of letters, and again we're very grateful that these survive. He wrote a liturgy, which in Orthodoxy, is second in influence only to the liturgy of Basil.

John also opposed the wholesale allegorization of scripture that had come to characterize the Alexandrian school. Whether there are connections between the Alexandrian school's tendency to allegorize scripture and that school's tendency to emphasize the divinity as against the humanity of Christ, that's an interesting question to think about. Anyway, John was a little worried about the allegorizing tendencies of the Alexandrian school and therefore he laid greater stress on the literal meaning. Does this have a connection then with Nestorius and the tendency in Antioch to place greater emphasis on the human side of Christ? That's interesting to think about, too. What emerges from the time of John Chrysostom on is that there is what is often called an Antiochene school of scriptural reading, a little more stress on the literal meaning, and an Alexandrian school of scriptural reading, a little more stress on the allegorical meaning of the text.

John was especially concerned about moral reform. He was actually pretty tactless in criticizing people's behavior, not least the behavior around the court. As a result the Empress Eudoxia finally got tired of him and ran him off. He was exiled and removed from office as patriarch of Constantinople.

If we turn to the Latin west and look for some representative figures, we would come first to Ambrose of Milan, born in 339, died in 397. Ambrose is an interesting figure in a number of ways. He was born at Trier, so that had been the great prefectural capital of the west. He was the son of the praetorian prefect of Gaul, so he's born into one of the highest possible Roman administrative families. He served for a time as a lawyer and governor in northwestern Italy. His seat was Milan, another of the great governing capitals of the Roman world. He acquired such a reputation for honesty, integrity, and so on that when the bishop of the city died, the people of the city spontaneously elected him bishop in 374, even though he was only a catechumen. He wasn't even a baptized Christian. He had to be baptized, ordained a priest, consecrated a bishop, boom, boom, boom, in very quick succession. This is not normally the practice in the Catholic Church, then or since, but Ambrose's case was kind of interesting in this regard.

Ambrose is important for a whole variety of reasons; let me mention just a few of them. It was Ambrose more than anyone else who mediated Origen's allegorical methods to the Latin west, this allegorical reading of scripture. It's interesting when we come to Saint Augustine we'll see that he learned from Ambrose that things that he read in the scriptures that struck him as meaningless or else as old wives' tales, now suddenly took on meaning. Augustine had been tempted simply to read what he found on the page in front of him and say, this is crazy, I can't possibly believe this, this doesn't make any sense to me. He listened to Ambrose and then he said, ah, now I understand.

Among Ambrose's biblical commentaries, his *Hexaëmeron*, six days, treated the six days of creation. You might think of Giovanni Boccaccio's *The Decameron*, 10 days. Boccaccio's title is a deliberate riff on Ambrose's title. This book was influential for centuries as a commentary on the opening of Genesis. His book *On the Duties of Christian Ministers* is a very interesting attempt to Christianize Cicero's great treatise on duties, *De officiis*. What it basically did is it created a Christianized ideal of public service. It took the fundamental ideas of Cicero about public service and rewrote them, as it were, rescored them we might say, in a Christian key. He also was a writer of poems and hymns, and his influence made hymns a regular part of the liturgy of the western church. Hymns had not been a part of western worship, at least not a regular part before Ambrose, and after him they pretty regularly were. Some of his hymns are still used today. *Deus Creator Omnium*, *Aeterne rerum conditor*, *Jam surgit hora tertia*, *Veni redemptor gentium*— these were ones that were my companions when I was a young boy, but some of them I haven't heard in a very long time.

Saint Jerome, 342–420 or thereabout, was born in northeastern Italy. He studied in Rome, traveled in Gaul, and became an ascetic. He joined for a period of time a very rigorous community in Syria before visiting Constantinople, and then returning to Rome where he became a secretary to Pope Damasus. Jerome's kind of a restless character as you can see, moving about all the time and associating with different people all of the time. We mentioned in an earlier lecture that Jerome became tutor and mentor to a group of aristocratic widows and virgins around Rome. This even brought him a certain amount of scandal and notoriety; it wasn't entirely clear that he should be involved with large numbers of women. Pope Damasus prompted Jerome to work on what eventually came to be called the "Vulgate Bible." It's important to see what this was. The Vulgate was the bible for the *vulgus*, the Latin word for the people, but more broadly it can have a negative connotation, sort of meaning the crowd. It can just mean the people. It can kind of mean sort of everybody, but the *vulgus* who spoke Latin. The Vulgate, it actually quite literally means the "vulgar bible," but it doesn't mean the profane or obscene bible. It means the "popular" one—popular in the sense of the bible for those whose language was Latin.

There had been a variety of biblical translations available up until this time. What really Pope Damasus seems to have had in mind is that it would be a good idea to kind of get a single and authoritative version into people's hands. Jerome followed a number of rather interesting practices in executing his Vulgate Bible. He held strictly to the Hebrew canon, for instance. In other words, he didn't use those few additional books that appear in the Septuagint in the Greek version of the Old Testament. He used only the Hebrew version. Generally speaking, through the Middle Ages, the other books of the Old Testament, that is to say the Greek ones, continued to be used. But eventually the Protestant reformers did cut back to only those books that had been in the Hebrew canon, so in an interesting kind of way, Jerome anticipated their point of view.

It's often said rather imprecisely that Jerome translated the Bible. He didn't in fact retranslate the whole Bible. He translated large parts of it, other parts he edited, in other parts he really just improved on the *Vetus Latina*. *Vetus Latina* means the "old Latin" version. *Vetus Latina* is itself a slightly deceptive term. There were various Latin translations in existence before Jerome's time and, from one point of view, these are referred to sort of generally as *Vetus Latina*. From another point of view, it is generally believed that there was a version that could be identified as *Vetus Latina*. There is at the Monastery of Beuron in Germany—there has been for many, many years—a project to go through the writings of the church fathers with meticulous care and lift quotations that are clearly not vulgate and therefore probably are *Vetus Latina*. Slowly but surely you've got this verse and that verse and this verse and that verse, and they're trying to reconstruct the *Vetus Latina*. In other words, nobody in the modern world has ever laid eyes on a *Vetus Latina*, but it was there and that was largely what Jerome was working with.

Jerome also wrote theological treatises, he wrote biblical commentaries, he wrote dozens of letters, so again, he's like these other church fathers. He is prolific in a variety of different genres; he's well known in a variety of different ways. His Latin style was very long-admired and imitated. We think sometimes of the Renaissance as people who looked back to the great secular authors, the profane authors of classical antiquity; that's true. But, among the authors most admired and most frequently imitated as a Latin stylist during the Renaissance was Saint Jerome. He also translated into Latin the works of various Greek fathers. Jerome was a little unusual, not in being very, very good in both Latin and Greek, although there were few and fewer people that had both languages, but in also knowing Hebrew, which he learned in Palestine when he lived there.

We can say, I think, that Jerome was the greatest scholar of all the church fathers. I didn't say the greatest intellect, I didn't say the most influential, but he is probably the greatest scholar in the sense of the most sort of learned and erudite and the one who did, we might almost say today, the most research.

Be that as it may, the towering figure among the church fathers, one of the most original and influential figures in the entire history of Christian thought is Saint Augustine. He was born in Thagaste, a relatively modest town in North Africa in 354, of modest but ambitious parents who sacrificed a great deal to get him a good education, at first locally, in the local schools, and then he went off to the schools in Carthage. Carthage was an important city in North Africa. It was a provincial city of the Roman world to be sure, but nevertheless a fairly important city. I've emphasized in earlier lectures just how rich and prosperous and luxurious really, in many ways, North Africa was, so Carthage was a big deal. It may not seem so obvious to us today looking back after 15 centuries, but this was a pretty big deal.

Then after his period of education in Carthage, he went off to Rome and later to Milan. He went onto Rome and basically sort of coming in from the provinces, the idea being, if I've made it in the provinces, can I make it in Rome? Then you might think, why does he leave Rome and go to Milan? Of course, this is in the period when, as we've had occasion to see in earlier lectures, Rome is no longer effectively the capital of the empire. Milan is the capital of the Western Empire, so Milan is really where the action was. In moving from Rome to Milan, we can see that Augustine was a figure who was reasonably ambitious. He was kind of looking for ways to make a name for himself. He was a professor of rhetoric, he was a wordsmith, he was a craftsman with words.

In Milan—and I alluded to this a few minutes ago—he fell under the influence of Ambrose. It's very interesting. He'd heard apparently stories about Ambrose being a great preacher, and he though, this Christian stuff, I've read some of this when I was younger, my mother was a Christian after all, she tried to get me to believe all this, and it just wasn't working very well. He goes along to listen to Ambrose and later on, he says, "I went to mock and came away converted." In part because, first of all, he found here a Christian writer who could command language in ways that were absolutely surpassing, but also he found someone who could explain the stories of the scriptures in ways that reveal their deeper spiritual truths.

By about 386, Augustine embraced Christianity. Of course, he portrays this in his later book the *Confessions* as a kind of a step-by-step process. It's invested with a kind of an air of inevitability. We have the wonderful story of Augustine in the garden thinking what he's going to do next, and he hears the voice of a child, *tole lege*, *tole lege*, pick it up and read. He picks up the scriptures. Not in hoarding and in vice and so on, give away all you have and join the church and so on. It's interesting, of course, that's the precise passage that Saint Anthony heard that drew him to the church. That's the same passage that Francis of Assisi would later hear to draw him to the church. One begins to think there may be a certain literary trope operating here. Be that as it may, Augustine does come to join the church.

He had intended to become an ascetic, but after his return to Africa in 388, he became a priest. In 391, he was ordained a priest. In 395, he was elected bishop of the city of Hippo, Hippo Regius, and he served the rest of his life, 35 years, as bishop of this city.

Augustine was the most prolific author. This is important to say. He was the most prolific author in all of Latin letters, Christian or classical. It's also important to say he was never a systematic thinker. If Augustine were a boxer, we would say he was a great counterpuncher. That is to say, he addressed problems as they came up. Then, late in his life, he wrote a long work called the *Retractationes*—the "retractations," the going back over my tracts—in which he reviewed and revised many of his earlier opinions. Some have said, you see, he was confused or he couldn't make up his mind. Others say he was very courageous. He was willing to admit that he'd changed his mind on various kinds of things. He remains one of the great fathers of the church, one of the doctors of the Roman Catholic Church, seemingly a perfectly safe and standard Catholic theologian. Yet, at the same time, John Calvin once said, "Augustine agrees with us completely." I think probably Augustine didn't agree with him completely, but he certainly agreed with him on an awful lot of things.

Shortly after returning to Africa, Augustine wrote his *Confessions*. The *Confessions of Augustine*, a wonderful book, a very influential book, is quite a beautiful book to read in lots of ways. It's cast in the form of a prayer. It is Augustine, in a sense, offering himself to God or almost imagining God as a mirror in which Augustine can see himself as he grows from youth. He begins at his mother's breast when he says that he was greedy. He goes all the way through his life, through the events of the garden when he hears the child's voice telling him to take and read. Then, the last books of the *Confessions* begin actually, in certain ways, some of his theological reflections. I'll offer it's not his first theological work. His work on freedom of the will was actually written before the *Confessions*, but we find theological reflections at the end of the *Confessions*.

The work is extremely valuable to us because Augustine spent time as a Manichee. Augustine spent time as a follower of various philosophical cults and intellectual fashions of his day, and he goes along and he explains for us. He's writing from the perspective of a man of middle age of what was attractive to him when he was a teenager and a man in his twenties. We have to be a little careful with that. Reminiscence from certain points in one's life about other points in one's life are not always strictly accurate, but the point is that Augustine does tell us in some very interesting ways why certain kinds of intellectual movements, cultural movements, religious movements, and philosophical movements were attractive to him, and what he eventually found to be failing in them, to be lacking in them. This is an extremely valuable book to have. It is really, in lots of ways, the first great work of introspection in Western literature. For anyone who likes reality television or confession shows and this sort of thing today, Augustine's *Confessions* would disappoint you. It's not that kind of work at all. It's a much more serious work, indeed, and a work that demands to be taken seriously. A thousand years later, of course, Petrarch, the great Renaissance Humanist, writes his secret book, in which basically Augustine interrogates Petrarch and Petrarch produces a second work much like Augustine's *Confessions* and, again, a work of profound introspection.

Let me give you three examples of how Augustine addressed specific issues, because I want to reveal something about his method, something about his thought, something about the way he went about things. Remember a second ago I said if he were like a boxer he'd be a counterpuncher. He'd spent some time as a Manichee. We talked about Manichaeans on an earlier day. He was particularly concerned to refute them. Indeed, in the *Confessions*, there's quite a long discussion of why the Manichaeans were attractive to him and why he eventually found that he had to reject Manichaean teaching, but his attempt to refute the Manichaeans led him to reflect on the problem of good and evil. I think most people would agree, the problem of good and evil is a pretty serious one.

What Augustine wants to know—remember Manichaeanism is one of these dualist sects, light, dark, good, evil, flesh, spirit, etc.—Augustine wants to know is the world torn between two primordial forces, one good and one evil? Is evil authentic? Is it "something" that actually exists, that has an impact? Augustine thought very long and hard on this, and he eventually comes to the conclusion that no, God created everything good. Evil therefore is an absence of good. It is a deprivation of the good. It has no reality in and of itself. One might say, good heavens! Look around us in the world. Surely, there is evil out there! Augustine would say, yes, of course there is. As a moral matter, the existence of evil is not part of the immutable order of things; it is a consequence of sin and free will. Evil is our fault. We do evil things; evil was not created as something in and of itself. That answer may or may not be satisfactory to most people, but there it is.

Augustine wrote against the Donatists. Remember, the Donatists were the rigorous sect in North Africa who had not collaborated with the imperial authorities during the Great Persecution of Diocletian, and therefore wouldn't accept anybody they felt had collaborated. The Donatists had separated from the Catholics in North Africa for a long time, and this has probably been going on for a century by the time Augustine comes along. Augustine rejected the rigorism and purism of the Donatists, arguing that human society and the church are communities of sinners, not communities of saints. It's a very, very interesting and important point—the sacraments of the church, the teaching of the officers of the church—that holiness does not depend upon individual human beings, all of whom are sinners. Holiness depends upon God, not upon the likes of us.

In replying to a man by the name of Pelagius, Augustine had to think about divine grace and original sin. What is it about us that make us inclined to want to do what is wrong—in other words, to sin? Pelagians believed that people could take their own steps on the way to their own salvation, that they were perfectly capable of saving themselves. Be perfect as my father is perfect: for heaven's sake, if Jesus said that, can't we all do that? Augustine said no, that's probably not going to work very well. Humans are burdened from birth, he said, by the stain of Adam, and they can only, with the help of God's grace, escape that stain. But, Augustine said—and here's the crucial point: Humans are endowed with free will and they can choose to call upon God for help. They are unable to help themselves, but they can call upon help, and in calling upon help, they exercise their will.

Humanity matters, choice matters, our capacity to act as full human beings matters, but we are not capable of doing good left to our own devices.

The pagan world in classical learning attracted Augustine's attention many times. Actually, I have more to say about this subject generally in my next lecture, but for now I want to draw your attention to his book *On Christian Teaching*, *De doctrina christiana*. It's especially revealing. Augustine proposes in this book to lay out a set of rules for understanding the scriptures. Augustine understands that the Bible is full of very difficult and obscure language, that it contains tropes, that it contains metaphors, that it exhibits many levels of meaning. But, he says, understanding the Bible requires prodigious learning, but is absolutely essential to salvation. It is in the Bible that one finds the path to salvation. How then is one going to equip oneself to read this very difficult book? One is going to have to master all the arts of classical education. What's very interesting here is that Augustine has effectively made classical education, everything we think of as the classical tradition, purely instrumental. It is purely preparatory. It is propaedeutic. He teaches by way of the metaphor of "spoiling the Egyptians." You take what you need; you take what is useful. The classics have no independent value. They can simply help you to read the Bible and save your soul. I'll come back at the very end to reiterate that point.

Augustine's greatest work was the *City of God, De civitate Dei*, his massive theology of history. This is a long book, a complex book, and an extremely intricate and difficult book. It is folly of the highest order for me to try, in a minute or two, to tell you what it's like, but I'm going to commit the folly anyway. When the Goths sacked Rome in 410, many people were shocked, many people were outraged. How could this happen to the Roman world? Augustine took a very different view. He started writing the *City of God* in response to the sack of Rome by the Goths in 410, something we've talked about. Augustine's basic point is that states have come and gone and come and gone and come and gone repeatedly throughout time. What had happened to Rome was part of an age-old pattern. This sort of thing is probably going to happen again. The danger, as Augustine saw it, was to depend too much on Rome itself, or even to equate Rome and the church. He doesn't like, for example, the historian Eusebius's way of thinking about the Constantinian and post-Constantinian church as a sort of a realization, as it were, of the city of God here on earth. Augustine said, no, the church is a flawed institution, the empire is a flawed institution, and they are part of God's providential purposes.

For Augustine, people live at some indeterminable point on a line that starts with creation and ends with the last judgment. We cannot know where we are on that line. We cannot know, but by the same token, all events in this world are in some sense ephemeral and inconsequential. Let's just repeat that point and pick up the point I made about *De doctrina christiana*. We take our leave of Augustine and remark the astonishing fact that he had rendered classical culture instrumental and Rome itself irrelevant. If Romans knew anything, they knew that line from Virgil's *Aeneid*—and Augustine knew it perfectly well, as he taught the book for years and studied it as a boy—that the world would last exactly as long as Rome did. Augustine has said that Rome is irrelevant. I'm minded to wonder what Dido would have thought. That's Dido, of course, who fell in love with Aeneas, but he had to leave her to go and found Rome. She commits suicide and in her long speech she asks for someone from these shores to rise up and avenge her. I daresay she didn't have in mind the African theologian Augustine, but if anyone avenged her against the founder of Rome, I daresay it was Augustine.

Lecture Twenty Four
"What Has Athens to Do with Jerusalem?"

Scope:

Tertullian asked the famous question that appears in this lecture's title. By looking at key figures from the period 400–600 A.D., we will watch as Christians colonized, so to speak, of all the great literary forms of classical antiquity. We will focus on great preachers such as Augustine and Caesarius, on great poets such as Sedulius and Prudentius, and on great schoolmasters such as Cassiodorus and Isidore. We will observe the substitution of a Christian education for Rome's traditional secular one. The lecture will conclude with a discussion of the prolific and influential Pope Gregory the Great, who mused on the qualities of saints, the condition of ordinary Christians, and the duties of the clergy.

Outline

I. Whereas Augustine was agitated about Christianity's often antagonistic relationship with classical culture, two centuries later the issue had vanished. The dominant culture was thoroughly Christian and the "classics" a fading memory. This is one of late antiquity's greatest transformations.

    A. We have seen that the church fathers substituted fundamental explorations in theology for the traditional speculations of secular philosophy.

    B. Transformations in philosophy show the new directions of thought.

        1. Dionysius the Pseudo Areopagite was long considered (incorrectly) a disciple of Saint Paul. He wrote works in a Neoplatonic mode.

            a. The aim of all his work was to show how the whole created order would eventually attain union with God through processes of purification, illumination, and union.

            b. His work was profoundly influential for centuries and lay behind a millennium of mystical theology.

2. Boethius was from a senatorial family, held the consulship in 510, saw his sons hold the consulship together in 522, and served as master of the offices in Theodoric's regime at Ravenna—which brought a charge of treason down on him.

    a. He was interested in mathematics and logic and translated important works of Aristotle (for centuries the west's only access to these works).

    b. Boethius discussed predestination and free will, good and evil, justice, and virtue (among other things).

C. History writing, an old and accomplished literary art in antiquity, is also revealing.

    1. Eusebius, bishop of Caesarea, who suffered under persecutors, was caught up in Arian politics but was befriended by Constantine and invented church history with his *Ecclesiastical History* in 10 books, the last 3 treating his own times.

        a. He begins with the times of Christ and marches through accounts of the martyrs (146 of them) who suffered for the faith and the bishops who built the church.

        b. His theme is the providential hand of God moving through human affairs.

    2. Paul Orosius was a young Spaniard who moved to Africa and was befriended by Augustine.

        a. When Augustine began his *City of God*, he commissioned Orosius to write a detailed, narrative counterpart.

        b. Orosius wrote *Seven Books of History Against the Pagans*, beginning with King Ninus of Assyria and coming down to his own times.

        c. His theme was that despite the rise and fall of great kingdoms and empires, one could discern the hand of God in human affairs and that the only history that mattered was providential.

D. The rise of Christian poetry marks yet another "takeover" of a major literary form.

    1. Sedulius was an obscure figure who set portions of the Bible to verse in his *Paschal Song*.

2. The Spaniard Prudentius had a fine public career and then retired to write, among other things, poems. His *Psychomachia*, in hexameters, recounts an epic struggle between virtue and vice.

II. In crucial respects this remarkable cultural transformation was made possible by changes in education.

    A. Traditional Roman education was elite and literary. It formed a class of men who governed the world and enjoyed their leisure. As their world passed away, so too did their education.

        1. Pupils began with a tutor at about the age of 7, then moved to a *grammaticus* at 12, and then to a *rhetor* at 15; "advanced" study in philosophy was possible.

        2. The basic curriculum is spelled out in Martianus Capella's *Marriage of Mercury and Philology: The Seven Liberal Arts*.

    B. Christianity, as a "religion of the book," required learning, but for a long time it had no access to basic literary culture except through the pagan classics.

    C. Crucial steps toward the medieval school were taken by Cassiodorus. He came from a senatorial family, served as quaestor in 507–511, consul in 541, master of the offices in 523–527, and praetorian prefect for Italy in 533–c. 540.

        1. He retired from public life during the Gothic wars and settled at a family estate near Squillace, which he called "Vivarium" ("Fish Ponds").

        2. He desired to create a sort of institute for Christian studies at Vivarium.

        3. Cassiodrous's works, plus the list of famous Christian authors begun by Saint Jerome and continued by others, became the basic bibliography for a millennium.

    D. Isidore of Seville came from a noble family disrupted by the Justinianic wars in Spain. He was a major ecclesiastical statesman who presided over church councils and required the establishment of schools in every diocese.

        1. Isidore was immensely learned but not original.

2. He wrote histories, polemical treatises against heretics and Jews, biblical commentaries, two books on ecclesiastical offices, and a continuation of Jerome's *On Illustrious Men*.

3. He is most famous for his *Etymologies*, an encyclopedic compendium of all knowledge based on Pliny the Elder and grounded in the assumption that the meanings of words reveal many truths.

4. Isidore transmitted to the Middle Ages a vast amount of ancient learning, but he pruned away what was manifestly pagan.

III. The themes we have been pursuing in this lecture come together in Pope Gregory I "the Great." Gregory was born into a senatorial family and served as prefect of Rome in 573 but retired and became a monk in his family house in Rome

A. Gregory, who was ill most of his adult life, desired nothing more than to be a monk and to pursue his reading and writing.

B. He had that remarkable Roman sense of duty, so when he was elected pope in 590, he did not object.

C. Gregory was a prolific author.

1. His *Pastoral Rule* was a how-to book for bishops. He wrote in the tradition of Cicero and Ambrose and was deeply imbued with a Christianized version of traditional Roman public ethics.

2. *Moralia on Job* was basically a commentary on the book of Job that addressed the human condition generally and particularly the problems of justice and suffering.

3. His *Homilies on Ezechiel* were deep reflections on his own times inspired by the book of Ezekiel.

4. He wrote many biblical commentaries, always primarily in the allegorical mode. They were influential in the Middle Ages.

5. His *Dialogues* were four books on the saints of Italy.

6. His more than 860 letters reveal an extraordinarily conscientious man going about his required routines.

D. Gregory had a sense that the world was drawing to a close, but he sent missionaries to England.

E. There is in Gregory a serenity that is missing in Augustine. Whereas Augustine sensed a still-living pagan tradition that threatened and challenged Christianity, Gregory saw only a Christian world that sometimes failed to live up to its own ideals.

Suggested Reading:

Cochrane, *Christianity and Classical Culture.*

Markus, *The End of Ancient Christianity.*

Questions to Consider:

1. What parts of the classical tradition did Christian writers accept and reject?

2. How did education change in late antiquity?

Lecture Twenty-Four—Transcript
"What Has Athens to Do with Jerusalem?"

Hello and welcome once more to our series of lectures on late antiquity. This time, in Lecture Twenty-Four, we ask, "What has Athens to do with Jerusalem?" That's not my question; it's actually a question of Tertullian who've we've bumped into a number of times in the course of these lectures, "What has Athens to do with Jerusalem?" He, of course, took the view that Athens had nothing to do with Jerusalem and Athens was best thrown overboard and left entirely on one side. But, as we've seen, Augustine, for instance, was agitated about Christianity's often antagonistic relationship with classical culture. What's interesting is that two centuries later, this issue has effectively vanished. The dominant culture was thoroughly Christian. The "classics" are a fading memory. That is one of the great transformations of late antiquity. To go from a world where Christianity didn't exist much at all and was persecuted, and certainly had no visibility or prominence, to a world where it had effectively taken over.

That's really the subject of this lecture, "What has Athens to do with Jerusalem?" Tertullian would have said nothing at all; by the end of the lecture, we'll be able to say nothing at all. But, in the middle, we'll be able to say Jerusalem took over Athens, and that is no small accomplishment. We've seen that the church fathers, for example, substituted fundamental explorations in theology for the kinds of traditional speculations of secular philosophy: philosophers that asked questions about the nature of reality, the nature of the universe, the nature of humanity, the kinds of obligations we have to one another, the nature of matter and so on, fair enough. Transformations in philosophy under the new Christian aegis show us some of these new directions of thought and show us how much they were also indebted to older ways of thinking. Clearly, this is not the time or place for a full course in the history of early Christian philosophy, but let's just mention a few examples.

For instance, there was Dionysius the Pseudo Areopagite. We call him the "Pseudo Areopagite" because we actually don't know who this guy was. Whoever he was, he wrote about the year 500. For a very long time, indeed probably we could say until the 12th century, it was pretty generally believed that this was a figure taught by Saint Paul in Athens. It couldn't have been this figure taught by Saint Paul, but as I said, for a very long time that's what's believed of him. He was a Neoplatonic philosopher, Pseudo-Denis. He wrote, in other words, in the way that Plato was interpreted and understood in Roman imperial times. He wrote four major books, *The Celestial Hierarchies*, *The Ecclesiastical Hierarchy*, *The Divine Names*, and *The Mystical Theology*. In one way or another, the aim of each one of these works was to show how the whole created order would eventually attain union with God through discernible processes. These were purification: We must purify ourselves, we must somehow purge ourselves, and we must somehow eliminate from ourselves all of those things that attach us to this dross world. Illumination: We must be open to the inflowing of the divine light. It's the cartoon trope, isn't it, that when the light bulb is over somebody's head and when the bulb goes on, they've got the light, *iluminacio*. They have been opened to the light. Finally, having been illumined, one can achieve union with God.

We can say just by way of conclusion that Pseudo-Denis was profoundly influential for centuries. Broadly speaking, he lay behind a millennium of mystical theology. There are many other kinds of theology, but mystical theology would eventually come to occupy a very prominent place in the Christian tradition, but not really before the 12th and 13th centuries, and that's long after the period that concerns us here.

Let's say a little about Boethius. Born about 480, died in 524. He came from a senatorial family, a very high-born Roman. He himself held the consulship in 510. He saw his sons hold the consulship together in 522. He served as master of the offices in Theodoric's regime at Ravenna. Unfortunately, he got mixed up in some kind of affair to do with Theodoric's religious problems. Theodoric, of course, and the Goths were Arian, with Constantinople, and he eventually was imprisoned and died in prison, perhaps indeed there executed. He was presumably put to death for treason. Boethius is an interesting figure in lots of ways. He's kind of a polymath. He was interested in mathematics and in logic. He translated important works of Aristotle. For centuries, this was the west's only access to these particular works. Some of Aristotle's mathematical treatises and some of his logical treatises are what are at stake here.

His greatest work was a book called the *Consolation of Philosophy*. It was written while he was in prison awaiting death, so he was seeking consolation and it was Lady Philosophy who brought him consolation. It is a "prosimetric" dialogue. What does that mean? It's partly in prose and partly in verse. This is an old ancient form and it's a form that would be used from time to time later on in Western literature. Boethius was very much a master of this particular form. Lady Philosophy and Boethius sort of had a long, extended conversation, and she brings him consolation by assuring him that wealth, fame, and the whole material order are transitory. It is not upon these things that one should place one's hope or one's expectations. In the course of the treatise the *Consolation of Philosophy*, Boethius discusses predestination, he discusses free will, he discusses good and evil, justice, and virtue, among many other things. What's remarkable about this book is that it's a philosophical book by a Christian that never once contradicts Christian teaching and never once makes reference to it. You would never know from reading this book that Boethius was a Christian. Yet, in reading it, you would never find there, as I said, anything that actually contradicts Christian teaching. We have begun to see that perhaps Christian philosophy by the end of antiquity has either moved in a direction we will call "mystical," or perhaps has moved in a direction that will achieve synthesis, a synthesis of various ways of thinking among the great ancient thinkers.

History writing was an old and accomplished literary art in antiquity. It reaches all the way back to the Greeks of the 5th century B.C.—Herodotus, Lucidities, and so on. Eusebius was born about 260, died about 340, we've mentioned him a number of times, bishop of Caesarea, who suffered under the persecutors. He was caught up in Arian politics, he was befriended by Constantine, and he effectively invented church history with his *Ecclesiastical History*. It was written in 10 books, the last 3 books of which actually treat Eusebius's own lifetime. He begins with the times of Christ and then he marches through an account of the martyrs, 146 of them, who suffered for the faith, and the bishops who built the church. You may recall we talked about Eusebius in an earlier lecture when we talked about his stress on the bishops and the succession of the bishops. But crucial is Eusebius's emphasis, his central theme, the providential hand of God moving through human affairs. This is how he understands history. This is how he understands history to move. History is not random by any stretch of the imagination.

Paul Orosius is another interesting figure. He was a young Spaniard who moved to Africa and was befriended by Augustine. When Augustine began writing his *City of God*, which was his great theology of history where he was going to lay out sort of the big points, the big issues, he commissioned Orosius to write, in a sense, a detailed narrative counterpart. In other words, he left it to Orosius to kind of write the ordinary nuts-and-bolts history. Orosius produced a work called *Seven Books of History Against the Pagans*; his title is rather interesting. He's fully Augustinian in his way of thinking about what history means, what history is for, why we would remember it, but he is actually going to tell the tale. He begins with King Ninus of Assyria and comes all the way down to his own times. His theme—and again it's very much Augustine's theme, but as I say, he provides the details—is that despite the rise and fall of great kingdoms and empires, one could discern the hand of God in human affairs, and that the only history that mattered was providential history. The ordinary affairs of individual people don't really matter much. They may be subjects of interest; they may not be. What one is looking for in the course of history are certain signs of the hand of God. That's what mattered. Here is a very interesting way in which we could say that ancient writers sort of camped upon a classical form of writing history, and transformed it and made it something different, and turned it to their own purposes.

Poetry is another example of the same kind. I mentioned in my last lecture, for instance, in connection with the church father Ambrose, that he wrote poems and hymns, that he contributed hymns to the church. Let's take a couple of other examples of figures who are mainly known to us as poets, not figures who mainly did lots of things, among which was write poems. What I'm suggesting, again, is we have another kind of "takeover" of a major Christian literary form or a colonization of a major literary form. We could view it from a number of different points of view. First of all, Sedulius—I daresay for most people Sedulius is not exactly a household name. He was a man who wrote in the early 5th century, a fairly obscure figure, who set portions of the Bible to verse in his *Paschal Song*, his *Carmen Paschale*. Let's just hear a few of his verses. This is a very familiar scene, the parting of the Red Sea.

The dark waters of the sea parted and opened, offering a
  way through
As they rolled back on either side; the earth was exposed,
Stripped of its familiar waters and on foot the mass of people
Entered the sea, though the sea was gone, and the dry waters
Were stunned to see strange feet walking through the deep.
Nature changed its course and the people went right in
Through the middle of the sea, already undergoing a
  primitive baptism,
For Christ was their leader, as the reading clearly proclaims:
The voice of the Lord is over many waters, and the voice is
  the Word.
Christ the Word is present; he who governs the
  two Testaments
Of the Law existing in harmony, opened up the
  ancient abyss,
So that the teaching that followed might walk on dry and
  level land.

That's not great poetry, but it's not bad. It is rather better in Latin
than it is in English, but I do want to draw your attention to a couple
of things there. You note the typological reading, the waters of the
Red Sea baptized the Hebrews going through. It foreshadows the
New Testament and the baptism of Christ. It doesn't actually mean
anything by itself. We noticed that Christ is the Lord of the two
Testaments. We can see a way of reading the Old Testament that in
Sedulius's account has been theologized. There's a lot there that you
wouldn't find in Exodus, the book of the Old Testament that actually
recounts the Hebrews going through the Red Sea. We can see some
of these theological themes that I've drawn your attention to in
earlier lectures.

The Spaniard Prudentius was in lots of ways actually a better poet;
348 to about 410 is when he lived. He had a fine public career and he
then retired to write, among other things, poems. His *Psychomachia*,
a *conflictus*, is a battle poem. It's a battle between states of mind,
habits of mind, that sort of thing. I think you'll see in just a minute
when I read a little bit kind of how it works. *Psychomachia* is a battle
of states of mind. It's written in hexameters, six-foot lines, the
classic epic meter of antiquity. It recounts an epic struggle between
virtue and vice. Here's a section of his account of Avarice and
Generosity. It's a rather long poem and it goes on like this at very

great lengths, so this is just by way of giving you an example of Prudentius. Then, also we can read poetry like this as an example of providing kind of basic ethical teaching for people who were sufficiently elite and sufficiently alert and interested to want to get such teaching from sources like poetry.

> It is said that Avarice, whose dress had a large pocket in front,
> Snatched with her hooked hand everything valuable
> Left behind by voracious Indulgence; with mouth wide open
> She looked covetously at the pretty trifles as she collected bits of gold
> Lying among the heaps of sand; but not content to fill her pocket
> She took delight in stuffing the filthy lucre into bags
> And making purses swell, heavy with stolen goods
> Which she covered with her left hand to conceal them, hiding them
> Under her cloak; for her right hand quickly snatches up her loot,
> Using her nails as hard as bronze to pick up the spoils.
> Worry, Hunger, Fear, Anxiety, Perjury, Pallor,
> Corruption, Trickery, Lies, Insomnia and Meanness,
> All the different furies push forward, accompanying this monster.

The battle rages and Generosity appears:

> When suddenly Generosity, gnashing her teeth, rushes forward
> Into the midst of battle, engaging in the fight to help her allies.
> She had been placed at the back of the army but was destined
> To put an end to battle, making sure nothing bad remained.
> She had thrown from her shoulders all that she carried, [and] she marched on
> Stripped of all clothing, having relieved herself of many bags.
> For she had been burdened by riches and the weight of money

But she was unencumbered now, having shown pity to
    the poor,
Caring for them with kindness and generosity, sharing her
    family wealth.
Rich in faith now, she looked at her empty wallet,
Counting up the sum from the return of interest which would
    last forever.
At the sight of this invincible Virtue's destructive power
Avarice stood still, paralyzed with shock, out of her mind.

I think you can see that's a very interesting way to teach the Christian vices or the Christian virtues and how they combat, how they fight, how they *machia*, how they battle against vice.

In crucial respects, this remarkable cultural transformation was made possible by changes in education. Let's devote a little bit of time to thinking about education and schooling in this late antique world, and get a feel for how it is that we can move from a world of secular profane classical literature to a world in which Christian literature has come to take first place. Traditional Roman education was elite and literary. It was not something that penetrated widely through society. It would have made no particular sense to the Romans that there should be free public education for everybody, and it was not an education that addressed in any meaningful sense that we can think of today as practical skills. It was literary education. It was education; it was not training. You got on-the-job training to do all kinds of things, but you didn't go to school to be trained. You went to school to be educated. This is sometimes a lesson that we have to relearn all the time.

It formed a class of men who governed the world. That's what Roman education did, it formed a class of men who governed the world and who enjoyed their leisure. It's interesting to think, for example, of the 19th century in Britain where the whole idea was that if you went up to Oxford or Cambridge and read the classics, you were perfectly well trained to run the British Empire. That's what you needed to do know. You needed to read Lucidities and Livy and Cicero and so on, and then you could run the world. The Romans understood that same very basic point.

Here's the crucial point: As that Roman Empire and the world it supported passed away, the kind of educational system that sustained that empire and that taught the men who ran that empire also passed away. This didn't succumb to barbarian invasions or growing ignorance. It happened as a result of a very broad transformation in the social system nurtured by and that nurtured a certain kind of education. What was that education like? A pupil would begin with a tutor and, at about the age of seven, would learn basic language. About age 12, he—generally speaking he, it was possible for women to get some education, particularly in the households, particularly in the more elite households of antiquity, but generally speaking, boys were the ones receiving education—they would then move on to a *grammaticus*. That means you would study grammar, but it means you would really study the Latin language or the Greek language, or both, in a more "advanced" and a more sophisticated way. At about age 15 or thereabouts, one would move on to a *rhetor*. A *rhetor* would teach the art of speaking, which is what rhetoric is. We think rhetoric is a word that nowadays has kind of an unhappy connotation. It's sort of lies that people in public office tell us or something. Rhetoric is in Quintilian's definition, the great author of *The Great Manual of Rhetoric*, a good man speaking well. The idea of rhetoric was to be able to speak elegantly and persuasively, so you were meant to be able to speak elegantly and persuasively.

In imperial antiquity, as opposed to republican antiquity where Rome is concerned, people spoke much less. The world is run by military dictators, emperors. There is less place for free citizens to speak freely, although there are still places in individual cities where people could debate. There were places in the church where, for example, bishops could preach, so there was still reason to be able to speak well, but it was also true that rhetoric was gradually slipping into what we would think of today as literary criticism. For instance, the despair of every high school child who has to go home at night and find three examples of onomatopoeia in a poem. Onomatopoeia is meant to be heard, not to be read on the page. But little by little, many of the great tropes that attach to the spoken word wound up attaching to the written word, so that we wind up with the peculiar examples like the one that I just gave.

Advanced study in philosophy was possible; not everyone went on to advanced study. The basic curriculum was spelled out eventually, not invented by, but sort of spelled out in a book by a man named Martianius Capella, who wrote in the late 5th century. He wrote a book called *The Marriage of Mercury and Philology*; the curriculum was the *Seven Liberal Arts*. The book itself is an allegory in which

Mercury marries Lady Philology. Seven attendants each come along, one after the other, and bring a gift to the wedding. The gift is one of the arts, and that attendant goes on a long disquisition about his art, the art that he is presenting. What were these? There was grammar, the basic study of language. There was rhetoric, as I said before, in principle the notion of speaking well, but also the ability, in a sense, to analyze, or criticize, a literary text. There were dialectic and logic. I leave it to everyone to decide on the backwardness of these ancient people who thought that persons trained for public life and responsibility should have to make sense; that's kind of an interesting puzzle. There was arithmetic, the basic command of numbers. There was geometry, measuring the earth, very practical for surveying, very practical for military affairs, and very practical for sailing. There was astronomy. An awful lot of what in antiquity passed for astronomy we would today regard as astrology, but of course that's another thing that we in our sophisticated modern world have gotten rid of. We don't have any trope or stuff like that any longer, so pity these poor ancient people who did so. Then, there was music. Music was not being taught how to play a musical instrument; it was actually understanding things that the Pythagorean philosophers in Greece had understood, the Law of Percent Consonances. The relationship between, for example, vibrating strings or vibrating columns of air can be expressed absolutely mathematically. Studying music was actually a way to study sort of what we would think of as physics, something about how the world works out there.

That was the basic educational structure they'd obtained in the ancient world. Christianity, as a "religion of the book," required learning, but for a long time, of course, it had no access to the basic literary culture, to any kind of basic literary culture, except through the pagan classics. If you were going to acquire an education, you got an education in the pagan classics. Writers like Tertullian, of course, were rigorous about this: Don't mix yourself up with that kind of stuff! Augustine in his Christian teaching *De doctrina christiana* we saw in the last lecture said, you can use that stuff to teach you what you need to know, spoil the Egyptians. You can learn what you need to know so that you can read your Christian texts. But as I said at the outset of this lecture, Augustine was worried about this. The first 10 books of his great book the *City of God* addressed themselves again and again and again to pagan learning, to pagan culture. He's worried about this.

Crucial steps toward the medieval school, toward the Christian school, and toward a different kind of school are taken by a number of figures. Augustine I think is actually one of them, but we can particularly instance Cassiodorus, 485/490 to about 580, lived to be a very old man. He came from a senatorial family. He served as quaestor in Italy 507–511. He served as consul in 541. He was master of the offices under Theodoric from 523–527. He was praetorian prefect for Italy certainly from 533, and seems to have retired perhaps about 540—that is to say, he retired during the Gothic wars. He was just disgusted. We've mentioned him earlier. He wanted really a reconciliation between the Gothic regime of Theodoric and the Roman regime, and he was unable to achieve that.

He retired and he settled on his family estate near Squillace in the south of Italy. He renamed it "Vivarium," which means "Fish Ponds." We saw in an earlier lecture that he wrote histories. We talked about his *Variae*; he kind of kept the official correspondence with Theodoric's court. What I want to draw attention to now is that he desired to create a kind of an institute for Christian studies at Vivarium, at his Fish Ponds. His most influential work, in his own time and for centuries after this, was *The Institutes of Divine and Human Readings*. It was a very interesting way he went about his work. In *The Divine Readings*, he went through the Bible, book by book by book, and then listed all of the great commentaries that he knew, that he could get any information about, on each one of those books, with some comments on those commentaries. It was a kind of massive bibliography of Christian discussion of the books of the Bible. In *The Human Readings*, he went through the seven liberal arts, and he listed the best works on each one of the arts. Wherever possible, he would try either to draw in Christian works or to indicate how a Christian interpretation could be offered, or how the particular text in question would not endanger a Christian reader.

Cassiodorus's works—plus a list of famous Christian authors' *On Illustrious Men* that was begun by Saint Jerome and was continued by a whole series of others—became interestingly, the basic bibliography for a millennium—monastic schools, cathedral schools, and so on, even sometimes royal courts. You took *The Divine and Human Readings* and the *De viris illustribus, On Illustrious Men*, and those were the books you wanted to go find. Those were the manuscripts you wanted to get copied and have in your library.

Isidore of Seville is another interesting figure. He's born about 560, died in 636. He came from a very noble Hispano-Roman family, one of those families that was actually disrupted by Justinian's wars in Spain. He was a major ecclesiastical statesman. He presided over church councils. He required the establishment of schools in very diocese in Spain. We don't know whether that was carried out successfully, but it's very interesting that he attempted to do this. He was immensely learned, but he was not a particularly original man. He was kind of an encyclopedist in a way. He wrote histories; he wrote polemical treatises against heretics and against Jews. You may recall my mentioning in the Visigothic Spain that things were not always very comfortable or friendly for Jews. He wrote two books on ecclesiastical offices, he wrote a continuation of Jerome's *On Illustrious Men* that I mentioned just a moment ago, kind of bringing it up to date a little bit, but he's most famous for his *Etymologies*, an encyclopedic compendium of all knowledge that he based on the encyclopedia of Pliny the Elder, 23–79 A.D. Pliny lived, who was the one of course who was killed because he got too close to the eruption of Mount Vesuvius. He was going to see what a volcanic eruption was like.

Isidore's work is grounded in the assumption that the meanings of words revealed many truths. I'm very much grounded in that same assumption myself. Sometimes Isidore's *Etymologies* are fantastic. Sometimes they're really very cunning and very clever. Let me give you just two examples that sort of illustrate how he went about his work, bearing in mind that this is a very long book, it goes on and on and on. Here's his entry for history:

> History is the story of what has been done, and by its means what has taken place in the past is perceived. It is called in Greek *historia*, that is from seeing and learning. For among the ancients no one wrote history unless he had been present and witnessed what was to be described. For we understand what we see better than we do what we gather by hearsay.

That's very interesting in a whole bunch of ways. You notice that he sees history as an active intellectual process of engagement by the historian. History is not sort of a quarry from which we go and hew facts. We make history in our own minds, but he also says that we can only write history of what we've seen. We actually can't write the history of the remote past. We managed to not pay too much attention to Isidore on that particular point. On medicine:

> Medicine is that which guards or restores the health of the body, and its subject-matter deals with diseases and wounds. ... Its name is believed to have been given to medicine from *modus*, that is, moderation, so that not enough but little be used. For nature is made sorrowful by much and rejoices in the moderate. Whence also they who drink in quantities and without ceasing of herb juices and antidotes are troubled. For all immoderation brings not welfare but danger.

His etymology on that particular score is utterly bogus. Nevertheless, it's interesting, isn't it, how he's teaching little truths while he's teaching the meaning of words. Isidore transmitted to the Middle Ages a vast amount of ancient learning, but he tried to prune away the stuff that was manifestly pagan.

The themes that I've really been talking about in this lecture, in some very interesting ways, come together in Pope Gregory I. Gregory "the Great," born about 530, became pope in 590, died in 604. He was born to a senatorial family. He served as prefect of Rome. In 573, he retired and became a monk in his family house in Rome. He served as papal envoy to Constantinople for about six years. He was ill almost the entirety of his adult life. He wanted nothing more than to be a monk and to live a life of quiet repose, but when he was elected pope, he served. He had that remarkable Roman sense of duty. He was a prolific author, Gregory was. His *Pastoral Rule* was a how-to book for bishops. He wrote in the tradition of Cicero and Ambrose. We've talked about them in earlier lectures, deeply imbued with the Christianized version of the traditional Roman public ethic. A tremendously influential book, the *Pastoral Rule* was in the Middle Ages. His *Moralia in Job*, was a long commentary on the book of Job that addressed the human condition generally, and the problems of justice and suffering. Why do the just suffer and the wicked prosper? His *Homilies on Ezechiel* were reflections on his own times, inspired by this remarkably pessimistic (in lots of ways) book of Ezekiel. He wrote biblical commentaries, always primarily in the allegorical mode, very influential in the Middle Ages, copied again and again and again. He wrote his *Dialogues*; we talked about these, remember, in connection with Saint Benedict. More than 860 of his letters survive, revealing not somebody who's thinking great high thoughts all the time, but somebody who is managing to administer the affairs of the Roman Church. He's living up to his own ideal.

Gregory, quite simply, had a sense that the world was drawing to a close, but he sent missionaries to England. There is in Gregory, I suggest, a kind of serenity. Augustine was agitated and worried. Gregory could now take things for granted. He lived in a Christian world where people didn't live up to their values. Augustine was worried about pagans contending with Christians.

Timeline

454	Murder of Aetius.
455	Murder of Valentinian III.
471–526	Reign of Theodoric as Ostrogoth king. (Assumed power in Italy 493–526.)
476	End of the Western Empire.
c. 480–c. 550	Life of Saint Benedict.
481–511	Reign of Clovis.
492–496	Pontificate of Gelasius I.
493	Ostrogoths take charge of Italy.
507	Franks defeat the Visigoths at Vouillé.
527–565	Reign of Justinian.
529–532	*Corpus Iuris Civilis.*
532	Nika revolt.
533–534	Justinian's reconquest of North Africa.
535–554	Justinian's reconquest of Italy.
542–544	Bubonic plague.
570–632	Life of Muhammad.
590–604	Pontificate of Gregory the Great.
622	Hijra of the Prophet.
630s	Heraclius defeats the Persians.
632–634	Ridda Wars.
632–661	"Rightly Guided" caliphs.
634–660	Muslim conquests of Syria, Palestine, Iraq, and Egypt.
661–748	Umayyad caliphs.
660–750	Continued Muslim expansion across North Africa and into central Asia.

Glossary

Abbasids: Dynasty of caliphs from 750 to 1258. Moved the Islamic capital to Baghdad and fostered a brilliant culture. Gradually declined in power as regions broke away and Turkish mercenaries acquired real power.

Anglo-Saxons: Catchall name for various peoples from northern Germany and southern Denmark who settled in England from 450 to 600 and built small kingdoms.

apologists: Christian writers of the 2nd and 3rd centuries who tried to differentiate between Christianity and Judaism, to demonstrate some compatibility between Christianity and classical culture, and to point out to Christians how to live in a pagan world.

Arianism: See Arius in Biographical Notes.

barbarians: To the Greeks, babblers, people who did not speak Greek; to the Romans, people outside the empire. The word gradually acquired more acutely negative connotations.

basilica: A rectangular building used by the Romans for many purposes and adapted by Christians for their churches. Its name derives from Greek *basileus* ("king"), hence a "royal hall."

bishops: "Overseers" in Greek, the chief religious and administrative officers of the Christian church.

Burgundians: Barbarian people who settled in (today's) Savoy in the 5th century and built an effective kingdom; conquered by the Franks.

caliph: Successor to the Prophet in Islam. Originally held only Muhammad's secular authority, but over time acquired some responsibility for custody of the faith.

Cappadocian Fathers: Basil the Great (c. 330–379), his brother Gregory of Nyssa (c. 330–395), and Gregory Nazianzus (c. 329–389), who were among the greatest Greek church fathers. They wrote especially on Trinitarian and Christological issues.

Carolingians: Dynasty of Frankish rulers whose most famous member was Charlemagne (Carolus Magnus). Became kings in 751 and ruled until 911 in Germany and 987 in France.

Christology: The branch of Christian theology that explores how Jesus Christ can be true God and true man.

church fathers: Greek and Latin Christian writers (from the period of 300–750, but especially 350–450) who set norms for biblical interpretation and explained key Christian doctrines.

Corpus Iuris Civilis: Massive codification of Roman law carried out (529–532) by a commission headed by Tribonian under the aegis of Justinian (see Biographical Notes).

Council of Chalcedon: Summoned by Pulcheria and Pope Leo I in 451 to address the Monophysite heresy.

Council of Nicaea: Summoned by Constantine I in 325 to address the Arian heresy.

dioceses: Twelve, later 14, administrative districts of the Roman Empire; the division below the prefectures and above the provinces.

Dominate: Name for the Roman imperial regime beginning with Diocletian, from *dominus*, "lord and master," emphasizing enhanced imperial authority and Persian-style ceremony.

Edict of Milan: Decree in 313 whereby Constantine I granted legal toleration to Christianity.

ethnogenesis: Name for the complex process of "the makings of a people"; stresses identity more than ethnicity.

evergetism: Name for the highly competitive civic benefactions that governed public life and construction in cities of the Roman Empire.

federates: People who had a *foedus*, a treaty, with Rome; usually along frontiers.

Franks: Germanic peoples who gradually moved south from the mouth of the Rhine toward Paris and built powerful kingdoms under the Merovingian and Carolingian families of kings.

Hadith: The sayings of the Prophet, Muhammad. Collected and written down, they are studied in the Islamic world as a source of religious guidance, although not on a par with the Qur'an.

Hagia Sophia: The church of "Holy Wisdom" built in Constantinople on Justinian's orders. Owed much to traditional Roman architecture but also innovated. Isidore of Miletus and Anthemius of Tralles were the principal architects.

hijra: The "flight," or pilgrimage, of Muhammad from Mecca to Medina in 622. Taken in the Islamic world to inaugurate a new era.

Huns: Fierce nomadic warriors from the frontiers of China who appeared on the Roman scene around 370 and pressured the western empire until their defeat in 451.

iconoclasm: Official religious policy of the Byzantine Empire from 730 to 787 that rejected all figural religious art and any acts of devotion performed in connection with works of art.

Isaurians: Ruling dynasty in Byzantium from 717 to 802. Defended frontiers, issued new laws, carried on with development of the *theme* system, and promoted iconoclasm (the removal or destruction of devotional images).

Islam: From *al-Islam*, "the surrender," the customary name for the faith taught by Muhammad, the Prophet, and involving a complete surrender of the self to Allah.

Lombards: Germanic people who entered Italy in 568 and gradually built a strong kingdom with rich culture, especially in law, only to fall to the more powerful Franks in 773–774.

Manichaeanism: Widespread religious sect that emphasized dualism: good-evil, flesh-spirit, light-dark, etc.

monk: Christian ascetic who in principle lives alone but in practice lives in some form of community.

Monophysitism: Christian heresy prominent in the eastern Mediterranean holding that Jesus Christ had only one true (divine) nature. Condemned by the Council of Chalcedon in 451. Still influential among Christians in western Asia.

monotheism: The belief in the existence of only one God.

Nestorianism: Christian heresy prominent in the eastern Mediterranean that emphasized Jesus human nature.

Notitia Dignitatum: A massive register kept at the Roman imperial court showing all the officials in the administrative hierarchy. A copy survives from the early 5th century.

Ostrogoths: Germanic people who, under Theodoric (r. 471–526), built a kingdom in Italy in 493, which eventually fell to the armies of Justinian (see Biographical Notes).

Papal State: Lands in central Italy ruled by the papacy beginning in the 8th century.

patristic era: The period of the church fathers (*patres*).

Petrine theory: Idea advanced by Roman bishops that as Peter was leader of the Apostles, the successor to Peter is the leader of the Catholic Church. Based on Matthew 16:16–19.

Pillars of Islam: Five practices that characterize the Islamic faith: profession of faith, fasting, daily prayer, generous almsgiving, and pilgrimage to Mecca.

polytheism: The belief in the simultaneous existence of many gods.

pope: The bishop of Rome who, on the basis of the Petrine theory, the historical resonances of Rome, and various historical circumstances, achieved a leading position in the Catholic Church.

prefectures: The four great administrative districts created under the tetrarchy by Diocletian; administered by the praetorian prefects.

Principate: Name for the Roman regime inaugurated by Augustus Caesar as *princeps*, or "first citizen." Contrasted with the Dominate of Diocletian (see Biographical Notes).

Qur'an: The sacred book of Islam. A series of recitations, gathered in chapters called "suras," given by the angel Gabriel to the Prophet.

Septuagint: Greek version of the Hebrew Bible, allegedly prepared by 70 translators in 70 days in Alexandria. Seven books longer than the Hebrew version. Authoritative still in Orthodox churches.

Sueves: A barbarian people who crossed the Rhine in 406, moved across Gaul to Spain, and built an effective kingdom in Iberia, later conquered by the Visigoths.

Sunna: The "good practice," or the habits and customs of the Prophet, studied in the Islamic world as a guide to life but not on a par with the Qur'an.

syncretism: The tendency, often manifest in religion, to adopt and adapt ideas and practices from neighbors, conquerors, or even those whom one has conquered.

Synod of Whitby: Church council in the north of England (664) that decided for Roman instead of Irish customs.

tetrarchy: "Rule by four" instituted by Diocletian. Two augustuses and two caesars would jointly rule the empire and provide for orderly succession. Only partially successful in practice.

Torah: The first five books of the Hebrew scriptures, traditionally ascribed to Moses.

Trinity: The Christian doctrine according to which one God exists in three distinct persons (Father, Son, and Holy Spirit).

typology: The typical Christian way of reading the Hebrew scriptures (the Old Testament). Stories in those scriptures had value only in so far as they foreshadowed developments in the New Testament.

Umayyad: Dynasty of caliphs from 661 to 750 who moved the capital of the caliphate to Damascus and did much of the work of building institutions.

umma Muslima: The community of all those who have made *al-Islam*, not confined to any political or ethnic boundaries.

Vandals: Germanic people who crossed the Rhine in 406, raided in Spain for a generation, crossed to North Africa, practiced piracy in the Mediterranean, and fell to Justinian (see Biographical Notes) in 532–534.

Visigoths: Germanic federates who crossed the Danube into Roman territory in 376, defeated a Roman army in 378, sacked Rome in 410, settled in Gaul under Roman auspices in 418, lost to the Franks in 507, migrated into Spain, and created a kingdom that finally fell to the Muslims in 711.

Vulgate: Latin translation of the Bible prepared by Saint Jerome (see Biographical Notes) on the order of Pope Damasus.

Zoroastrianism: Principal religion of the ancient Persians. Revealed in songs (*gathas*) in the Avesta, the holy books of the religion. Consisted of the teachings of Zarathustra (dates controversial), who stressed dualities.

Biographical Notes

Ambrose (339–397): High-born citizen of Milan who became bishop of the city and wrote extensively, bringing to Latin theology the conceptual frameworks of Greek thought. He is considered a church father.

Anthony (c. 251–356): Egyptian solitary who established the ideals of eremitic (solitary) monasticism.

Arius (c. 250–336): Priest of Alexandria who, in an attempt to preserve absolute monotheism, taught that Jesus Christ was slightly subordinate to God the Father. Condemned by Council of Nicaea in 325 but influential among Germanic peoples who were converted to Arianism.

Attila (r. c. 434–453): Charismatic leader of the Huns who exacted tribute from the Romans but eventually lost a great battle in Gaul.

Augustine (354–430): Prolific Christian theologian and greatest of Latin church fathers. One of the most influential writers in Christian history.

Basil (330–379): Greek church father who wrote influential theological, liturgical, and monastic works; one of the Cappadocian Fathers.

Bede (673–735): Anglo-Saxon monk and scholar at Wearmouth-Jarrow who wrote biblical commentaries, a book on time reckoning, and history. Greatest scholar of his day.

Benedict of Nursia (c. 480–c. 550): Italian ascetic who founded a community at Monte Cassino where he wrote his *Rule*, eventually the most influential of all monastic rules.

Boethius: (c. 480–c. 524): Neoplatonic philosopher put to death by Theodoric. He wrote *Consolation of Philosophy* and translated mathematical and logical works of Aristotle from Greek to Latin.

Cassiodorus (c.480–c. 585): High-born Italian who served Theodoric; author of historical and educational works.

Clovis (r. 486–511): Greatest Frankish king of the Merovingian dynasty who consolidated Frankish rule in Gaul, defeated the Visigoths in 507, and accepted Roman Catholicism.

Constantine I (the Great) (r. 306–337): Roman emperor who continued the reforms of Diocletian, restructured the Roman army, granted toleration to Christianity, and became Christian himself.

Diocletian (r. 284–305): Roman emperor who instituted the tetrarchy (see Glossary), reformed the Roman administration, and persecuted Christians.

Gelasius I (r. 492–496): Pope who spelled out respective spheres of authority of kings and priests.

Gregory I (r. 590–604): Pope who wrote influential books and ruled Rome as temporal overlord in the absence of effective Roman rule.

Heraclius (r. 610–641): Byzantine emperor who defeated the Persians, only to lose to the Arabs. Failed to achieve religious unity. Began to promote a more Greek culture. Initiated the theme system as a new form of administration.

Ignatius of Antioch (c. 35–107): Author of letters to Christian communities that show the emerging structure of the Christian church.

Jerome (342–420): High-born Roman citizen who became a Christian ascetic, wrote many letters, and translated the Bible into Latin (the Vulgate; see Glossary). He is considered a church father.

Justin Martyr (c. 100–c. 165): Christian apologist who wrote *Dialogue with Trypho the Jew* to differentiate between Christianity and Judaism.

Justinian (r. 527–565): Byzantine emperor who reconquered some western provinces, overhauled the administration, issued the *Corpus Iuris Civilis* (see Glossary), failed to institute religious unity, and built the Hagia Sophia.

Leo I (r. 440–461): Pope, gifted writer, and great theoretician of the powers of the papal office.

Muhammad (570–632): Meccan merchant who became the Prophet of Islam.

Offa of Mercia (r. 757–796): Anglo-Saxon *bretwalda* who was first to call himself "King of the English."

Pachomius (290–346): Egyptian monk credited with preparing the first monastic rule and thus formulating cenobitic (common-life) monasticism.

Pippin III (r. 751–768): First Carolingian (see Glossary) to become king. He allied with the popes, defeated the Lombards in Italy, and fostered church and cultural reform.

Theodosius I (r. 378–395): The last emperor to rule a unified Rome. An effective military leader, he pacified the Balkans after the Visigothic incursion of 376–378.

Valens (r. 364–378): Roman emperor who was defeated and killed by the Visigoths at Adrianople.

Bibliography

Amory, Patrick. *People and Identity in Ostrogothic Italy, 489–554.* Cambridge: Cambridge University Press, 1997. Challenging but up-to-date and provocative.

Barnes, T. D. *Constantius and Athanasius: Theology and Politics in the Constantinian Empire.* Cambridge, MA: Harvard University Press, 1993. Complex, but excellent as a discussion of the religious cross-currents of the 4th century.

————. *The New Empire of Diocletian and Constantine.* Cambridge, MA: Harvard University Press, 1982. A masterful study by a scholar with an unmatched command of the sources.

Berkey, Jonathan P. *The Formation of Islam: Religion and Society in the Near East, 600–1800.* Cambridge: Cambridge University Press, 2003. An excellent account of early Islamic thought and practice.

Bowersock, G. W. *Julian the Apostate.* Cambridge, MA: Harvard University Press, 1978. Brief, but still the best treatment of Julian.

Bowersock, Glenn, Peter Brown, and Oleg Grabar, eds. *Interpreting Late Antiquity.* Cambridge, MA: Harvard University Press, 2001. Accessible essays by masters on many key topics.

Brown, Peter. *Augustine of Hippo: A Biography.* 2nd ed. Berkeley: University of California Press, 2000. Simply magisterial.

————. *Poverty and Leadership in the Later Roman Empire.* Hanover, NH: University Press of New England, 2002. A brilliant evocation of social attitudes in late antiquity.

————. *The World of Late Antiquity.* 1971. Reprint, New York: Norton, 1989. The fundamental introduction to the subject.

Browning, Robert. *Justinian and Theodora.* rev. ed. London: Thames and Hudson, 1987. A great read, and useful for its emphasis on Theodora.

Cameron, Averil. *Christianity and the Rhetoric of Empire: The Development of Christian Discourse.* Berkeley: University of California Press, 1991. An excellent discussion of how Christian writers adopted and adapted the chief literary forms of antiquity.

Caner, Daniel. *Wandering, Begging Monks: Spiritual Authority and the Promotion of Monasticism in Late Antiquity.* Berkeley: University of California Press, 2002. An evocative treatment focusing on the eastern Mediterranean.

Charles-Edwards, T. M. *Early Christian Ireland.* Cambridge: Cambridge University Press, 2000. Although long and difficult, this is nevertheless a magnificent work of scholarship.

Chitty, Derwas J. *The Desert a City.* Crestwood, NY: St. Vladimir's Seminary Press, 1966. Still unsurpassed as a treatment of monasticism's origins in Egypt.

Christie, Neil. *The Lombards.* Oxford: Blackwell, 1995. Lively and interesting for all its archaeological evidence.

Clark, Gillian. *Women in Late Antiquity: Pagan and Christian Lifestyles.* Oxford: Oxford University Press, 1993. A fine survey of a fascinating and important topic.

Cochrane, Charles Norris. *Christianity and Classical Culture.* rev. ed. Oxford: Oxford University Press, 1944. Still the classic treatment of this fascinating, important topic.

Collins, Roger. *The Visigoths in Spain, 409–711.* Oxford: Blackwell, 2004. The most recent and authoritative survey.

Crone, Patricia. *God's Rule: Government and Islam.* New York: Columbia University Press, 2004. The fundamental treatment of the governmental structures of the caliphate.

Dark, Ken. *Britain and the End of the Roman Empire.* Charleston, SC: Tempus, 2000. Fascinating account based heavily on archaeological sources.

Dietz, Maribel. *Wandering Monks, Virgins, and Pilgrims: Ascetic Travel in the Mediterranean World A.D. 300–800.* University Park, PA: Penn State Press, 2005. A good read that helps to explain how ascetic ideas proliferated.

Dignas, Beate, and Engelbert Winter. *Rome and Persia in Late Antiquity.* Cambridge: Cambridge University Press, 2007. An interesting account of Persia itself and of Rome's tortured relations with its greatest foe.

Dodds, E. R. *Pagan and Christian in an Age of Anxiety.* 1965. Reprint, New York: Norton, 1970. A penetrating analysis of the moral and spiritual crisis of the 3rd century.

Donner, Fred M. *The Early Islamic Conquests.* Princeton: Princeton University Press, 1981. This remains the basic study of an incredibly dynamic process.

Downey, Glanville. *Constantinople in the Age of Justinian*. Norman: University of Oklahoma Press, 1960. Dated now, but still a fine introduction.

Dunn, Marilyn. *The Emergence of Monasticism*: *From the Desert Fathers to the Early Middle Ages*. Oxford: Blackwell, 2000. Readable and reliable.

Elm, Susanna. *"Virgins of God." The Making of Asceticism in Late Antiquity*. Oxford: Oxford University Press, 1994. A long and complex but fascinating treatment of female monasticism within the total context of the phenomenon.

Elsner, Jaś. *Imperial Rome and Christian Triumph*. Oxford: Oxford University Press, 1998. Superb survey covering the period 100–450 A.D.

Fox, Robin Lane. *Pagans and Christians*. New York: Alfred A. Knopf, 1987. Long and detailed but utterly splendid.

Garland, Lynda. *Byzantine Empresses: Women and Power in Byzantium, A.D. 527–1204*. New York: Routledge, 1999. Lively and readable biographical sketches of Byzantium's key women, emphasizing their personal stories and political significance.

Geffcken, Johannes. *The Last Days of Greco-Roman Paganism*. New York: North Holland, 1978. A brilliant treatment of a complex subject by a master scholar.

Gibbon, Edward. *The Decline and Fall of the Roman Empire*. 3 vols. New York: Modern Library, 1932. Brilliantly written and still influential.

Goffart, Walter. *Barbarian Tides*: *The Migration Age and the Later Roman Empire*. Philadelphia: University of Pennsylvania Press, 2006. Brilliant, argumentative, and controversial.

Grisar, Hartmann. *A History of Rome and the Popes in the Middle Ages*. 3 vols. London: K. Paul, Trench, Trübner & Co., 1911. Old, but a wide, wonderful, sweeping survey.

Haldon, J. F. *Byzantium in the Seventh Century: The Transformation of a Culture*. Cambridge: Cambridge University Press, 1990. A comprehensive survey by an acknowledged authority.

Halsall, Guy. *Barbarian Migrations and the Roman West, 376–568*. Cambridge: Cambridge University Press, 2007. Lively and opinionated, this is the most comprehensive treatment in many years.

Hanson, R. P. C. *The Search for the Christian Doctrine of God: The Arian Controversy, 318–381.* 1988. Reprint, Grand Rapids, MI: Baker Academic, 2005. Learned and very detailed, but still a fine introduction to a complex and important topic.

Heather, Peter. *The Fall of the Roman Empire: A New History of Rome and the Barbarians.* Oxford: Oxford University Press, 2006. A detailed account of how Rome's encounters with the barbarians led to the "fall" of the Western Empire.

————. *Goths and Romans, 332–489.* Oxford: Oxford University Press, 1991. Learned and accessible, this is the best introduction to the Goths.

Herrin, Judith. *The Formation of Christendom.* Princeton: Princeton University Press, 1987. A brave and stimulating attempt to capture all three of Rome's heirs.

Hodges, Richard, and David Whitehouse. *Mohammed, Charlemagne and the Origins of Europe.* London: Duckworth, 1983. A "catastrophist" interpretation of the late antique economy based heavily on archaeological sources.

Holum, Kenneth. *Theodosian Empresses: Women and Imperial Dominion in Late Antiquity.* Berkeley: University of California Press, 1982. Intensely interesting, revealing, and readable.

Jensen, Robin Margaret. *Understanding Early Christian Art.* London: Routledge, 2000. A fine, clear book that delivers on the words of its title.

Jones, A. H. M. *The Late Roman Empire, 284–602.* 2 vols. 1964. Reprint, Baltimore: Johns Hopkins University Press, 1986. Massive and detailed, yet absolutely fundamental on government and institutions.

Kaegi, Walter E. *Heraclius: Emperor of Byzantium.* Cambridge: Cambridge University Press, 2003. An excellent account of a fascinating man and ruler.

Kelly, Christopher. *Ruling the Later Roman Empire.* Cambridge, MA: Harvard University Press, 2004. Emphasizes the 6th century and well-grounded in the sources.

Kelly, J. N. D. *Early Christian Doctrines.* 5th rev. ed. San Francisco: Harcourt, 1978. The fundamental survey of all the key issues.

————. *Golden Mouth: The Story of John Chrysostom—Ascetic, Preacher, Bishop.* Ithaca, NY: Cornell University Press, 1995. A beautifully written account of this remarkable personage.

————. *Jerome.* London: Duckworth, 1975. The best introduction to the church father by a real master.

Kennedy, Hugh M. *The Prophet and the Age of the Caliphates.* Harlow, UK: Longman, 1986. Detailed, but readable and authoritative.

Kirby, D. P. *The Earliest English Kings.* rev. ed. London: Routledge, 2000. A balanced and reliable account of a complex, controversial period.

Krautheimer, Richard. *Three Christian Capitals: Topography and Politics.* Berkeley: University of California Press, 1983. A splendid comparative account of Rome, Constantinople, and Milan, with glances at other cities.

Lançon, Bertrand. *Rome in Late Antiquity.* London: Routledge, 2001. A brief, clear, and wide-ranging introduction.

Lenski, Noel. *Failure of Empire: Valens and the Roman State in the Fourth Century A.D.* Berkeley: University of California Press, 2002. The most recent and scholarly treatment.

Levy, Reuben. *The Social Structure of Islam.* Cambridge: Cambridge University Press, 1957. Although dated in parts, this work is still unsurpassed as a general, thematic social history.

Liebeschuetz, J. H. W. G. *The Decline and Fall of the Roman City.* Oxford: Oxford University Press, 2001. Richly detailed, clearly argued, and packed with interesting details.

Maas, Michael, ed. *The Cambridge Companion to the Age of Justinian.* Cambridge: Cambridge University Press, 2005. Readable, commissioned essays by experts on almost all aspects of the period.

Markus, Robert. *The End of Ancient Christianity.* Cambridge: Cambridge University Press, 1990. A stunning treatment of the period from Augustine to Gregory by a gifted scholar and writer.

————. *Gregory the Great and His World.* Cambridge: Cambridge University Press, 1997. The greatest biography of the greatest of popes.

MacCormack, Sabine G. *Art and Ceremony in Late Antiquity.* Berkeley: University of California Press, 1981. A penetrating analysis of textual and visual expressions of Roman power.

Mathews, Thomas F. *Clash of Gods: A Reinterpretation of Early Christian Art*. rev. ed. Princeton: Princeton University Press, 1999. Readable, controversial, and stimulating.

McCormick, Michael. *Origins of the European Economy: Communications and Commerce, A.D. 300–900*. Cambridge: Cambridge University Press, 2001. A magisterial account of the transformation of the late antique economy.

McLynn, Neil B. *Ambrose of Milan: Church and Court in a Christian Capital*. Berkeley: University of California Press, 1994. Clear, readable, and comprehensive, this book is strong on the overall context.

Millar, Fergus. *The Emperor in the Roman World, 31 B.C.–A.D. 337*. Ithaca, NY: Cornell University Press, 1977. The best overall treatment of the actual roles and importance of the emperors.

Noble, Thomas F. X., ed. *From Roman Provinces to Medieval Kingdoms*. London: Routledge, 2006. A collection of essays by major scholars reflecting the current state of understanding.

Pelikan, Jaroslav. *The Emergence of the Catholic Tradition (100–600)*. Chicago: The University of Chicago Press, 1971. The first volume of a five-volume history of Christian thought, this book is *the* starting place for late antiquity.

Pirenne, Henri. *Mohammed and Charlemagne*. 1939. Reprint, Cleveland: World, 1965. One of the most brilliant and influential of all history books written in the 20th century.

Rees, Roger. *Diocletian and the Tetrarchy*. Edinburgh: Edinburgh University Press, 2004. Current and accessible; on the same scale as Williams.

Salzman, Michele Renee. *The Making of a Christian Aristocracy: Social and Religious Change in the Western Roman Empire*. Cambridge, MA: Harvard University Press, 2002. A sparkling account of how the Roman elite became Christian.

Schimmelpfennig, Bernhard. *The Papacy*. New York: Columbia University Press, 1992. A readable, concise survey.

Thompson, E. A. *The Goths in Spain*. Oxford: Oxford University Press, 1969. Somewhat overtaken by more recent work, this is still a masterful account.

Van Dam, Raymond. *The Roman Revolution of Constantine.* Cambridge: Cambridge University Press, 2007. Readable, insightful, stimulating.

Ward-Perkins, Bryan. *The Fall of Rome and the End of Civilization.* Oxford: Oxford University Press, 2005. A classic "catastrophist" argument.

Wilken, Robert Louis. *The Christians as the Romans Saw Them.* New Haven, CT: Yale University Press, 1984. A stunning presentation of the pagan critique of Christianity.

―――. *The Spirit of Early Christian Thought: Seeking the Face of God.* New Haven, CT: Yale University Press, 2003. A moving and sensitive appreciation of the patristic era.

Williams, Stephen. *Diocletian and the Roman Recovery.* London: Routledge, 1985. Readable and concise, an excellent introduction.

―――. *A History of the Later Roman Empire A.D. 284–641.* Oxford: Blackwell, 2007. A fine, readable, political overview of the whole period, but not strong on society or religion.

Williams, Stephen, and Gerard Friell. *Theodosius: Empire at Bay.* New Haven, CT: Yale University Press, 1994. Excellent, readable, and comprehensive.

Wolfram, Herwig. *The Roman Empire and Its Germanic Peoples.* Berkeley: University of California Press, 1997. Dense, learned, and controversial, but highly stimulating.

Wood, I. N. *The Merovingian Kingdoms, 450–751.* Harlow, UK: Longman, 1994. An outstanding introduction to the history of the Franks.

Notes

Notes